Collins
English for Exams

SKILLS FOR THE TOEFL iBT® TEST
Reading and Writing

Collins

HarperCollins Publishers
77-85 Fulham Palace Road
Hammersmith
London W6 8JB

First edition 2012

Reprint 10 9 8 7 6 5 4 3 2 1 0

© HarperCollins Publishers 2012

ISBN 978-0-00-746059-5

Collins * is a registered trademark of HarperCollins Publishers Limited.

www.collinselt.com

A catalogue record for this book is available from the British Library.

Editorial Services: Content*Ed Publishing Solutions, LLC

Writing Services: Creative Content, LLC

Typeset in India by Aptara

Printed in Italy by Lego

HarperCollins does not warrant that www.collinselt.com or any
other website mentioned in this title will be provided uninterrupted,
that any website will be error free, that defects will be corrected, or
that the website or the server that makes it available are free of viruses
or bugs. For full terms and conditions please refer to the site terms
provided on the website.

Academic Word List © Coxhead, Averil (2000)

Contents

How to Use This Book

Skills for the TOEFL iBT® Test: Reading and Writing, and its companion edition, *Skills for the TOEFL iBT® Test: Listening and Speaking* offer a comprehensive guide to the TOEFL test. If you use this series to prepare for the test, you will earn a top score on the TOEFL test and improve your chances at getting accepted by a great university.

No matter the level of your English, *Skills for the TOEFL iBT® Test: Reading and Writing* provides you with all the tools you need to succeed on the test. Here's a glimpse of the learning tools included in this book:

» **Skill-specific *Challenges and Solutions* sections.** These sections offer strategy and skills reviews to help you learn how to overcome the most common challenges in each section of the test.

» ***Quick Guide* question overviews.** Each lesson provides a brief summary of the question type in an easy-to-read chart, making it simple for you to quickly understand what is important to know to answer the question correctly.

» ***Walk Through* samples.** Clear, visual examples show you the types of questions, passages, and responses you can expect to find on the test. Knowing what to expect is an important part of preparing for the test.

» ***Get It Right* presentations.** These presentations give an overview of the most important steps for doing well on each question. It provides Tips and Tasks for noticing and understanding the important elements of each question type.

» ***Progressive Practice.*** For each question type, carefully designed activities gradually prepare you for the TOEFL test. This step-by-step practice builds the knowledge and skills you need for a high score and encourages independent learning while working up to TOEFL testing levels.

   • *Get Ready* activities require you to look and listen for certain pieces of information, practice structured activities, and notice why answers are correct or incorrect.

   • *Get Set* activities encourage even more practice working with the question types and answers and will help you gain the skills and confidence you need.

   • *Go for the TOEFL Test* activities provide you with authentic test questions to practice what you have learned and further prepare you for the test.

» ***Answer Analysis* presentations.** The answer analyses will teach you how to eliminate incorrect answer options and select the best answers for various question types.

» **Skill-specific *Review Test* sections.** At the end of each section, you'll be able to put your skills to the test by taking a practice test. The review sections will help you identify your weaknesses so you can know what areas to focus on before the test.

» ***Test Tips.*** Throughout the book, you'll see *Test Tips*, which offer best practice strategies and useful advice on how to approach certain activity types.

» **Dictionary definitions.** *Collins Cobuild Advanced Dictionary* definitions and web links are provided throughout the book to help you understand words and build your knowledge of academic vocabulary often found on the TOEFL test and in U.S. university texts and lectures.

» **Academic Word List.** The Academic Word List, compiled by Coxhead (2000), consists of 570 word families that occur frequently over a wide range of academic texts. Knowing and practicing these words will help you build your vocabulary base to understand and use more academic English words.

» **Audio Script and Answer Key.** Found at the back of this book, these tools will help you practice and check your answers as you prepare for the TOEFL test. The Writing section also includes two sample responses per question type.

» **Audio CD.** The CD included with this book provides you with all of the listening passages for the Writing lessons and review test.

Tips for Success

Make a plan to succeed, and start by following these tips:

» **Register for the test early**. Check the application deadlines for the universities you are applying to. Make sure that you register to take the test well before the deadline to ensure that your scores arrive on time. For information on how to register, see page xi of this book.

» **Learn the score requirements for the universities you want to apply to.** Degree programs that have minimum score requirements typically post them on their admissions websites.

» **Start to study early.** The more you practice, the more you will improve your skills. Give yourself at least one month to review the materials and complete <u>all</u> of the practice activities in this book and in the companion edition: *Skills for the TOEFL iBT® Test: Listening and Speaking* offer. Spend at least one hour a day studying and don't give up. Remember, by using this book, you are on your way to high scores on the TOEFL test!

» **Time yourself** when you complete the exercises and practice tests.

» **Complete the exercises** on the page. Also, don't be afraid to make your own notes on the page. For example, writing down the definitions to words you don't know on the page will help you remember them later on.

» On the reading sections, read the passages and the model responses as many times as you need to in order to understand the concepts taught in this book

» On the writing section, return to the prompts and try to come up with new responses. Practice until creating responses within the time limits becomes easy for you.

Overview of the TOEFL® Test

The TOEFL® iBT test (Test of English as a Foreign Language) measures your proficiency in English. The TOEFL test does not evaluate your knowledge of the English language. Rather, it measures your ability <u>to use</u> English in a variety of academic settings.

The test is divided into four timed parts: Reading, Listening, Speaking, and Writing. Each section tests key skills that you will need in order to succeed as a student at an English-speaking university.

Reading Section

The reading section is the first section on the test. It measures your reading comprehension abilities by presenting you with a series of academic passages. Then you will answer a set of questions based on each reading. The questions in this section test your ability to:

» identify the main idea

» understand the main details

» make inferences

» understand the organizational structure of the passage

» use context clues to determine the definitions of key words

There are three to five academic reading passages per reading section. Each passage is between 600 and 750 words long. After each reading passage, you will answer a set of questions. There are usually 12 to 14 questions per passage. In the reading section, you are allowed to go back to previously-answered questions in the section to review or change your answers. For a detailed discussion of the reading section, including more information on the specific question types, see pages 1–93.

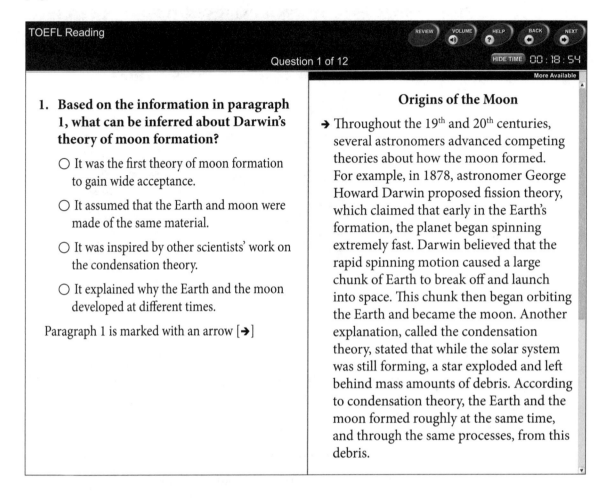

Listening Section

The listening section is the second section on the test. In order to evaluate your listening comprehension abilities, you will first listen to a lecture or conversation through your headphones. Then you will answer a set of questions based on each listening. The questions in this section will test your ability to:

» identify the main idea or purpose of the listening

» understand the main details

» make inferences

» indentify the speaker's purpose

There are six to nine listening passages per listening section. Each listening is between five to seven minutes long. After each listening passage, you will answer a set of questions. There are usually five to six questions per passage. In the listening section, you are <u>not</u> allowed to review questions that you have answered previously. For a detailed discussion of the listening section, including more information on the specific question types, see *Skills for the TOEFL iBT® Test: Listening and Speaking.*

Speaking Section

The speaking section is the third section on the test. In this section, you will speak your response to a variety of tasks into the microphone. The tasks test a number of speaking abilities, including:

» giving opinions

» understanding and responding to questions in the classroom

» participating in discussions on academic subjects

» synthesizing (combining) information from two sources

» reporting the opinions of others

» interacting with university employees

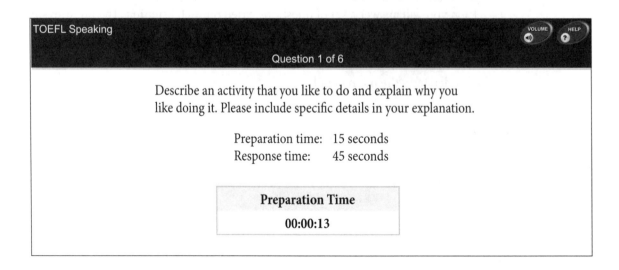

There are six speaking tasks in the speaking section: two independent tasks and four integrated tasks. Each item requires different skills, including: speaking only; reading, listening and speaking; and, listening and speaking. For more information about the speaking section, see *Skills for the TOEFL iBT® Test: Listening and Speaking*.

Writing Section

The writing section is the fourth section on the test. In this section, you will type your responses for each item on the computer. The tasks measure your ability to:

» plan and organize an essay

» develop a written response by using examples or specific details

» use a variety of grammatical structures and vocabulary

» use correct spelling and punctuation

There are two writing tasks in the writing section: one integrated writing task and one independent writing task. For more information about the writing section see pages 95–140.

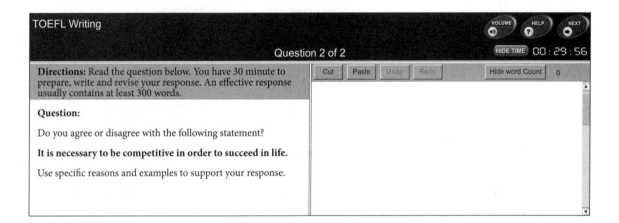

Experimental Sections

In order to field test new materials, ETS always includes an experimental section in <u>either</u> the reading or listening section of each test. That means that on the day of the test, you will see extra passages and questions in either the reading section or the listening section. If the experimental section is part of the reading section, you will have to read an additional two passages and answer the accompanying questions for them. If the experimental section is part of the listening section, you will have to listen to an additional three listening (two lectures and one conversation) and answer questions that are based on them.

Please note that the experimental section is not graded. However, you will have no way of knowing which section is experimental, so it is very important that you try your best on <u>all</u> of the sections of the tests.

QUICK GUIDE: TOEFL® Test

Section	Tasks	Timing	
Reading Section	Reading Passages: 3–5 Number of Questions: 39–70	Part 1 (1 Passage + Questions)	20 minutes
		Part 2 (2 Passages + Questions)	40 minutes
		Part 3* (2 Passages + Questions)	40 minutes
		Total Section Time: 60–100 minutes	

Listening Section	Listening Passages: 6–9
	  4–6 Lectures
	  2–3 Conversations
	Number of Questions:
	34–51
		Part 1 (2 Lectures, 1 Conversation + Questions)	

			30 minutes
		Part 2 (2 Lectures, 1 Conversations+Questions)	
			30 minutes
		Part 3* (2 Lectures ,1 Conversations+Questions)	
			30 minutes
		Total Section Time: 60–90 minutes	
	10 Minute Break		

Speaking Section	Number of Questions: 6
	  2 Independent
	  4 Integrated
		Total Section Time: 20 minutes	

Writing Section	Number of Tasks: 2
	  1 Integrated
	  1 Independent
		Integrated Task:	20 minutes

		Independent Task:	30 minutes
		Total Section Time: 50 minutes	

*These parts are experimental and will appear on <u>either</u> the Reading or Listening Section.

Scoring

You will receive a score for each section of the test. The score ranges per section are as follows:

Reading	0–30
Listening	0–30
Speaking	0–30
Writing	0–30

In order to calculate your total score, the score for each section are added together. Thus, the highest score you can possibly achieve on the TOEFL test is 120.

The reading and listening sections are both scored by computer. However, in order to determine your scores for the speaking and writing sections, your responses are saved and sent to ETS, where they are scored by certified raters. Each of the six responses in the speaking section are assigned a score of 0–4. The scores for each task are added together and converted into a score on the 30-point scale described above. Similarly, the two tasks on the writing section are given a score of 0–5. Again, the scores for both tasks are added together and then converted to a score of 0 to 30.

Score Reports

There are several ways to review your scores. First, you may view your scores online 15 business days after the test. All you have to do is visit the TOEFL website (http://www.ets.org/toefl) and sign into the "My TOEFL iBT account" with the username and password that you created when you registered for the test. Your online score report will show the following information:

» The date that you took the test

» Your scores for each section

» Your total score

» Performance evaluations for each section that describe whether your performance was low, medium, or high

You may access your scores online for tests that you have taken within the past two years. Please note that the universities and/or institutions that you have selected to receive your scores will also be able to view your scores online.

In addition to being able to access your scores online, you will receive a paper score report via mail two to three weeks after the test date.

TOEFL Test: What You'll See and Hear on the Day of the Test

Registration

There are a number of ways to register for the TOEFL iBT test.

» **Online Registration:** Visit the TOEFL website at http://www.ets.org/toefl and follow the instructions for registering. You will be able to find the nearest test center near you on the website, as well as dates for upcoming tests. Seats at test centers are limited, so be sure to register for the test early! You must register seven days before your desired test date. Late registration is also available up to three days before your desired test date, but you will be charged a late registration fee.

» **By Phone:** Visit the TOEFL website and download the registration form. Then, call your regional registration center (check website for phone numbers) and a representative will help you register. Late registration by phone is available until 5 p.m. the day before your desired test date.

» **By Mail:** Visit the TOEFL website and download, print and complete the registration form. Send your completed form with payment to your regional registration center four weeks before the desired test date.

For payment information and other details about the registration process, visit the TOEFL website at http://www.ets.org/toefl.

Before the Test Starts

When you arrive at the test center, you will sign in and give your identification document, such as a passport, to a test center employee (for information about accepted identification documents, see the ETS website at www.ets.org). Make sure that the name on your identification document matches the name under which you registered! If it does not match, you will not be allowed to take the test.

After you sign in, the employee at the test center will instruct you to put your personal belongings such as jackets, car keys, or cell phones into a storage area. Review the TOEFL website for rules about personal items. You will also be given a document that outlines the rules of the test. At the end of the document, you will see a statement of confidentiality. You are required to write this statement at the bottom of the page. Then you will sign and date the document and submit it to the employee.

Next, an employee at the test center will call your name. You will be asked to pose for a photograph in order to ensure that you are the person who signed up to take the test (this photo will appear on the paper copy of your score report). At this point, the employee will return your identification document. The employee will also give you two pencils and several sheets of blank paper for notes. You may be asked to show the employee the inside of your pockets to verify that you are not taking any unauthorized materials into the test room. Then, an employee will escort you to the computer on which you will be taking the test.

Screen-by-Screen Process

1. **Confirmation of Identity:** On the first screen, you will see your name and the photo that you took before you entered the test room. Before you proceed, you must confirm that the information is correct.

2. **Copyright Screen:** The next screen contains copyright information about the TOEFL test materials. To proceed, click "Continue".

3. **Test Introduction:** You will see a screen that contains general information about the test, including:

   - a general description of the TOEFL test

   - a short description of all four parts of the test

   - timing guidelines

   Once you have finished reading the introduction, click "Continue" to proceed to the next screen.

4. **Test Rules:** The next screen will describe the test policies. Be sure that you read the rules carefully and that you understand them, as breaking any of the rules may result in cancellation of your scores and you may lose your test fee. Click "Continue" when you've read and understood the rules.

5. **Confidentiality Statement:** You will see a confidentiality agreement on the next screen. The confidentiality agreement states that you will not share information about the test such as passages or questions with anyone. Read the statement carefully. By clicking "Continue" on this screen, you are agreeing to the terms of the confidentiality statement.

6. **Headset Instructions:** On the following screen, you will be instructed to put on your headset. The headset includes noise-cancelling headphones and a microphone. You are allowed to wear the headset throughout the entire test.

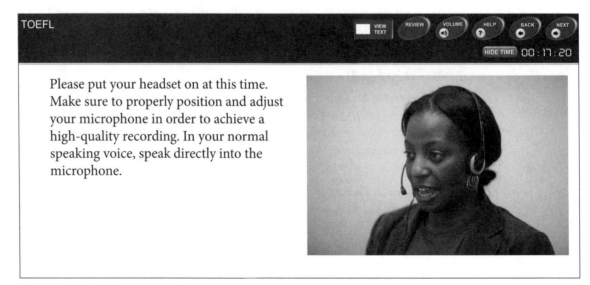

Please put your headset on at this time. Make sure to properly position and adjust your microphone in order to achieve a high-quality recording. In your normal speaking voice, speak directly into the microphone.

7. **Microphone Adjustment:** Next, you will see a screen that gives you instructions on how to adjust your microphone. You will be asked to speak a response to the following question: *Describe the city that you live in.* Please note that this portion is not graded and is only used to adjust your microphone. Just be sure to speak clearly and in your normal speaking voice.

You will continue to speak until a window appears that says "*Success: Your microphone is functioning properly*" appears.

If your microphone adjustment is not successful, readjust the microphone so that it is closer to your mouth and try again. If you continue having problems adjusting your microphone, raise your hand to get help from an employee at the test center.

Section Screens

At the beginning of each section, you will see a screen that gives you directions about that particular section. Please note that the on-screen tools will vary according to the section. For more information about the screen-by-screen process for each section, see the Overviews and Walk-throughs for the questions types.

On-screen Tools

Throughout the test, you will have access to a number of on-screen tools. The tools vary slightly by section. For example, in the reading section, you will have a button that allows you to review your answers. In the listening section, you will have buttons that allow you to confirm your answers before you proceed. For more information about the specific on-screen tools, please see the Overview for each section.

"Help" Button

During the reading and listening sections, you will see a "Help" Button on the toolbar at the top of the screen. By clicking on the "Help" button, you will be given instructions for:

» Using the on-screen tools

» Marking your answers

» Section directions, and

» Test directions

Please note that when you access the "Help" materials, the clock will keep running. If you must refer to the "Help" materials, be sure to do so quickly or you may waste precious time.

About the Break

After you've finished with the Listening Section, you are required to take a 10-minute break. The break screen will appear on the monitor. At this time, you may leave the test room. You will have to take your identification document with you. When you leave the test room, be sure to notify the test center employee. You may be required to sign out during the break.

When you are ready to return to the test room, you will have show the test employee the contents of your pockets once again. You may also have to sign back in. Then, the test center employee will escort you back to your seat and unlock the screen so you can continue the test.

Please note that while you are allowed to use the bathroom at any point during the test, the clock will <u>not</u> stop unless it is your designated break time. Therefore, to ensure that you have enough time to finish each section, it is wise to only leave the test room during the break.

When You're Done

1. **Score Reporting:** After you've completed the final task of the writing section, you will see the Score Reporting screen, which will give you the option of reporting or cancelling your scores. If you choose to cancel the scores, you will not be able to see your scores. Furthermore, you will not receive a refund of the test fee.

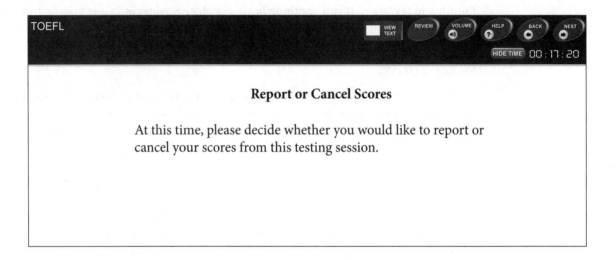

2. **Checking Out:** When you are finished, you may leave the test room. Be sure to bring your note paper and pencils and personal identification document. The test center employee will take back the pencils and note paper. You will sign out and indicate the time that you finished the test. Then you can get your personal belongings from the storage area and leave the test center.

Overview of the Reading Section

The reading section is the first part of the TOEFL® test. It tests your comprehension of written English by presenting you with a series of reading passages and then asking you a set of questions based on each one.

QUICK GUIDE: TOEFL Test Reading Section

Definition	The reading section tests your ability to understand written academic English. The section includes different types of reading passages that are based on a variety of academic subjects.
Targeted Skills	In order to do well on the reading section, you must be able to: • understand basic academic vocabulary in context. • quickly scan a written passage and understand its main ideas and supporting details. • understand how information is organized. • understand inferences, relationships, paraphrases, and the purpose of a passage. • answer questions within the given time.
The Reading Passages	The reading section includes three to five reading passages. Each passage is usually 650–700 words long. A typical reading section consists of three reading passages, each of which will appear on your screen and remain there while you answer the questions based on that passage. Please note that, on some occasions, the testing company ETS will include two additional reading passages as sample material. This sample material is not scored. However, you will not know which passages are sample materials, so you should try your best on <u>all</u> of the passages. There are three different types of passages in the reading section: expository, argumentative, and historical. In addition, each passage is arranged according to a particular organizational style, which include compare and contrast, cause and effect, problem and solution, theory and support, and classification. For more information about passage types and organizational styles, see pages 1–80.
Questions	There are typically 12–14 questions per reading passage. The questions are multiple choice and can usually be classified as one of the following question types: • Detail • Vocabulary • Referent • Sentence Summary • Negative Fact • Passage Summary • Function • Add Text • Inference • Table Completion
Timing	You will have **60 minutes** to read and answer the questions for a set of three reading passages. If you receive sample material for the reading section, which will add an additional two reading passages, you will have **100 minutes** to read and answer the questions for all five reading passages.

Reading Section: What You'll See and Hear

On-screen Tools

In the reading section, the information on the computer screen is slightly different than in other parts of the test. Study the sample screen below to familiarize yourself with the on-screen tools for the reading section.

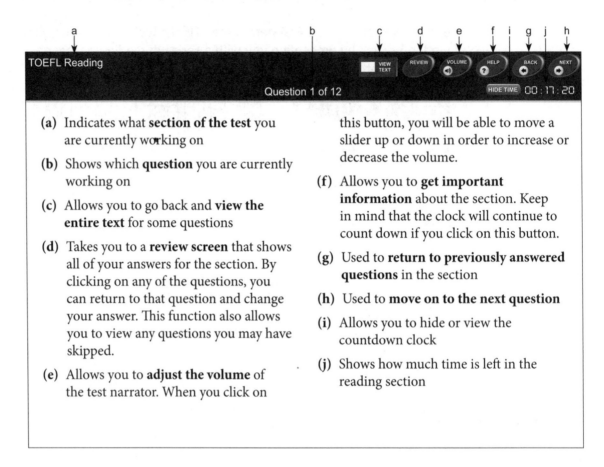

(a) Indicates what **section of the test** you are currently working on

(b) Shows which **question** you are currently working on

(c) Allows you to go back and **view the entire text** for some questions

(d) Takes you to a **review screen** that shows all of your answers for the section. By clicking on any of the questions, you can return to that question and change your answer. This function also allows you to view any questions you may have skipped.

(e) Allows you to **adjust the volume** of the test narrator. When you click on

this button, you will be able to move a slider up or down in order to increase or decrease the volume.

(f) Allows you to **get important information** about the section. Keep in mind that the clock will continue to count down if you click on this button.

(g) Used to **return to previously answered questions** in the section

(h) Used to **move on to the next question**

(i) Allows you to hide or view the countdown clock

(j) Shows how much time is left in the reading section

Screen-by-Screen Process

In the reading section, you will see a number of screens. By familiarizing yourself with the screens and the instructions, you will know exactly what to do on the day of the test.

1. **Instructions:** First, you will see a screen that gives you general information about the section, including information about how the section is organized and how much time you will have to complete the entire section. This screen also gives information about scoring and how to use the on-screen tools for the section. You must wait until the narrator has finished reading the instructions before you are allowed to move on to the next screen.

2. **Reading:** Once the section begins, a reading passage will appear on the right half of your screen. Note that the entire passage will not be viewable on the screen—you will have to use the scroll bar to view the rest of the passage. When you first see the passage, you should only scan it. In other words, you should quickly read through the passage, paying special attention to the important ideas and details. When you have finished scanning the passage, click on the "Continue" button.

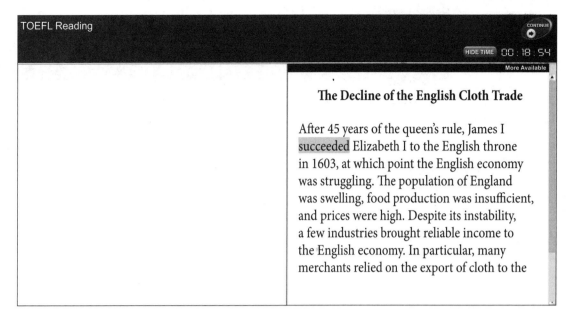

3. Questions: The questions for the passage will appear one at a time on the left side of the screen. Note that the paragraph that the question is based on will be marked with an arrow (→) in the passage. To mark your answer, click on the circle next to the answer option you want to choose. The circle will turn dark when it has been selected. To deselect an answer, click on the circle again. After selecting an answer option, click on the "Next" button to proceed to the next question. You may also click on the "Back" button in order to view the previous question and change the answer.

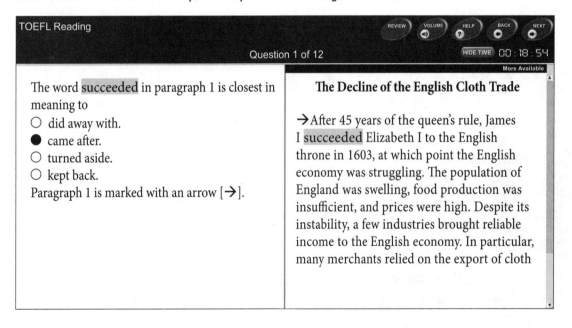

4. End of Section / Confirmation Screen: When the given time for the reading section is over, you will see a screen alerting you that the time is up. If you have viewed all of the questions in the reading section before the given time is over, you will see a confirmation screen that informs you of your options. If you want to continue working, you should click on the "Return" button. If you want to see the review screen in order to check your answers, click on the "Review" button. If you are finished and wish to proceed to the next section, click on "Continue." Remember, if you choose to continue, you will <u>not</u> be able to return to the section at a later time. Carefully consider whether you want to proceed or return to the questions in the section.

Review Screen

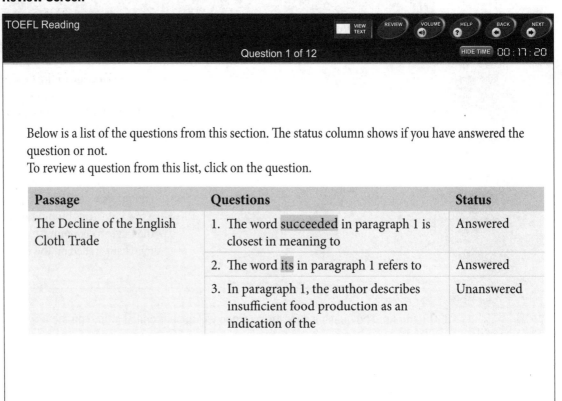

Reading Section: Passage Types

In the reading section, you will be presented with reading passages that are similar to texts that a student may encounter at a North American university. The topics for the reading passages are drawn from a wide range of academic subjects, including the following:

- anthropology
- archaeology
- art history
- astronomy
- botany
- biology
- education

- engineering
- environmental science
- history
- geology
- geography
- literature
- marketing

- music
- paleontology
- photography
- psychology
- sociology
- urban studies

There are three types of passages on the reading section: expository, argumentative, and historical. Typically, a reading section will consist of at least one of each passage type.

Passage Type	Definition	Sample Topics
Expository	Provides a general explanation of a topic	• Types of Camouflage • Adaptations of Deep Sea Fish • Important Traditions of the Bambara Culture
Argumentative	Provides a point of view and gives several reasons to support that point of view	• Evidence of Contact Between Pacific Cultures and Indigenous Americans • Recuperation Theory vs. Circadian Theory of Sleep • How Non-Native Species Hurt Local Habitats
Historical	Focuses on past events	• History of the Telescope • The Effects of the Norman Conquest • Journalism and Social Change in the Twentieth Century

Organizational Styles

Each passage will usually feature a specific organizational style. An organizational style describes how the ideas in a passage are arranged.

Common Organizational Styles of Reading Passages	
Organizational Style	**Description**
Classification	Describes two or three different categories of something
Compare / Contrast	Discusses similarities and differences between two or more things
Cause / Effect	Explains the causes and effects of something
Theory / Support	Presents a theory and provides support for it
Problem / Solution	Presents a problem and discusses solutions

Challenges and Solutions

» **CHALLENGE 1: "I don't know a lot of the words that I see in the passages or in the questions."**

SOLUTION: Expand your vocabulary. There are several tools that you can use to increase your vocabulary. For one, there are several word lists available that present the most common words found in academic settings. The Academic Word List, developed by Averil Coxhead, is a list of 570 words that are commonly included in introductory college texts. Getting to know these words will likely help you perform better on the test and prepare you for entering English-language courses. For more information on the Academic Word List, see page 170.

SOLUTION: Use a learner's dictionary when you study. Dictionaries such as the *Collins Cobuild Advanced Dictionary* offer clear definitions, sample sentences, grammar, illustrations, and photographs to help you expand your knowledge and use of everyday and academic vocabulary. In this book, you will find definitions for challenging or unfamiliar words, much like you would in the TOEFL reading passages. These definitions come from the *Collins Cobuild Advanced Dictionary*.

SOLUTION: Use context clues. Context clues are the words and phrases that surround key words. Using these clues will help you determine the meanings of unfamiliar words. The author may use a number of strategies to provide context clues for key words, including giving examples of the key word, contrasting the meaning of the key word with an opposite idea, or giving an indirect definition of a key word. For more information about these strategies, see the table in Lesson 3B on page 44. To practice finding and using context clues, try reading a 300-word excerpt from a newspaper or a college textbook. Pay attention to the strategies that the authors use to help you figure out the definitions of difficult words.

Strategies for Using Context Clues		
Strategy	**Key Words**	**Example**
Pay attention to **examples** that appear near the highlighted word. If you are familiar with the examples, you can use them to determine the meaning of the highlighted word.	such as including consists of this includes like	The photographs show banal activities, like going to the grocery store or doing household chores.
Look for key words that signal a **contrast** from a previous idea. If you know the meanings of the words from surrounding sentences, you'll know that the highlighted word has an opposite meaning.	Unlike X . . . On the other hand, X . . . While . . . But . . . However . . .	Unlike most mammals, few of which are venomous, the platypus produces a **noxious** substance that can cause extreme pain in humans.
Look for **indirect definitions** of terms in the sentences that surround the highlighted word. These definitions may include an easier synonym of the highlighted word or information that helps clarify its meaning.	and meaning that	In the southwestern United States, the sunflower is ubiquitous, and it is difficult to find a garden that doesn't include the plant.

SOLUTION: Learn how to look at word parts, like prefixes and suffixes, to determine the meanings of unknown words. Many English words are formed through the use of prefixes, which go at the beginnings of words, and suffixes, which go on the ends of words. By learning the meanings of common English prefixes and suffixes, you will be able to guess the definitions of unknown words. For more information, see the table in Lesson 3B on page 45.

» **CHALLENGE 2: "I often run out of time before completing all of the questions."**

SOLUTION: Use skimming and scanning skills to find the answers to the questions. Skimming is when you quickly read a passage, paying attention only to the most important ideas. By skimming, you can often identify the key ideas that many questions are based on in a short amount of time. This way, you can avoid running out of time during the test.

In order to skim effectively, make sure you know where to find the most important ideas. Regardless of the different organizational styles for passages, important ideas often appear in the same places. See the table below for information on where to find a passage's most important ideas.

Part of the Passage	Skimming Strategy
Introduction	• Read **the last two–three lines** in the introductory paragraph. These lines will typically describe the main idea of the passage.
Body Paragraphs	• Read **the first two–three lines** in the body paragraphs. These sentences will describe the main ideas of the paragraphs. • Read **the last two–three lines** in the body paragraphs. These lines will often explain how each paragraph relates to the main idea of the passage. These lines will also help you understand how the body paragraphs are related to one another.

Scanning is when you read the passage quickly in order to find specific key words or ideas. After you've read a question and its answer options, you should make note of any key words or ideas, like names, terms, or numbers, that will help you answer the question. Then, scan the passage, looking specifically for those key words.

Remember, you don't need to understand every word perfectly while you skim or scan a passage. The most important part is to find the information you need in order to answer the questions quickly and correctly.

To practice skimming and scanning, find an article with 600–700 words in a college textbook. First, skim the article and write down the most important ideas on a piece of scrap paper. Then, try scanning the article for key words and dates. The more you practice skimming and scanning, the faster and more accurate you will get, so try to practice every day.

SOLUTION: Pay attention to the on-screen clock. This clock displays how much time you have left in the section. You should not spend more than 20 minutes on each reading passage. While you work on the questions, be sure to glance at the clock. On the reading section, you are able to return to unanswered questions later, so be sure to take advantage of this feature. If you take more than two minutes on a question, skip it and return to it later. This will help you avoid getting stuck on one question and wasting your time.

» **CHALLENGE 3: "The passages are often complicated and confusing—sometimes I get lost as I'm reading them."**

SOLUTION: Understand the basic organizational styles found on the reading section of the TOEFL test. If you lose concentration or become confused while you are reading, you just have to think about how the passage is structured in order to get back on track. See the table below for the most common organizational structures of the reading passages and how the information in these passages is often arranged.

	Classification	Compare / Contrast	Cause / Effect	Problem / Solution	Theory / Support
Introduction	Introduces what will be classified in the passage	Introduces two ideas, things, or events	Introduces an event or process	Introduces a problem	Introduces a theory
Body Paragraphs	Present 2–3 **different types or features** of the subject being classified	The first body paragraph describes several **features of the first subject**. In the following paragraphs, the author presents **corresponding features of the second subject**, pointing out how these are **similar to or different from** those of the first subject.	The first body paragraph describes 1–2 **causes** for an event or process. Then, the author describes the **effects**, or consequences, of the causes.	Provide 2–3 **solutions** to the problem	Provide 2–3 **pieces of evidence** to support the theory

To practice, read each of the passages in this book. See if you can identify the organizational structure of each passage. Make note of how the body paragraphs are organized.

SOLUTION: Look for transition language as you read. Transition language includes words and phrases that are used to connect the ideas in different sentences. For example, some transition words signal the introduction of a new topic (e.g., "Another example of X is . . ."), while others signal a process or sequence of events (e.g., "First . . ."). Transition words often appear at the beginning of a new paragraph, though they can appear in the middle part of a paragraph as well. By paying attention to transition words and how they are used, you can get a better sense of what is happening in the passage. In turn, this will help you avoid becoming confused by the information in the passage. For a more detailed discussion on transition words and to practice identifying them, see page 67.

» **CHALLENGE 4: "There's too much information to remember!"**

Solution: Don't worry about remembering every detail from the passage. In the reading section, the passages will <u>always</u> appear on the right side of the screen while you answer the questions. The paragraph that the question is based on will be marked with an arrow [→], and you will be able to scroll through the paragraph as you answer the question in order to find any information you may need.

SOLUTION: On your scrap paper, create a quick outline of the passage. Just because you have access to the passage while you answer the questions doesn't mean that it's not helpful to write down notes in certain instances. For example, while you skim the passage, you can create a quick outline of the basic points in the reading. You should try to use abbreviation strategies so you don't spend too much time writing your outline. Then, you can use this outline as a quick reference while you answer the questions. The outline does not need to contain all of the details from the passage, but it should contain the main ideas, which can be helpful when answering nearly all of the question types. See below for a sample outline for a reading passage. This outline is based on the passage on page 23.

- Age of Bradshaws: unsure, wasp nest
- 2 theories about who created Bradshaws
  - Australian Aborigines
    - similar to Aboriginal artwork
  - 1st humans in Aust.
    - human migration studies
    - canoes, animals in paintings

Note that while the outline is very brief, it still contains the most important ideas from the passage. Furthermore, the outline reflects the basic organization of the passage, which would be especially helpful for table completion or passage summary questions. Regardless of what question type you are working on, by writing this information down, you may find that you understand the basic ideas of the passage better and remember them more clearly.

SOLUTION: Write down key words and ideas as you read the questions and answer options. Some people find it helpful to highlight key words while they read. However, on the day of the test, you will <u>not</u> be able to highlight any portion of the text on the computer screen. Instead, you can use your notepaper to write down any key words that will help you remember important ideas from the questions or the answer options. Then, you can refer to your list of key words and quickly scan for them in the reading passage.

» **CHALLENGE 5:** "I have a hard time telling the difference between major supporting details and minor facts."

SOLUTION: Try to understand the role of the details in the passage. By understanding how the details that you are confused about relate to the ideas in the passage, you will be able to sort the major details from the minor ideas. Use the steps in the table below to start understanding the roles of details in a passage.

	Steps For Differentiating Between Major Supporting Details and Minor Facts
Step 1	Skim the first paragraph to find the topic sentence. Topic sentences are sentences that express the main topic of a passage or paragraph. Regardless of the passage type or organizational style of a passage, each reading will have a major point that it is trying to make.
	The introduction will usually provide a brief background of the main topic and then present a topic sentence that summarizes the main point of the passage.
Step 2	Skim the body paragraphs to find the topic sentence for each paragraph. The topic sentences are usually located within the first two or three lines of the body paragraphs.
	By locating the topic sentences, you can start to understand what the main argument of the passage is and how the author has organized the flow of ideas.
Step 3	Once you've located the topic sentences and the main point of the passage is clear to you, quickly review the details that you are unsure about. Again, when you review details, make sure you scan the passage for the key words associated with those details in order to save time.
Step 4	When you read a sentence containing a detail you are unsure about, ask yourself the following question: If you were to leave out that particular detail, would the main point of the passage be weakened?
	If the answer is yes, the detail in question is probably a major detail. On the other hand, if leaving out the detail would not majorly change or weaken the main point of the passage, then the detail is a minor fact.

» **CHALLENGE 6: "None of the answer options 'feels' right."**

SOLUTION: Familiarize yourself with the question types and the skills required to answer each one. On the reading section, there are 10 possible question types. By learning which skills each question type tests, you will better understand what to look for in a correct answer, which should help improve your intuition about the correct answers. Study the *Quick Guides* for each question type, located at the beginning of each lesson.

SOLUTION: Understand how correct answer options are created. While the correct answers on the reading section will vary in many ways, remember that one common feature of correct answer options is the rewording of key information. A correct answer option will <u>always</u> contain key information that you've read in the passage. However, the information is typically mixed up so that the correct answer option doesn't use the exact wording from the reading. In other words, the correct answer option will include paraphrased information from the reading passage. Information in answer options may be paraphrased by:

- changing out key words (i.e., using synonyms).
- including general information about a concept that is described in detail in the passage.
- changing the voice of the information from active to passive (or vice versa). The passive voice is formed by using the verb *be* + past participle.

To practice recognizing paraphrased information, complete an activity in the reading section of this book, then try to identify the paraphrase types used in some of the answer options. This may help you improve your ability to recognize correct and incorrect answers.

SOLUTION: Use a process of elimination. A process of elimination involves reading each answer option carefully and eliminating options that are incorrect. Typically, you can eliminate answer options that contain:

- information that contradicts the facts and details presented in the passage.
- information that does <u>not</u> answer the question.
- the exact wording from the passage. Remember, the correct answer typically paraphrases information from the passage, so an answer option that includes the same wording is probably incorrect.

SOLUTION: Skip questions you are unsure about. Remember, you are allowed to return to previous questions on the reading section. However, you have only 60 minutes to answer all of the questions in this section. For some people, it's easier to answer difficult questions once they've had some time to think about them. So if you find that you're spending too much time on one question and you aren't certain of the answer, move on to the next question or the next passage. You may find that it's easier to answer a difficult question when you return to it later.

Overview of Question Types on the Reading Section

Question Type	Description	Frequency Per Reading Passage
Detail	Asks you about factual information presented in a reading passage.	3–5
Referent	Asks you to identify the word or phrase that another word refers to—usually a pronoun.	1
Negative Fact	Asks you to recognize the answer option that is not true according to the passage.	1
Function	Asks you about the rhetorical strategies used by the author. Is the author trying to give an example, explain or clarify something, challenge a point, etc.?	1
Inference	Asks you to draw a conclusion based on the information presented in the passage.	1
Vocabulary	Asks you to choose the definition that best describes how a highlighted word or phrase is used in the passage.	2–4
Sentence Summary	Asks you to choose the answer that provides the best summary of a highlighted sentence from a passage.	1
Passage Summary	Presents you with an introductory statement for the passage, then asks you to choose three answer options that best summarize the main idea of the passage.	1
Add Text	Asks you to determine where a given sentence will fit best in a passage.	1
Table Completion	Asks you to categorize information into a table format.	1

Detail Questions

Detail questions ask you about factual information presented in a reading passage. They are the most common type of question in the reading section, and you can expect three to five detail questions per reading passage.

Detail questions may be worded as follows:

» *According to paragraph 1, what is true about X?*

» *According to paragraph 2, why was the discovery of X significant?*

» *What do X and Y have in common?*

» *According to paragraph 3, which of the following was responsible for X?*

» *In paragraph 4, what does the author say about X?*

QUICK GUIDE: Detail Questions

Definition	Detail questions ask about important facts presented in the reading passage that support the main points of the reading. They are often based on supporting facts, definitions of key terms, and the order of events described in the passage.
Targeted Skills	In order to answer a detail question correctly, you must be able to: • identify the main points of the reading and the details used to support them. Be prepared to answer questions about secondary details as well. • understand the relationships between two events or concepts (Is one caused by the other? Did one occur after the other? Is one more important than the other?). • read the question carefully and understand what information it is asking for. • scan the passage for specific details that you can use to determine the correct answer.
The Correct Answer	The correct answer for a detail question contains factual information that was presented in the reading. Correct answers can usually be found in one or two sentences in the passage and typically contain reworded information from the reading.
Wrong Answer Options	Watch out for answer options that: • include information that contradicts the information given in the reading. • use the exact wording from the reading but don't answer the question. The correct answer usually rewords the information. • include information that is <u>not</u> mentioned or supported by the reading.

WALK THROUGH: Detail Questions

A Quickly read the sample detail question below. Underline any key words in the question and the answer options that will help you determine the correct answer.

TOEFL Reading

VIEW TEXT | REVIEW | VOLUME | HELP | BACK | NEXT

Question 1 of 12

HIDE TIME 00:17:20

1. According to paragraph 2, what is true about the repetition strategy used in ancient India?
   ○ It allowed users to add new details to narratives.
   ○ It is more complex than other repetition methods.
   ○ It was only used to memorize sacred texts.
   ○ It required users to remember entire paragraphs at a time.

B Now read part of a passage about literature. While you read, underline words or phrases that you think will help you answer the question in Part A. When you are done, mark the correct answer for the question above.

Oral Narratives

[1] Oral narratives are stories that are communicated through speech and not through the written word. Most cultures have important oral narratives that allow them to pass on traditional stories to younger generations. Amazingly, these can survive for many years without experiencing significant changes. Oral narratives remain unchanged for many years due to specific memorization techniques that help storytellers preserve the original form of the narrative.

[2] One such technique is repetition, which involves saying the words of a story many times. For instance, a storyteller might repeat the same sentence many times until he or she remembers it. Once one sentence is memorized, the storyteller repeats the next sentence until it, too, is committed to memory. Thus, sentence by sentence, one can learn a complete narrative. Of course, some forms of repetition are more complicated than the method just described. For example, in ancient India, people memorized sacred texts by repeating the words in a different order. If a sentence read, "She went to the river to wash her clothes," a person might memorize the sentence by repeating the words like this: "She went she, went to went, to the to, went to the to," and so on.

[3] Another important way to memorize oral narratives is through the use of musical memory, which refers to a person's ability to remember pitch. Like notes in a song, some words in a story have higher or lower pitch than the surrounding words. Someone listening to an oral narrative might remember these changes in pitch, and this can help the person remember the changes in the story. If one part of the story is exciting, the storyteller's voice may become higher in pitch. The listener will record this in his or her musical memory, and when the listener retells the story, his or her voice will become higher at the same moment.

Glossary:

ⒺⓌ POWERED BY COBUILD

sacred: something that is believed to be holy and to have a connection to God

pitch: how high or low a sound is

GET IT RIGHT: Tips and Tasks for Answering Correctly

» **TIP 1: Read the question carefully.** The wording of detail questions varies widely, so make sure you read the question carefully and understand exactly what it is asking for. Is it asking about a main detail or a secondary detail? Does it ask when an event occurred, or is it asking about the cause and effect relationship between two events?

TASK 1: Underline the words or phrases in the question on page 14 that help you understand what information you need to answer the question.

» **TIP 2: Scan the paragraph that the question is based on**. The answer for detail questions can typically be found in one or two sentences from the reading passage. When you scan the paragraph the question is based on, look for key words that will help you answer the question.

TASK 2: Scan paragraph 2 in the passage on page 14 and draw a box around words or expressions that will help you choose the correct answer.

» **TIP 3: Watch out for answer options that use the same wording as the passage**. Correct answers for detail questions usually contain reworded information from the reading. Be cautious of answer choices that contain exact wording from the reading—they may not include the information that the question is asking for.

TASK 3: For the question on page 14, draw a line through one answer option that uses exact wording from the reading.

» **TIP 4: Eliminate answer options that are inaccurate according to the passage**. Detail questions are always based on facts from the passage. Therefore, any answer option that is false according to the information in the passage is incorrect.

TASK 4: Draw a line through two of the remaining answer options on page 14 that are inaccurate according to the information in the passage.

» **TIP 5: Guess wisely!** Detail questions are often asked about supporting details for main points. If you are having a difficult time choosing the correct answer, choose the answer option that coincides with the main idea of the paragraph that the question is based on.

TASK 5: Circle one sentence in paragraph 2 in the passage on page 14 that summarizes the main idea of the entire paragraph. Does the answer you marked as correct support this topic sentence?

TEST TIP!

Don't spend too much time on one question. Remember, on the reading section of the TOEFL test, you are allowed to return to previous questions in the section as long as you have time. Therefore, if you are having trouble with one question, don't be afraid to move on to the next one. Just be sure to make a note of the question number so you remember to return to it later.

Referent Questions

A referent question asks you to identify the word or phrase that another word refers to. The most common type of referent question will include a pronoun. A pronoun is a word that takes the place of a noun or noun phrase in a sentence. On the TOEFL test, personal pronouns are most commonly tested, though on occasion referent questions may be based on relative, demonstrative, or reflexive pronouns, in addition to other words. See the table below for some examples.

Pronouns or Other Words	Examples
Personal Pronouns: I, you, he / she / it, we, they, me, him / her, us, them	**Susie** went to the lab. <u>She</u> didn't come back until later.
Relative Pronouns: which / that, who / whom / whose, whatever, what	Rick replaced the **window** <u>that</u> was broken during the storm.
Demonstrative Pronouns: this, that, these, those	The **apples** were in the bowl. Alan used <u>these</u> to bake a pie.
Reflexive Pronouns: myself, yourself, herself, himself, itself, ourselves, themselves	The **baseball players** entertained <u>themselves</u> by singing.
Other Words: any, so, one	Sarina and Ben went to buy **supplies** at the store. They couldn't find <u>any</u>.

Note: In these examples, the pronoun is <u>underlined</u> and the referent is in **bold**.

There is typically no more than one referent question per reading passage.

Referent questions may be worded as follows:

» *The word X in paragraph 2 refers to . . .*

QUICK GUIDE: Referent Questions

Definition	Referent questions will specify a pronoun in the passage by highlighting it in gray. The answer options will be words or phrases from the passage. You must choose the answer option that indicates the referent of the highlighted pronoun.
Targeted Skills	In order to correctly answer a referent question, you must be able to: • understand grammatical agreement between nouns and pronouns. • identify the referent of a pronoun that is highlighted in a passage.
The Correct Answer	The correct answer for a referent question correctly identifies the referent of the highlighted pronoun. The referent will agree with the highlighted pronoun in number, gender, or case. In most cases, the referent will appear before the pronoun in the passage.
Wrong Answer Options	Watch out for answer options that: • do not agree with the highlighted pronoun in number, gender, or case. • appear immediately before the highlighted word. While the correct answer usually appears before the pronoun, the referent is not usually the noun that immediately precedes the pronoun. • change the meaning of the sentence so that it contradicts the facts presented in the passage.

WALK THROUGH: Referent Questions

A Quickly read the sample referent questions below. Underline any key words in the questions and the answer choices that will help you determine the correct answers.

TOEFL Reading

VIEW TEXT   REVIEW   VOLUME   HELP   BACK   NEXT

Question 1 of 12

HIDE TIME   00:17:20

1. The word it in paragraph 1 refers to
   ○ the fifteenth century.
   ○ Venice, Italy.
   ○ Europe.
   ○ a top producer.
2. The word they in paragraph 2 refers to
   ○ the city's legacy.
   ○ printers.
   ○ books.
   ○ historians.

B Now read the sample passage. While you read, underline the sentences that contain the answer options for the questions above. When you are done reading, mark the correct answers for the questions above.

Printing in Venice

¹ In 1455, a German goldsmith named Johannes Gutenberg invented the printing press, changing the way that people received new information thereafter. Not long after that, hundreds of print shops had opened throughout Europe. However, one city in particular emerged as the leader in printing by the end of the fifteenth century: Venice, Italy. Printing nearly a quarter of all books in Europe during the 1490s, it was a top producer of books. This success, which continued well into the 1500s, was due to several factors.

² Long before the first print shop opened in Venice in 1469, the city was known as a major trade capital in Europe. For centuries, Venice had been an important stop on many trade routes, allowing Venetian merchants to establish partnerships with businesses based in many international locations across Europe and Asia. The city's legacy as a trade hub proved useful for printers in the fifteenth century because it was relatively easy to sell and distribute the books that they produced. According to historians, many printers in Venice created books specifically for export to other countries.

³ Another factor that allowed Venetian printers to flourish was the abundance of skilled and educated workers who resided in the city. Indeed, throughout the 1400s, Venice was home to a large and diverse population of scholars. These scholars not only provided manuscripts for printing, but were able to edit works created by other people as well. As a result, editing and printing a manuscript in Venice was relatively inexpensive. In some cases, printing costs in Venice were a third of what they were in other printing centers in Europe.

Glossary:

POWERED BY COBUILD

hub: an important center for activity

flourish: to be successful and develop quickly and strongly

GET IT RIGHT: Tips and Tasks for Answering Correctly

» **TIP 1: Reread the paragraph in which the highlighted word appears.** When you do this, be sure to pay attention to the nouns that are used as answer options for the question. Also, look for context clues that will help you eliminate incorrect answer options.

TASK 1: Scan paragraphs 1 and 2 in the passage on page 17. Underline four words or expressions in paragraph 1 that are used as answer options for question 1. Underline four words or expressions in paragraph 2 that are used as answer options for question 2.

» **TIP 2: Try replacing the highlighted word with each of the answer options.** When you do this, you can eliminate answer options that:

- contradict the facts in the passage. You may find that more than one answer option works. However, one of them may change the meaning of the sentence so that it is no longer accurate according to the passage.

- don't agree with the pronoun in terms of number, gender, or case. See the table below for a brief explanation of grammatical agreement.

Type of Agreement	Explanation	Examples
Number	Refers to whether the noun and the corresponding pronoun are singular or plural	*Correct:* The **students** sat in the classroom. They didn't know when the class would start. *Incorrect:* The **students** sat in the office. He didn't know when the class would start.
Gender	Refers to whether the noun and the corresponding pronoun are masculine or feminine	*Correct:* The **man** left his keys on the table, where he could find them easily. *Incorrect:* The **man** left his keys on the table, where she could find them easily.
Case	Refers to whether the noun and the corresponding pronoun are the object or subject	*Correct:* **Peter** arrived late, so he couldn't find a seat. *Incorrect:* **Peter** arrived late, so him couldn't find a seat.

Note: In these examples, the pronoun is underlined and the referent is in **bold**.

TASK 2: For **question 1** on page 17, draw a line through one answer option that contradicts the facts from the passage when used in place of the pronoun. For question 2 on page 17, draw a line through one answer option that doesn't agree with the number of the pronoun.

PROGRESSIVE PRACTICE: Get Ready

A Scan the short passage about theater. Underline the main idea of each paragraph.

English Renaissance Theater

[1] As European societies changed dramatically in the sixteenth and seventeenth centuries, artistic expression changed as well. England offers a clear example—in the early sixteenth century, a new type of theater, called English Renaissance theater, flourished there. English Renaissance theater was popular through the mid-seventeenth century and featured the work of famous playwrights like Christopher Marlowe and William Shakespeare. This new theatrical style, which was more for entertainment and less for promoting religious values, developed because of a number of changes in England.

[2] One major reason for the popularity of English Renaissance theater was that it reflected the cultural changes that were occurring in England at the time. One such change was the ongoing attempts to distinguish the practices and beliefs of the English from those of cultures in mainland Europe. In the theater, this was accomplished by breaking from the types of plays that were trendy at the time throughout Europe. These typically featured religious themes and were intended to teach the audience moral lessons. They were common in English theater until the early sixteenth century. However, as social change occurred in the 1500s, morality plays became less prevalent in England. Instead, theater companies borrowed heavily from classical Greek tragedies and comedies to create new Renaissance-style pieces. The plays of William Shakespeare are well-known examples—he wrote about tragic love stories, comedic love stories, and the histories of royal families. These themes, which prioritized entertainment over moral lessons, became widespread throughout England.

[3] During the same period, English theater companies and performance spaces also underwent a number of changes that helped bolster English Renaissance theater. Before the sixteenth century, theater groups in England consisted of traveling companies that went from town to town performing the same morality plays. But starting in the mid-sixteenth century, English nobility began funding the construction of theaters throughout the country. These public spaces housed companies of actors, who enjoyed the support and sponsorship of different noble families. Many theaters became recognized as public spaces devoted to entertainment, and gradually, the traveling companies of morality actors disappeared completely. Moreover, because many acting companies received financial support from noble families, they had the resources to create more and more Renaissance pieces and perform them in these spaces.

Glossary:

POWERED BY COBUILD

trendy: something that is fashionable and modern

bolster: to increase or strengthen something

B Read the questions carefully. What types of questions are they? Underline any key words in the questions and answer options that you will look for while you review the passage. Then, answer the questions. Note the correct answers and read why the answer options are correct or incorrect.

1. According to paragraph 2, which of the following best describes popular theater in mainland Europe during the 1500s?

   ○ It was based on Greek plays.

   ○ Its primary goal was to teach lessons.

   ○ It featured the work of William Shakespeare.

   ○ It was developed in churches.

ANSWER ANALYSIS ▶

Question Type: **Detail**

    ✗ The author states that English Renaissance theater, not European theater, borrowed from Greek plays.

    ✓ **The passage mentions that morality plays were popular in Europe and that they taught lessons.**

    ✗ The passage says that English Renaissance theater featured works by William Shakespeare.

    ✗ The author mentions that morality plays featured religious themes, but it does not say where the plays developed.

2. The word those in paragraph 2 refers to

    ○ cultural changes.

    ○ ongoing attempts.

    ○ practices and beliefs.

    ○ the English.

ANSWER ANALYSIS ▶

Question Type: **Referent**

    ✗ If "cultural changes" replaced the highlighted pronoun, the sentence would not make sense.

    ✗ If "ongoing attempts" replaced the highlighted pronoun, the sentence would not make sense.

    ✓ **The pronoun is referring to practices and beliefs.**

    ✗ Remember, the answer for referent questions is rarely the noun that is closest to the pronoun.

3. According to paragraph 3, what role did noble families play in the growth of English Renaissance theater?

    ○ They discouraged the production of morality plays.

    ○ They formed traveling companies that could perform new plays.

    ○ They provided inspiration for new types of plays.

    ○ They paid to have public theater spaces built.

ANSWER ANALYSIS ▶

Question Type: **Detail**

    ✗ The author says that noble families supported English Renaissance theater, not that they tried to prevent morality plays.

    ✗ The author says that traveling companies disappeared because noble families supported local acting companies.

    ✗ In paragraph 2, the author says that English Renaissance theater featured stories about royal families, but these are not the same as noble families. Also, the question indicates that the answer appears in paragraph 3.

    ✓ **The author says that noble families funded the construction of public theaters.**

4. The word they in paragraph 3 refers to

    ○ public spaces.

    ○ morality actors.

    ○ acting companies.

    ○ noble families.

ANSWER ANALYSIS ▶

Question Type: **Referent**

    ✗ Public spaces are referred to at the end of the sentence ("these spaces"), so this cannot be the answer.

    ✗ The author says that morality actors disappeared. If this choice replaced the pronoun, the sentence would not make sense.

    ✓ **The pronoun is referring to acting companies.**

    ✗ While "noble families" agrees in number with the pronoun, this choice does not make sense.

PROGRESSIVE PRACTICE: Get Set

A Scan the short passage about music. Write the main idea of each paragraph.

1. _____

2. _____

3. _____

4. _____

Ástor Piazzolla and Nuevo Tango

[1] Tango is a type of music that originated among immigrant communities in Argentina and Uruguay during the mid-1800s. Today, tango remains iconic in its countries of origin and can still be heard in the homes of many Argentines and Uruguayans, though some musicians have made efforts to modernize the genre. One such artist was Ástor Piazzolla, who based his *nuevo tango*, or new tango, on traditional Argentine tango. Piazzolla's nuevo tango retains elements of traditional tango, but it is also distinct in several ways.

[2] Piazzolla was born to Italian parents in Argentina. However, he spent most of his childhood in New York City. Throughout his early years, Piazzolla missed Argentina and felt a connection to his native country's tango music, the lyrics of which often describe nostalgia for one's home country. Piazzolla began to explore traditional Argentine music by learning how to play the *bandoneón*, an accordion-like instrument that is often employed in tango music. At sixteen, Piazzolla returned to Argentina, where he was widely considered a highly skilled bandoneón player. In fact, he was often invited to play with Argentine orchestras and bands before his own music gained popularity. The bandoneón also featured prominently in his nuevo tango music.

[3] While there were clear influences of traditional Argentine tango in his work, Piazzolla's nuevo tango also reflected the other types of music he was exposed to as a young man. For example, growing up in New York, he developed an interest in jazz. Not surprisingly, he often incorporated rhythms from this music into many of his pieces. Furthermore, he learned about classical music by composers like Johann Sebastian Bach through his parents and later through his musical studies. Piazzolla used classical ideas in his work, such as counterpoint, which is when two or more voices sing using different rhythms but work together to create the harmony of a piece. Between jazz and classical influences, Piazzolla's tango was very different from the traditional tango of Argentina.

[4] Another unique element of Piazzolla's nuevo tango music is its experimental tendency. Piazzolla was always looking for new and interesting pieces to incorporate into his own music. In 1956, Piazzolla released an album that combined his music with the poetry of writer Jorge Luis Borges. Throughout the album, Borges's romantic and emotional poetry was narrated over Piazzolla's nuevo tango music. This unique collaboration sparked outcries from traditional tango musicians, who considered Piazzolla's style to be too experimental.

Glossary:

POWERED BY COBUILD

iconic: to be a symbol of something

genre: a particular type of literature, music, film, or other art that has special characteristics

B Read the questions carefully and note whether they are referent or detail questions. Then, answer the questions. Write the letter of each answer option next to the reason in the *Answer Analysis* box explaining why it is correct or incorrect.

1. The word it in paragraph 1 refers to

   ○ origin. [A]

   ○ the genre. [B]

   ○ nuevo tango. [C]

   ○ traditional tango. [D]

ANSWER ANALYSIS ▶

Question Type: **Referent**

_____ ✗ The author is referring to nuevo tango, not to traditional tango.

_____ ✗ If "origin" replaced the pronoun, the sentence would not make sense.

_____ ✓ **The pronoun is referring to nuevo tango.**

_____ ✗ Replacing the pronoun with "the genre" would change the meaning of the sentence.

2. According to paragraph 2, what aspect of Piazzolla's nuevo tango is directly inspired by traditional Argentine tango?

○ His use of the bandoneón [A]

○ The lyrics of his music [B]

○ His tendency to write music for large orchestras [C]

○ The focus on childhood experiences [D]

ANSWER ANALYSIS ▶

Question Type: **Detail**

_____ ✗ The passage mentions Piazzolla's childhood, but there is no mention of this being a part of Piazzolla's music.

_____ ✓ **The author says that the bandoneón is often used in tango music and that Piazzolla used the instrument.**

_____ ✗ The author mentions this as a feature of Argentine tango, but there is no indication that Piazzolla used it in his own music.

_____ ✗ The passage says that Piazzolla played with Argentine orchestras, but not whether he wrote for them.

3. The phrase this music in paragraph 3 refers to

○ Argentine tango. [A]

○ nuevo tango. [B]

○ jazz. [C]

○ classical music. [D]

ANSWER ANALYSIS ▶

Question Type: **Referent**

_____ ✗ Piazzolla's pieces are what created the nuevo tango genre, so this cannot be the correct choice.

_____ ✓ **The pronoun is referring to jazz.**

_____ ✗ "Classical music" could replace the pronoun, but it would change the meaning of the sentence.

_____ ✗ While "Argentine tango" could take the place of the pronoun, the meaning of the sentence would change.

4. According to paragraph 4, the experimental quality of Piazzolla's work resulted in

○ the inspiration of a work of poetry. [A]

○ disapproval from traditional Argentine musicians. [B]

○ collaborations with musicians in various genres. [C]

○ his lasting popularity in his home country. [D]

ANSWER ANALYSIS ▶

Question Type: **Detail**

_____ ✗ The author says that Piazzolla worked with a writer, not with other musicians.

_____ ✗ The author does not say that the poetry was inspired by Piazzolla's experimental music.

_____ ✓ **The last sentence says that Piazzolla's experimental style sparked outcries from traditional musicians, which means that they disapproved.**

_____ ✗ While Piazzolla was popular in his home country, the experimental quality of his music caused some people to dislike it.

PROGRESSIVE PRACTICE: Go for the TOEFL Test

Read the passage about a topic in art history.

TOEFL Reading

VIEW TEXT   REVIEW   VOLUME   HELP   BACK   NEXT

Question 1 of 12

HIDE TIME 00 : 17 : 20

Bradshaw Rock Paintings

[1] In 1891, Australian farmer John Bradshaw discovered a rock painting in the Kimberley region of western Australia while taking his cattle out to graze. The rock painting that he uncovered turned out to be only one of 100,000 that were scattered throughout the region. This collection, which came to be known as the Bradshaw rock paintings, has gained the attention of art historians and archaeologists alike. Art historians marvel at the realistic representations of humans and animals that are featured in the paintings. These representations are interesting in that these subjects are extremely rare in ancient art. Archaeologists, meanwhile, are more concerned with identifying the artists who were responsible for creating the Bradshaws. This task has proven to be a difficult undertaking and has led to the formulation of two competing theories about who created the ancient rock paintings.

[2] In order to find out more about who painted the Bradshaws, scientists first needed to get an idea of approximately how old they are. Unfortunately, archaeologists have mostly been unsuccessful in determining when the Bradshaws were painted, due to the chemical changes that the rocks have experienced. Over time, iron oxide and other chemicals have blended with the rocks on which the paintings were created. These changes have made it impossible for scientists to use their usual dating methods, which in normal cases would involve testing the age of the paint.

[3] Still, due to a curious accident, archaeologists are not without any information about the age of the paintings. In one extraordinary case, the fossil of an ancient wasp nest was found covering a painting. While the painting itself could not be analyzed, scientists could determine the age of the nest, which would help them estimate how old the painting beneath was. After testing the wasp nest, scientists discovered that it was more than 17,000 years old. This breakthrough suggested that the painting underneath the wasp nest was at least this old, and some scientists argued that it could very well be much older. Though scientists need more information to determine the exact age of the Bradshaws, there is enough proof to demonstrate that the Bradshaws are among the oldest pieces of art in the world.

[4] Because archaeologists cannot determine the definite age of the artwork, no one can be sure who painted the Bradshaws. This issue has become a major controversy in the archaeological community. On one side of the argument are those who believe that these paintings were created by the Australian Aborigines, the largest indigenous group in Australia. In support of this theory, many archaeologists point out that there are many examples of indigenous artwork in the Kimberley region that closely resemble Aboriginal works created elsewhere in Australia. This resemblance, they say, indicates that the Bradshaws were likely created by the Aborigines.

[5] However, other archaeologists contend that the Bradshaws were painted by a cultural group that lived in Australia before the Aborigines. They suggest that the Bradshaws could even have been painted by the first groups of humans to arrive in Australia. This theory is supported by studies of human migration, which indicate that the first humans reached the coast of Southeast Asia between 70,000 and 60,000 years ago. Based on historical fluctuations in sea level, scientists believe that it was possible for these groups to have crossed from the southern tip of Southeast Asia to Australia about 65,000 years ago.

Glossary:

POWERED BY COBUILD

graze: to eat plants or grass

resemble: to be or appear similar

[6] Furthermore, the images depicted on the Bradshaws hint that the artists who created them were not originally from Australia. For example, some of the paintings include portrayals of ancient canoe-like boats. Some experts believe that these boats may be representations of the type of boat used to cross the sea from Asia to Australia. Other paintings show animals that look like deer. However, there are no deer, or any creatures related to the deer, in Australia. To explain these images, some scientists suggest that the artists who created the Bradshaws had seen these animals elsewhere before their arrival in Australia.

Now answer the questions.

1. According to paragraph 1, what makes the Bradshaws interesting to art historians?
   ○ The number of pieces found in the Kimberley region
   ○ The subjects of the paintings
   ○ The location where they were created
   ○ The possible age of the paintings

2. The word they in paragraph 2 refers to
   ○ theories.
   ○ the Bradshaws.
   ○ scientists.
   ○ archaeologists.

3. According to paragraph 2, why can't scientists use typical dating methods to determine the age of the Bradshaws?
   ○ The artists used an unknown type of paint.
   ○ Chemicals have damaged the paint.
   ○ Iron oxide was used in the creation of the works.
   ○ The paintings were created on different types of rocks.

4. According to paragraph 3, how were scientists able to find the minimum age of one of the Bradshaw paintings?
   ○ By testing the age of an object that was covering the painting
   ○ By determining how long a species of wasp has lived in Australia
   ○ By analyzing the age of the materials used to create the painting
   ○ By comparing the painting to similar creations found elsewhere

5. According to paragraph 4, what proof is there to support the argument that Australian Aborigines are responsible for the Bradshaws?

   ○ The paintings were created at the same time that the Australian Aborigines arrived in Australia.

   ○ The Australian Aborigines continue to create artwork today that resembles the Bradshaws.

   ○ The Bradshaws look similar to paintings created by Australian Aborigines in other parts of the country.

   ○ Artwork by Australian Aborigines has been found in different parts of the country, including the Kimberley area.

6. The word their in paragraph 6 refers to

   ○ images.

   ○ the artists.

   ○ the Bradshaws.

   ○ animals.

Negative Fact Questions

A negative fact question asks you to recognize the answer option that is <u>not</u> true according to the information in the reading passage. It may take you longer to answer negative fact questions compared to other question types because you have to confirm the accuracy of three details instead of just one. Expect to see no more than one negative fact question per reading passage.

Negative fact questions may be worded as follows:

» *The passage describes all of the following EXCEPT:*

» *According to paragraph 2, which of the following is NOT true about X?*

» *In paragraph 3, which of the following is LEAST likely?*

QUICK GUIDE: Negative Fact Questions

Definition	A negative fact question asks you to choose one of four answer options that presents <u>incorrect</u> information according to the passage. The question is usually based on one paragraph of the reading, although in some cases, negative fact questions can be based on multiple paragraphs from the passage. Negative fact questions are often based on information that appears as part of a list.
Targeted Skills	In order to correctly answer a negative fact question, you must be able to: • understand the main ideas and main supporting details in the reading passage. • quickly scan the passage in order to find facts that support three out of the four answer options. • recognize one answer option that contains incorrect information according to the passage.
The Correct Answer	The correct answer for a negative fact question is the answer option that contradicts information in the passage. Often, it uses key words or phrases from the text but changes a key detail, making it incorrect according to the passage. In cases where the question is based on a list, the correct answer is the item that is not included in that list.
Wrong Answer Options	Watch out for answer options that include: • rephrased information from the passage. An answer option might rephrase a fact from the passage so that it looks like it is incorrect when it's actually accurate according to the passage. Remember, for this question type, you are looking for the answer that is <u>not</u> true. • a shift from the active voice to the passive voice (or vice versa). For example, the passage might say, "The man ate the apple." In the answer option, it shifts to the passive voice, reading, "The apple was eaten by the man." Notice that the meaning is the same in both cases.

WALK THROUGH: Negative Fact Questions

A Quickly read the sample negative fact question below. Underline any key words in the question and the answer options that will help you determine the correct answer.

TOEFL Reading	VIEW TEXT · REVIEW · VOLUME · HELP · BACK · NEXT
Question 1 of 12	HIDE TIME 00:17:20

1. According to paragraph 1, all of the following accurately describe dynamic pricing EXCEPT:
- ○ Its popularity started to decline at the end of the twentieth century.
- ○ It gives the buyer some control over the price of an item.
- ○ It is used by sellers in online auctions.
- ○ It means that sellers charge different prices according to the situation.

B Now read the sample passage. While you read, check (✓) the facts that are mentioned in the answer options in Part A. Remember, the answer option that is <u>not</u> a fact according to the passage is the correct answer. When you are done, mark the correct answer for the question above.

The Return of Dynamic Pricing

[1] Throughout the twentieth century, many businesses used fixed-price strategies, meaning that prices for goods or services are predetermined by the seller. If a store has fixed prices, customers are expected to pay the set price. More importantly, ☐ buyers do not have any direct input in regard to the price of the items that they wish to purchase. In recent years, however, many sellers have started using dynamic pricing, ☐ a strategy that involves changing the price of an item based on an individual buyer's needs and the circumstances of the purchase. Unlike fixed pricing, dynamic pricing is more flexible and allows buyers and sellers to work together to come up with prices that both parties can agree on. ☐ For example, online auctions, which allow buyers to place bids on items, use dynamic pricing. The rising popularity of dynamic pricing is, without a doubt, linked to the improvement of technology, such as the Internet.

[2] The Internet has made it easier for sellers to use dynamic pricing by giving them access to information that affects pricing decisions. For example, sellers can now access up-to-date market information at any time of the day by using the Internet. They might receive information that shows that the demand for an item is rising or that the cost to make a specific product has dropped. Both these factors influence the price of the item, so knowing this information allows sellers to update prices as often as they want in order to reflect market fluctuations.

[3] New technologies also allow companies to monitor the purchase history of individual buyers. Sellers can then use this information to make recommendations that are tailored to meet a particular customer's preferences. Furthermore, the seller can change prices according to the customer's desires. For instance, sellers might offer unwanted inventory at lower prices to customers who show interest in it. As a result, the buyer receives a better deal.

Glossary:

⊜ POWERED BY COBUILD

bid: an offer to pay a particular amount of money for something

inventory: a supply or stock of something

GET IT RIGHT: Tips and Tasks for Answering Correctly

» **TIP 1: Read the question and the answer options before you scan the passage.** For this question type, you will have to review the paragraph or paragraphs specified in the question in order to check the accuracy of each of the answer options. Before you review the paragraph(s), read the question and the answer options. You should try to understand the full meaning of each answer option. That way, you can determine whether or not it is accurate based on the facts in the passage. Also, make note of any key words or phrases in the answer options. Then, scan the appropriate paragraph(s) in the passage and look for these key words or phrases. This will help you find the information you need in order to answer the question quickly.

TASK 1: Look at the key words you underlined in the question and the answer options on page 27. Scan the passage on page 27 and circle four key words or expressions in paragraph 1 that relate to each of the answer options.

» **TIP 2: Check for rewording of language from the passage.** Answer options for this question type will often contain rephrased information from the passage in order to make correct answer options seem incorrect. If you see that an answer option has reworded information from the passage, compare it to the passage. Is the meaning the same? If the answer option is supported by the information in the passage, you can eliminate it.

TASK 2: Which two answer options on page 27 reword the information from the passage?

» **TIP 3: Look for answer options that use the passive voice.** In English, the passive form is constructed by using a *be* verb plus the past participial form of a verb. For example, the sentence "The company opened three new factories" is in the active voice. "Three new factories were opened by the company" is in the passive voice. Notice that the meaning of the sentence doesn't change regardless of the voice. For this reason, you should watch out for answer options that change the voice of the sentences they are based on. For example, if a sentence in the passage is in the active voice, and the answer option is in the passive voice, they could mean the same thing.

TASK 3: Which answer option on page 27 uses the passive voice to talk about an event that was originally described in the active voice?

TEST TIP!

Negative fact questions typically take more time to answer than other question types because you have to confirm the accuracy of each answer option. Expect to spend 2–3 minutes on each negative fact question.

Function Questions

A function question (also referred to as a rhetorical purpose question) asks you about the rhetorical strategies used by the author. A rhetorical strategy is a tactic used to accomplish a number of functions, including giving an example, explaining or clarifying a point, challenging or supporting a point, etc. Answers for this question type often start with *to* infinitives. For example, *to explain and to make a point about* are common infinitive phrases used to start answer options for function questions. There is typically no more than one function question per reading passage.

Function questions may be worded as follows:

» *Why does the author mention X in paragraph 1?*

» *Why does the author give an example of X?*

» *How does the information in paragraph 2 relate to paragraph 1?*

QUICK GUIDE: Function Questions

Definition	Function questions ask you to identify the purpose of a word, phrase, or even an entire paragraph in the passage. There are two types of function questions. One type will ask you to identify why the author mentions a specific piece of information in the passage. For example, you will be presented with a word or phrase, and you will have to identify the function of the word or phrase in relation to the sentences around it. The second type asks you why the author organizes the information in part of the passage in a certain way. For instance, you may have to explain how one paragraph relates to another.
Targeted Skills	In order to answer a function question correctly, you must be able to: • recognize common rhetorical strategies and the expressions associated with them. • determine the author's reasons for mentioning a piece of information. • identify the main idea in each paragraph in order to understand how the paragraphs are related. • understand how the word, phrase, or paragraph being asked about relates to the sentences or paragraphs around it.
The Correct Answer	The correct answer for a function question correctly identifies the author's motivations for mentioning a piece of information or for organizing the information in a paragraph in a certain way. Please note that the author will <u>not</u> state the function directly in the passage. Therefore, you must determine the function based on the clues in the passage and your overall understanding of the passage.
Wrong Answer Options	Watch out for answer options that include: • information that is mentioned in the passage but does not explain the speaker's function. • ideas that are not mentioned in the passage at all. • relationships that contradict the facts presented in the reading.

WALK THROUGH: Function Questions

A Quickly read the sample function questions below. Underline any key words in the questions and the answer options that will help you determine the correct answers.

TOEFL Reading | VIEW TEXT · REVIEW · VOLUME · HELP · BACK · NEXT

Question 1 of 12 | HIDE TIME 00:11:20

1. In paragraph 3, why does the author discuss the pyramid in Teotihuacan that featured the feathered serpent?
   ○ To argue that the Mayans inspired the use of the feathered serpent in Teotihuacan
   ○ To contrast the symbolic images used by the Teotihuacanos and the Maya
   ○ To give an example of an archaeological technique used by the Teotihuacanos
   ○ To point out that the symbol was popular in Teotihuacan before the Maya used it

2. How does paragraph 1 relate to paragraph 2?
   ○ Paragraph 1 gives examples of an idea that is explained in further detail in paragraph 2.
   ○ Paragraph 2 describes the background of one of the cultures mentioned in paragraph 1.
   ○ Paragraph 1 defines a key term that is central to the theory refuted in paragraph 2.
   ○ Paragraph 2 provides evidence to support a theory that is introduced in paragraph 1.

B Now read the sample passage. While you read, underline information that you think will help you answer the questions in Part A. When you are done reading, mark the correct answers for the questions above.

The Influence of Teotihuacan

[1] The city of Teotihuacan, located in the central region of modern-day Mexico, was one of the first urban civilizations in Central America. Due to its military strength and far-reaching trade partnerships, Teotihuacan became very influential, reaching the height of its power around the year 450 AD. During this time, the people of Teotihuacan had frequent and direct contact with the Maya, a civilization whose territory extended from southwestern Mexico to the regions of El Salvador. Evidence suggests that the Maya were greatly influenced by the Teotihuacanos, especially in the areas of architecture and ideology.

[2] The Maya used a variety of architectural styles. However, one that was likely inspired by Teotihuacan was a technique called the slope-and-panel style. This technique involved stacking rectangular stone panels on top of stone slabs that had inwardly sloped sides. The largest stone panels were located at the base, and the size of the panels decreased at each level, giving the resulting structures their characteristic pyramid shape. According to archaeological evidence, the slope-and-panel style was used in Teotihuacan as early as 200 AD. Experts observed the same style in several Mayan cities. Interestingly, the Mayan structures that used the slope-and-panel style were built much later than those at Teotihuacan. This suggests that the style developed first in Teotihuacan and that the Maya adopted the style as a result of direct contact with the Teotihuacanos.

[3] There is also evidence that the Teotihuacanos influenced the ideology of the Maya. This is particularly apparent in the use of certain religious symbols. For example, one of the most important religious symbols in Teotihuacan was the feathered serpent. Between the years 150 and 200, the Teotihuacanos even built a pyramid that featured the symbol extensively. The same symbol has been found in Mayan texts. However, the Maya didn't use it before 1000 AD.

Glossary:

≪ POWERED BY COBUILD

urban: belonging to a town or city

serpent: a snake

GET IT RIGHT: Tips and Tasks for Answering Correctly

» **TIP 1: Read the answer options before you scan the reading.** When you read the answer options, be sure to make note of key words. This will help you find important information faster when you scan the passage.

TASK 1: Look at the key words you underlined in question 1 and its answer options on page 30. Scan the passage on page 30 and circle four key words or expressions in paragraph 3 that relate to each of the answer options for question 1.

» **TIP 2: Learn the rhetorical strategies that are commonly used on the TOEFL test.** In the reading section, the authors will use a number of common rhetorical strategies in order to achieve a number of goals. The table below shows some common rhetorical strategies and the words you may see in the passage that signal the use of these tactics.

Common Rhetorical Strategy	Words You Might See in the Passage	How Answers May Be Worded
Give an Example	For example . . . That is to say . . . This shows how . . .	To provide / give an example of . . . To describe X in more detail To show / illustrate / demonstrate . . . To provide evidence of . . . To describe . . .
Compare or Contrast	In contrast . . . For the same reason . . . Another similarity / difference . . .	To contrast X and Y To show the similarity / difference between X and Y To argue that X is the same as Y
Emphasize a Piece of Information	In this sense, X could be seen as . . . Specifically . . . This is particularly apparent in . . .	To note that . . . To highlight that . . . To make the point that . . .

TASK 2: Draw a box around one phrase in the passage on page 30 that is related to the common rhetorical strategies mentioned above. Which answer option for question 1 on page 30 is related to this phrase?

» **TIP 3: Eliminate answer options that don't relate directly to the author's purpose.** In some cases, an answer option will mention information from the passage that does not correctly explain the author's function.

TASK 3: Draw a line through one answer option for question 1 on page 30 that contains information that's mentioned in the passage but does not indicate the author's purpose.

» **TIP 4: If a question asks how two paragraphs relate, find the main ideas of both paragraphs asked about.** Typically, each paragraph will have a topic sentence that describes the main idea of the paragraph. Comparing the topic sentences will give you clues about how the paragraphs are related. Does one paragraph refute or support a theory introduced in the other? Does one paragraph discuss an idea introduced in the other?

TASK 4: Underline the main ideas for paragraphs 1 and 2 in the passage on page 30. Based on these topic sentences, how are the two paragraphs probably related?

PROGRESSIVE PRACTICE: Get Ready

A Scan the short passage about architecture. Underline the main idea of each paragraph.

Active Design

[1] Daily physical activity is an important part of a healthy lifestyle. For this reason, many architects and designers are working to create buildings that encourage people to make exercise a part of their ordinary routine. The movement to promote healthy activity through architecture is called active design. It began in 1998 as part of a university public health program, and it has since gained popularity in cities around the world. Active design uses a number of techniques to encourage the occupants of a building to be more active.

[2] One of the most important strategies of active design is inspiring people to make walking part of their routine. A particularly successful tool for promoting walking is the skip-stop elevator. These elevators stop only on every second or third floor, leaving riders to take the stairs in order to reach their destination. Another strategy of active design is to make stairs more pleasant and inviting. Instead of creating dim stairwells that are located in isolated parts of buildings, active design uses well lit and centrally placed stairs to encourage more foot traffic. Skip-stop elevators and appealing stair design are both effective tools of active design because they offer incentive and opportunity for exercise. In fact, researchers studying a building that employs both skip-stop elevators and more attractive stair design said that 70 percent of building occupants reported using the stairs every day.

[3] Active design encourages physical activity using not only the interior features of a building, but the relationship between a building and its surroundings as well. A building that employs active design may integrate outdoor space in order to make the environment more engaging and promote physical activity. Some elements that architects use to incorporate the exterior with the interior are glass walls, interior gardens or park spaces, and courtyards with open ceilings, all of which de-emphasize the boundaries between inside and outside. These elements make the building more physically and mentally invigorating. Similarly, by increasing the number of entrances and exits to a building, architects can help keep a building's users interested in their surroundings by providing a variety of routes for them to use. If people continue to be stimulated by new sights or experiences, they are less likely to choose the quickest and easiest path to their destination and may instead choose a more physically challenging route.

Glossary:

POWERED BY COBUILD

incentive: encouragement to do something

incorporate: to include; to make a part of

B Read the questions carefully. What types of questions are they? Then, answer the questions. Note the correct answers and read why the answer options are correct or incorrect.

1. According to paragraph 1, all of the following are true about active design EXCEPT:

   ○ It began at the end of the twentieth century.

   ○ Promoting physical activity is its goal.

   ○ Architects and medical professionals created it.

   ○ It is becoming increasingly common in cities.

ANSWER ANALYSIS ▶

Question Type: **Negative Fact**

    ✗ The passage says the active design movement started in 1998, which is the end of the twentieth century.

    ✗ The passage says, "The movement to promote healthy activity through architecture is called active design."

    ✓ **While the passage mentions both architects and health professionals, there is no indication that architects and medical professionals worked together to create the active design movement.**

    ✗ The passage says, "It has since gained popularity in cities around the world."

2. Why does the author discuss dim stairwells in paragraph 2?

    ○ To demonstrate the differences between elevator and stairwell design

    ○ To make a point about why people don't use the stairs often

    ○ To describe one advantage of using skip-stop elevators in buildings

    ○ To argue that skip-stop elevators may lead to design failures

ANSWER ANALYSIS ▶

Question Type: **Function**

    ✗ The author does not mention the differences between the design of elevators and stairwells.

    ✓ **The author writes that well-designed stairwells encourage foot traffic. Dim stairwells are mentioned to give an example of why people avoid using the stairs.**

    ✗ While the author talks about the advantages of using skip-stop elevators, dim stairwells are not one of the benefits.

    ✗ The author implies that dim stairwells are a design failure not that skip-stop elevators cause this type of failure.

3. According to paragraph 3, which of the following is NOT a way that architects eliminate the boundary between indoor and outdoor spaces?

    ○ Creating spaces with open ceilings

    ○ Using see-through materials

    ○ Creating more routes for entering and exiting

    ○ Building gardens inside the building

ANSWER ANALYSIS ▶

Question Type: **Negative Fact**

    ✗ The author mentions "courtyards with open ceilings" when describing how to incorporate outdoor spaces indoors.

    ✗ The author mentions "glass walls," and glass is a see-through material.

    ✓ **The passage says that creating multiple exits and entrances is meant to keep building users stimulated, not to eliminate the boundary between indoor and outdoor spaces.**

    ✗ The passage mentions "interior gardens or park spaces."

4. How does paragraph 2 relate to paragraph 3 in the passage?

    ○ Paragraph 2 describes an early model of a design discussed in paragraph 3.

    ○ Paragraph 3 argues about the effectiveness of the technique from paragraph 2.

    ○ Paragraph 2 explains a technique, and paragraph 3 gives examples of how it is used.

    ○ Paragraph 3 introduces a different strategy than the one discussed in paragraph 2.

ANSWER ANALYSIS ▶

Question Type: **Function**

    ✗ The author does not discuss the early model of any design mentioned in the passage.

    ✗ Paragraph 3 does not mention the effectiveness of the strategy described in paragraph 2.

    ✗ Each paragraph describes a separate technique and gives examples. The same technique is not split over two paragraphs.

    ✓ **Both paragraphs discuss a distinct strategy that is used in active design.**

PROGRESSIVE PRACTICE: Get Set

A Scan the short passage about archaeology. Write the main idea of each paragraph.

1. _____

2. _____

3. _____

4. _____

Archaeological Dating

[1] In the past, archaeologists had few precise ways of determining the age of artifacts. Some methods they used included researching written records, comparing objects to similar items, or analyzing the depth at which an object was buried. The limitations of such methods were numerous. For instance, though it may seem logical to assume that relics buried deep underground are older than those found closer to the surface, earthquakes, floods, and even rodents can change the position of artifacts. Thus, these methods could not provide the exact information that archaeologists needed. However, advances in technology have provided modern archaeologists with several methods that give them the absolute age of an object.

[2] The most common absolute dating technique is radiocarbon dating. This process involves analyzing objects for a substance called radiocarbon. All organic material, or matter that was once part of a living organism, contains trace amounts of radiocarbon. For example, human remains, ash residue on cooking pots, or animal products used for clothing or tools all contain radiocarbon. Over time, the amount of radiocarbon in an object steadily decreases at a predictable and measurable rate. Thus, by determining the amount of radiocarbon present in a skull fragment, for example, archaeologists can calculate the age of that object.

[3] However, many of the artifacts that archaeologists study are not organic. They also study the inorganic remains of human culture, like architecture, tools, jewelry, and pottery. For some inorganic remains, like pottery, archaeologists use a technique called thermoluminescence dating. This process measures radioactive decay, which is the breakdown and loss of atomic material that many inorganic remains experience. In rigidly structured matter, like the minerals often found in pottery, radioactive decay also results in the storage of small amounts of energy. When the minerals are heated to high temperatures, they release this stored energy as light, or thermoluminescence.

[4] Thermoluminescence dating is particularly useful for dating pottery because of the process by which pottery is made. In order for clay to be converted into pottery, it must be fired. The clay is put into a special oven, called a kiln, and heated to very high temperatures. When pottery is fired, the minerals in the clay release the energy they have stored during radioactive decay. This resets the clock, and the minerals continue to undergo radioactive decay from the time of firing. When archaeologists heat a pottery sample, the amount of light it releases tells them how long ago it was fired. Because pottery is a common artifact of ancient cultures, thermoluminescence dating is a valuable tool for archaeologists.

Glossary:

⋐ POWERED BY COBUILD

relic: something that was made or used a long time ago

trace: very small amount

B Read the questions carefully and note whether they are negative fact or function questions. Then, answer the questions. Write the letter of each answer option next to the reason in the *Answer Analysis* box explaining why it is correct or incorrect.

1. The author discusses rodents in paragraph 1 in order to

○ explain the problem with one dating technique. [A]

○ argue that modern dating techniques are not accurate. [B]

○ describe how scientists use living organisms to date objects. [C]

○ give an example of a modern dating technique. [D]

ANSWER ANALYSIS ▶

Question Type: **Function**

_____ ✗ The author does not mention using living organisms to date objects in paragraph 1.

_____ ✗ When the author mentions rodents, the focus is on giving an example of earlier dating techniques, not modern ones.

_____ ✓ **The author says that rodents can change the position of artifacts, which would give an inaccurate age if an archaeologist used the depth of burial as an indication of age.**

_____ ✗ The author is arguing that earlier dating techniques, not modern ones, are inaccurate.

2. **Why does the author mention ash residue in paragraph 2?**

○ To illustrate the accuracy of radiocarbon dating [A]

○ To show how radiocarbon can be destroyed [B]

○ To provide an example of an organic material [C]

○ To differentiate between organic and inorganic objects [D]

ANSWER ANALYSIS ▶

Question Type: **Function**

_____ ✗ The passage does not mention ash residue in relation to the accuracy of radiocarbon dating.

_____ ✓ **In the previous sentence, the author defines organic material. The sentence in question starts with "For example."**

_____ ✗ The author does not specify if or how radiocarbon can be destroyed.

_____ ✗ The sentence in question mentions only organic materials, not inorganic ones.

3. **According to paragraph 3, which of the following is NOT true about thermoluminescence dating?**

○ It will likely replace radiocarbon dating methods. [A]

○ It measures how much radioactive energy has been stored. [B]

○ It works well for materials that have a rigid structure. [C]

○ It uses light as a measure of stored radioactive energy. [D]

ANSWER ANALYSIS ▶

Question Type: **Negative Fact**

_____ ✗ The author says that the age of pottery is based on how much light it releases when heated to extremely high temperatures.

_____ ✓ **The author says that radiocarbon dating doesn't work for inorganic materials, not that thermoluminescence dating will become more popular than radiocarbon dating.**

_____ ✗ The author says that radioactive decay results in "the storage of small amounts of energy."

_____ ✗ The author says that thermoluminescence dating is used on "rigidly structured matter," like the minerals in some pottery.

4. **According to paragraphs 3 and 4, which of the following is NOT a way that pottery is well suited to thermoluminescence dating?**

○ It is relatively easy to find compared to other artifacts. [A]

○ Pottery is made of inorganic materials. [B]

○ Pottery contains minerals that undergo radioactive decay. [C]

○ It has no stored radioactive energy from the time it is fired. [D]

ANSWER ANALYSIS ▶

Question Type: **Negative Fact**

_____ ✗ In paragraph 4, the author explains that when pottery is fired for the first time, it "resets the clock," meaning that it has no stored radioactive energy.

_____ ✗ In paragraph 3, the author says that thermoluminescence dating is good for some inorganic materials, like pottery.

_____ ✓ **While pottery is a common artifact, this doesn't relate to its appropriateness for thermoluminescence dating.**

_____ ✗ The author says that the minerals in pottery "continue to undergo radioactive decay" once the pottery has been fired.

PROGRESSIVE PRACTICE: Go for the TOEFL Test

Read the passage about a topic in psychology.

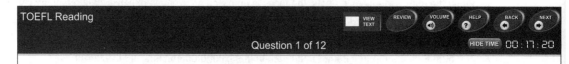

TOEFL Reading   VIEW TEXT   REVIEW   VOLUME   HELP   BACK   NEXT

Question 1 of 12   HIDE TIME 00:11:20

Nonverbal Communication

1 The ability to share complex, detailed information through spoken language is frequently cited as the primary factor that distinguishes humans from animals. However, in addition to using a highly developed language system, people also share information nonverbally, without using words at all. Though speech is often considered the chief form of human communication, people also depend heavily on many types of nonverbal communication.

2 One of the most common forms of nonverbal communication is body language. Body language can include facial expressions, gestures, and even eye contact. The human body is capable of a nearly limitless variety of expressions, postures, and gestures, all of which can carry meaning that can be used for the purposes of communication. Facial expressions are perhaps the most commonly recognized form of body language. Some studies even suggest that facial expressions showing feelings like anger, fear, surprise, happiness, and sadness could be universal, meaning that they are understood by people all over the world. For example, in some cases, even though two people may speak entirely different languages and come from widely divergent cultures, they can still share basic emotions by using facial expressions.

3 It is important to recognize, however, that not all body language is universal and that the attitudes and norms of a culture play a large role in how some kinds of body language are interpreted. For instance, putting one's hands in one's pockets might indicate feelings of relaxation to members of one culture, but it could signal disrespect to members of another. Thus, the meaning of body language is often dependent on culture or personality. Despite the difficulty of interpreting what particular types of body language mean, studies of human behavior indicate that it forms a significant part of human life. Some researchers suggest that 50–70 percent of human communication consists of body language.

4 In addition to communicating through movements, expressions, or other visible body language, human beings also communicate nonverbally through touch, which is often referred to as the haptic sense. Research indicates that haptic communication is especially important in the development of infants. Before children develop language, parents or other caregivers can use touch to convey a number of ideas, such as attention, care, and safety. Touch remains an important means of communication for adult humans as well. It is a central part of establishing friendships and other cooperative relationships. That's because touch often indicates and encourages trust. However, in some cases, the haptic sense can also communicate less positive messages. For instance, physical violence is a form of haptic communication in which a person expresses their state of mind by threatening or harming another.

Glossary:

POWERED BY COBUILD

divergent: things that are different from each other

convey: to cause information or feelings to be known or understood by someone

[5] Though a majority of the messages sent and received through body language and interpersonal contact are subconscious, human beings use nonverbal communication consciously as well. People often choose certain aspects of their appearance, like their clothes, their hairstyles, or other forms of personal decoration, very carefully, and these choices are another form of nonverbal communication. One of the primary purposes of nonverbal communication through appearance is to indicate wealth or status. For example, a person can communicate wealth by wearing expensive clothes. Similarly, a person can show his or her status by wearing specialized types of clothing, like badges or uniforms. Appearance can communicate information about whether a person wishes to be considered serious or playful, conventional or odd, professional or casual. For instance, though the types of clothing that are considered formal differ widely from culture to culture, most societies recognize some difference between formal and informal dress. Most commonly, formal dress is apparel that shows respect for an important occasion. While most people exert some degree of control over what they wear or how they present themselves, there are some types of nonverbal communication that are unintentional. Studies have found that, in some cultures, taller people are regarded as being more impressive and often receive promotions over their shorter colleagues. In this case, nonverbal communication is not intentional and may even convey false information.

Now answer the questions.

1. According to paragraph 2, which of the following is NOT true about body language?

   ○ It includes behaviors like gestures and facial expressions.

   ○ Some cultures use body language more than others.

   ○ It accounts for at least half of all human communication.

   ○ Some body language is thought to have the same meaning everywhere.

2. In paragraph 3, the author mentions putting one's hands in one's pockets in order to

   ○ explain a common way of using body language.

   ○ make a point about how body language can affect mood.

   ○ give an example of body language that can have multiple interpretations.

   ○ support the idea that the majority of communication is nonverbal.

3. How does paragraph 2 relate to paragraph 3?

   ○ Paragraph 2 presents a theory about some body language, and paragraph 3 demonstrates that the theory is not always true.

   ○ Paragraph 3 compares the two types of body language described in paragraph 2.

   ○ Paragraph 2 gives examples of body language, and paragraph 3 explains how body language is interpreted.

   ○ Paragraph 3 provides evidence for a theory about body language that was introduced in paragraph 2.

4. In paragraph 4, the author mentions all of the following functions of haptic communication EXCEPT:

   ○ Giving attention to infants

   ○ Promoting language development

   ○ Building trust among friends

   ○ Physically harming others

5. In paragraph 5, the author says that conscious nonverbal communication can be used for all of the following EXCEPT:

○ To indicate one's personality

○ To demonstrate how much money one has

○ To recognize members of the same group

○ To show respect in certain situations

6. Why does the author mention a study about height in the workplace in paragraph 5?

○ To illustrate how nonverbal communication can have unintended consequences

○ To suggest that people's impressions based on height are the same around the world

○ To provide evidence that most types of nonverbal communication are conscious

○ To show that using nonverbal communication can have a number of advantages

Inference Questions

An inference question asks you to draw a conclusion based on the information presented in the passage. The correct answer for an inference question will <u>never</u> be stated outright. Rather, you will have to connect information from the passage in order to make an inference. There is typically no more than one inference question per reading passage.

Inference questions may be worded as follows:

» *In paragraph 1, the author implies . . .*

» *According to paragraph 2, which of the following can be inferred about X?*

» *Which of the following is implied about X in paragraph 3?*

» *Based on the information in paragraph 4, what can be inferred about X?*

QUICK GUIDE: Inference Questions

Definition	Inference questions ask you to test your understanding of an idea or suggestion that is implied in the reading. While the answer will not be stated in the passage, you should be able to make a strong inference by using the information provided.
Targeted Skills	In order to answer an inference question correctly, you must be able to: • understand ideas that are implied but not stated directly in the reading. • interpret the idea in the passage based on context clues. • quickly scan the passage in order to find information that supports your conclusion.
The Correct Answer	The correct answer for an inference question correctly draws a conclusion. The inference will be supported by information in the passage but will not be stated directly.
Wrong Answer Options	Watch out for answer options that include: • a conclusion that is true but is not supported by the information in the passage. On the test, the correct answer to an inference question is <u>always</u> supported by the information given. You do not have to rely on previous or outside knowledge to answer a question. • information that contradicts the main idea or details of the passage. • the exact wording from the passage. The correct answer will usually reword information.

WALK THROUGH: Inference Questions

A Quickly read the sample inference question below. Underline any key words in the question and the answer options that will help you determine the correct answer.

TOEFL Reading	VIEW TEXT	REVIEW	VOLUME	HELP	BACK	NEXT

Question 1 of 12   HIDE TIME 00:11:20

1. According to paragraph 2, what can be inferred about the abacuses used in Babylon?
- ○ They were the earliest calculators.
- ○ They did not have any educational value.
- ○ They were not easy to move around.
- ○ They inspired the invention of the wire abacus.

B Now read the sample passage. While you read, underline key words and phrases from the passage that you think will help you answer the question in Part A. When you are done, mark the correct answer for the question above.

Early Calculators

[1] Modern electronic calculators perform many complex mathematical functions. However, any device that helps compute mathematical values is a type of calculator. The earliest form of calculator was the human hand. In fact, a medieval English monk developed a system for using one's fingers to count all the way up to one million. But advanced tools are necessary for math that requires more difficult calculations than simple counting. Ancient cultures all over the world developed a variety of early calculators.

[2] The most common type of early calculator was the abacus. An abacus is a device that uses stones or beads as markers to assist a person in basic calculations, like addition, subtraction, multiplication, and division. The earliest abacuses, which used grooves for holding stone markers, are also called counting trays. Merchants used them to determine prices, while government officials used them to keep official accounts and teachers used them to teach mathematics. Records suggest that the Babylonians created the first counting tray around 300. This type of abacus was used by Greeks, Romans, Egyptians, and other cultures for centuries. In the thirteenth century, Chinese thinkers invented the wire abacus, which uses beads mounted on wires and held within a frame. The wire abacus is more portable than the counting tray and can be used for more rapid calculations. In fact, despite advancements in technology, people all over the world still use the wire abacus.

[3] Trade between people in China, India, Europe, and Africa explains the spread of early calculators in many parts of the world. However, the early inhabitants of the Americas actually created a calculator without these influences. Some scholars propose that the Inca, a South American empire that was powerful from about 1430–1533, used a device called a *yupana* for calculations. The yupana is a block of stone carved into many sections and levels that resembles a miniature model of a city. This device was most likely used to calculate amounts of stored resources, like grain or livestock, and some historians speculate that it may have been used for astronomical calculations. Unlike the wire abacus, the yupana is no longer in use.

Glossary:

⊜ POWERED BY COBUILD

portable: something that is easily carried or moved

miniature: something that is very small; a smaller version of something that is normally bigger

GET IT RIGHT: Tips and Tasks for Answering Correctly

» **TIP 1: Read the question and answer options carefully.** When you read the question, pay attention to what you are supposed to make an inference about. Also, you should read the answer options carefully to make sure you understand the general point of each option.

TASK 1: Circle the five key phrases in the question and answer options on page 40. When you scan the passage, make sure you keep these words in mind to help you answer the question.

» **TIP 2: Watch out for answer options that contain key words from the reading!** The correct answer for an inference question won't be stated directly in the reading. Furthermore, the correct answer will usually reword any key ideas. Because of this, you should be careful with answer options that use the same language from the passage.

TASK 2: Draw a line through an incorrect answer option on page 40 that repeats key words from the reading.

» **TIP 3: Eliminate answer options that aren't supported by the information in the passage**. You might see an answer option that seems like it could be true. However, unless it is supported by the information in the passage, it <u>cannot</u> be the right answer. Also, you should be able to answer the question based only on the information in the passage. You do not need any background knowledge in order to answer questions in the reading section.

TASK 3: Draw a line through an incorrect answer option on page 40 that presents an inference that may be true but is not supported by the reading.

TEST TIP!

Inference questions are often based on dates and numbers. While you read a passage, pay attention to information relating to dates. You may have to draw a conclusion about events that occurred before or after the specified dates.

Vocabulary Questions

A vocabulary question asks you to choose the definition that best describes how a highlighted word or phrase is used in the passage. In most cases, you will be asked to choose the definition of a single word, though occasionally you may be asked about the definition of a short phrase. There are typically two to four vocabulary questions per reading passage.

Vocabulary questions may be worded as follows:

» *The word X in the passage is closest in meaning to . . .*

» *The phrase X in the passage is closest in meaning to . . .*

QUICK GUIDE: Vocabulary Questions

Definition	Vocabulary questions ask you to identify the definition of a word or phrase from a passage. The word or phrase will be highlighted in the passage. The vocabulary you are tested on may have multiple meanings. You must choose the definition that best describes how the word or phrase is used in the passage. For this reason, you cannot simply study a list of words in preparation for vocabulary questions.
Targeted Skills	In order to answer a vocabulary question correctly, you must: • be able to understand how words or phrases are used in a passage. • be able to use context clues to determine the meaning of a word or phrase. • know common English suffixes and prefixes and their meanings. • have a broad knowledge of English vocabulary.
The Correct Answer	The correct answer for a vocabulary question can replace the highlighted word or phrase without changing the meaning of the sentence or contradicting the main idea of the passage. The correct answer option is often a synonym of the highlighted word.
Wrong Answer Options	Watch out for answer options that include: • similar constructions as the highlighted word, such as the words *slather* and *gather*. Remember, just because two words look alike does not mean they have the same meaning. • the opposite meaning of another answer option. If two answer options have opposite meanings, it's likely that neither one of them is correct. • the correct definition of the word but for a different usage. You must choose the answer that best describes the meaning of the word as it's used in the passage.

WALK THROUGH: Vocabulary Questions

A Quickly read the sample vocabulary questions and answer options below. Write down brief definitions for the words you know.

TOEFL Reading | VIEW TEXT | REVIEW | VOLUME | HELP | BACK | NEXT

Question 1 of 12 | HIDE TIME 00:17:20

1. The word gradual in paragraph 1 is closest in meaning to
- ○ hurried.
- ○ continuous.
- ○ slow.
- ○ graceful.

2. The word imperceptible in paragraph 2 is closest in meaning to
- ○ dangerous.
- ○ insignificant.
- ○ unnoticeable.
- ○ impassible.

B Now read the sample passage. While you read, underline information that you think will help you answer the questions in Part A. When you are done reading, mark the correct answers for the questions above.

Fast-Moving Glaciers

[1] Glaciers are enormous rivers of ice that form in locations where snow accumulates more quickly than it can melt. These ice rivers are known for their gradual pace—on average, glaciers move a mere 30 centimeters a day. However, in some cases, glaciers move at a much faster rate. For example, one glacier travels at a speed of 111 feet a day. Fast-moving glaciers can have both local and more widespread consequences.

[2] One result of increased glacial speeds is glacial earthquakes. When a glacier experiences a dramatic increase in speed, it can cause seismic waves, or waves of energy that travel through the earth. Because glaciers are usually located in uninhabited areas, glacial earthquakes are not particularly destructive. Furthermore, the seismic waves produced by glacial earthquakes are usually imperceptible, even to someone standing on the glacier as the earthquake occurs. However, some scientists hypothesize that a significant glacial earthquake could cause oceanic disturbances and perhaps even tsunamis.

[3] While glacial earthquakes may currently have limited effects, fast-moving glaciers can also impact the environment in a more noticeable way. When a glacier moves at a fast pace, it loses massive amounts of ice. This causes the sea level to rise because the ice melts into the ocean. In fact, records show that melted ice from a single, particularly rapid glacier has caused the global sea level to rise by four percent. Higher sea levels can have disastrous effects not only for human beings, who frequently settle in coastal areas that could be flooded by rising oceans, but also for the complex ecosystems that are located in or near oceans and freshwater bodies. For example, many organisms live in tidal areas, or places that are underwater at high tide and above water at low tide. Rising sea levels could wash these habitats away altogether. Thus, by raising the sea level, increased glacier speed in extreme northern regions of the earth could be devastating for organisms in locations thousands of miles away.

Glossary:

⊆ POWERED BY COBUILD

mere: a small amount or number of something

hypothesize: to say what you think will happen because of various facts

43

GET IT RIGHT: Tips and Tasks for Answering Correctly

» **TIP 1: Review the paragraph in which the highlighted word or phrase appears.** Because you have to choose the answer that is closest in meaning to the word or phrase in the passage, you need to see exactly how the word or phrase is used. When you review the word or phrase and the surrounding sentences, make note of context clues that can help you figure out the meaning. See the table below for strategies for using context clues to determine the meaning of a word or phrase.

Strategies for Using Context Clues		
Strategy	**Key Words**	**Example**
Pay attention to **examples** that appear near the highlighted word. If you are familiar with the examples, you can use them to determine the meaning of the highlighted word.	such as . . . including . . . consists of . . . this includes . . . like . . .	The photographs show banal activities, like going to the grocery store or doing household chores.
Look for key words that signal a **contrast** from a previous idea. If you know the meanings of the words from surrounding sentences, you'll know that the highlighted word has an opposite meaning.	Unlike X . . . On the other hand, X . . . While . . . But . . . However . . .	Unlike most mammals, few of which are venomous, the platypus produces a noxious substance that can cause extreme pain in humans.
Look for **indirect definitions** of terms in the sentences that surround the highlighted word. These definitions may include an easier synonym of the highlighted word or information that helps clarify its meaning.	and meaning that	In the southwestern United States, the sunflower is ubiquitous, and it is difficult to find a garden that doesn't include the plant.

Task 1: Draw a box around one indirect definition and one contrasting word located near the word gradual in **the passage** on page 43. Based on these context clues, which of the answer options is probably correct?

» **TIP 2: Learn common English prefixes and suffixes.** By learning the meanings of common English prefixes and suffixes, you will be able to analyze an unfamiliar word and guess its meaning.

Common English Prefixes and Suffixes			
Prefix / Meaning	**Example**	**Suffix / Meaning**	**Example**
a- without	*amoral:* without morals	*-able* ability to do	*readable:* able to be read
de- remove	*defog:* to remove fog	*-acy* state	*privacy:* the state of being private
im- not	*improper:* not proper	*-ate* make	*activate:* to make active
mis- wrong	*misplace:* to put in the wrong place	*-er / -or* job	*actor:* a person who acts
pre- before	*predate:* to happen before a certain date	*-ful* full of	*merciful:* full of mercy
re- do again	*redo:* to do something again	*-ish* somewhat	*whitish:* somewhat white
sub- under or below	*subzero:* below zero	*-ment* state	*fulfillment:* the state of being fulfilled
un- not	*unhealthy:* not healthy	*-ness* state	*happiness:* the state of being happy

Task 2: Draw a box around the prefix in the word imperceptible in the passage on page 43. What does this prefix mean in English?

» **TIP 3: Try replacing the highlighted word with each of the answer options.** Then, try reading the sentence. When you insert the correct answer option, the sentence should be logical and should support the main ideas of the passage. Answer options that don't make sense when inserted should be eliminated.

Task 3: Draw a line through the answer options for questions 1 and 2 on page 43 that are illogical or contradict the main ideas of the passage when inserted in place of the highlighted words.

» **Tip 4: Increase your vocabulary knowledge before the test**. Use a dictionary and the Academic Word List on page 170 to learn the definitions of new words. The Academic Word List, created by Coxhead (2000), consists of 570 word families that occur frequently over a wide range of academic texts. Knowing and practicing these words will help you build your vocabulary.

Task 4: Use a dictionary to look up the highlighted words in questions 1 and 2 on page 43.

TEST TIP!

On the day of the test, you may notice that some of the words in the reading passages are underlined. These are typically technical words that are defined for you. To see the definition, just click on the underlined word.

PROGRESSIVE PRACTICE: Get Ready

A Scan the short passage about climate. Underline the main idea of each paragraph.

The Climate of the Atlantic Archipelago

[1] The Atlantic Archipelago is a group of islands located northwest of continental Europe. The largest island in the archipelago, Great Britain, covers nearly 90 thousand square miles and is one of the most heavily populated islands in the world, with nearly 60 million inhabitants. Ireland, located west of Great Britain, is the second largest island in the group, with a land area of about 32 thousand square miles and a population of 6.4 million. In addition to the two large islands, the Atlantic Archipelago consists of more than six thousand smaller islands. The entire archipelago covers more than 120 square miles, and its location plays a large role in the climate of the region.

[2] The latitude of the Atlantic Archipelago undoubtedly influences its climate. Latitude refers to how far north or south a place is in relation to the equator, the imaginary line that divides the north half of the world from the south half. Typically, the farther away from the equator a location is, the weaker the intensity of sunlight in that area. The Atlantic Archipelago is about 54 degrees north of the equator, similar to Russia and Canada. Yet, despite their northern location, the islands have a temperate marine climate that ranges from 32 degrees Fahrenheit in the winter to 90 degrees Fahrenheit in the summer.

[3] The islands enjoy mild temperatures largely because of their proximity to the ocean. Ocean water heats up and cools down more slowly than land, so areas by the coast usually experience less extreme temperature swings in summers and winters. Furthermore, the Atlantic Archipelago benefits from being near the Gulf Stream. The Gulf Stream is an ocean current that begins in the Gulf of Mexico, flows up the east coast of North America, then crosses the Atlantic Ocean and reaches the Atlantic Archipelago. The water transported by the Gulf Stream ranges in temperature from 45–72 degrees, which is about twice as warm as the water surrounding the Gulf Stream. The islands in the Atlantic Archipelago constantly receive this warm ocean water from the Gulf Stream, which makes the climate about 10 degrees warmer than it would be otherwise.

Glossary:

€ POWERED BY COBUILD

climate: general weather conditions

marine: relating to the sea

B Read the questions carefully. What types of questions are they? Underline any key words in the questions and answer options that you will look for while you review the passage. Then, answer the questions. Note the correct answers and read why the answer options are correct or incorrect.

1. Based on the information in paragraph 2, which of the following can be inferred about sunlight?

○ Its intensity is not affected by latitude.

○ Areas north of the equator receive less sunlight.

○ It is most intense near the equator.

○ Places near the ocean receive more sunlight.

ANSWER ANALYSIS ▶

Question Type: **Inference**

✗ The author says that the intensity of sunlight is weaker the farther away from the equator a place is. This means that latitude does influence the intensity of the sun.

✗ The author says that the farther away from the equator a place is, the less intense the sunlight is in that location. This does not mean that these areas receive less sunlight.

✓ **The author explains that the intensity of sunlight is weaker in areas far from the equator. Based on this information, you can infer that it is strongest at the equator.**

✗ While the islands of the Atlantic Archipelago are surrounded by the ocean, the author doesn't say that this factor accounts for the amount of sunlight that the islands receive.

2. The word temperate in the passage is closest in meaning to

○ moderate.

○ extreme.

○ varying.

○ humid.

ANSWER ANALYSIS ▶

Question Type: **Vocabulary**

✓ **The contrast words "yet" and "despite" in the same sentence signal that "temperate" is the opposite of what one would expect from northern locations (i.e., coldness). In the next sentence, the author writes that the islands have mild temperatures. "Mild" is another word for "moderate," or lacking serious extremes.**

✗ "Temperate" means lacking in extreme temperatures.

✗ While "varying" works in the sentence, it changes the meaning. The focus should be on the lack of extremes, not on the range of temperatures.

✗ The islands may have a humid climate, but "humid" does not have the same meaning as "temperate."

3. The word proximity in the passage is closest in meaning to

○ dependence.

○ introduction.

○ significance.

○ closeness.

ANSWER ANALYSIS ▶

Question Type: **Vocabulary**

✗ This answer option is illogical. While the islands could be said to be dependent on the ocean in some sense, this dependence would have no effect on temperatures.

✗ Replacing "proximity" with "introduction" creates a sentence with a confusing meaning. This answer is incorrect.

✗ While "significance" works in the sentence, it changes the meaning of the sentence so that it doesn't support the main ideas of the paragraph.

✓ **The author mentions that the Atlantic Archipelago is surrounded by water. Also, it makes sense that being close to the ocean would affect temperatures.**

4. Which of the following can be inferred about the Gulf Stream?

○ It leads to warm water temperatures in the Gulf of Mexico.

○ It keeps its warmth as it crosses the Atlantic Ocean.

○ It carries cooler waters during the summer.

○ It ends when it reaches the Atlantic Archipelago.

ANSWER ANALYSIS ▶

Question Type: **Inference**

✗ The author mentions that the Gulf Stream originates in the Gulf of Mexico, but there is no information that indicates how the current affects water temperatures there.

✓ **The author says that the current crosses the Atlantic Ocean and that the Atlantic Archipelago receives warm water from the current. From this information, you can infer that the current keeps its heat as it crosses the ocean.**

✗ The author mentions that the Atlantic Archipelago constantly receives warm water from the current. This suggests that the temperature of the water does not change in the summer.

✗ The author describes the movement of the current up until it reaches the Atlantic Archipelago. This does not mean that the Gulf Stream ends there.

PROGRESSIVE PRACTICE: Get Set

A Scan the short passage about biology. Write the main idea of each paragraph.

1. _____

2. _____

3. _____

4. _____

Poison Sequestration

[1] There are hundreds of thousands of poisonous organisms in the world, and many of these plants and animals are able to produce their own toxins. However, there is also a class of poisonous animals that cannot produce toxins independently. Instead, they use a process called poison sequestration in order to obtain toxins. By using this method, animals are able to save and use toxins that are produced by another organism, generally in order to defend themselves from predators. Given the advantages that toxins offer, many animals have developed multiple strategies for obtaining poison through poison sequestration.

[2] One method of poison sequestration involves obtaining toxins from plant sources. This strategy is especially common among insect species, such as butterflies, beetles, and ants, but it's also employed by several larger species. One such animal is the African crested rat, a species native to West Africa that can grow up to fourteen inches long. The rat's spine is protected by long, absorbent fur that sticks up when the rat is threatened. This strip of fur is covered with poison that the rat obtains by chewing on the bark and roots of the arrow poison tree and coating the hairs on its spine with the chewed material. Thus, if a predator attacks the rat, it inadvertently ingests the poison, which causes heart attacks in many organisms.

[3] Another poison sequestration strategy involves obtaining poison from other animals. Typically, this strategy is used by larger animals, like the European hedgehog, that are capable of hunting other organisms. In a manner similar to African crested rats, European hedgehogs chew the skins of poisonous toads and slather the remains onto themselves. However, some small species have developed methods of obtaining toxins from animals larger than them. For example, the blue sea slug, a creature that usually grows no larger than one inch, becomes poisonous by eating the tentacles of an aquatic animal called the Portuguese man-of-war. These tentacles are up to 100 feet long and contain a deadly poison. When blue sea slugs eat Portuguese man-of-wars, they store the poisonous parts of the animal in special pouches so they can use it for defense at a later time.

[4] It is also common for poison sequestration to progress up the food chain, meaning that many predators sequester poison from prey that have also sequestered poison. For instance, the tiger keelback, a species of snake, sequesters poison by eating poisonous frogs. In many cases, poisonous frogs become toxic by eating poisonous insects.

Glossary:

⊑ POWERED BY COBUILD

ingest: to eat or adsorb something

toxin: a poisonous substance

B Read the questions carefully and note whether they are inference or vocabulary questions. Then, answer the questions. Write the letter of each answer option next to the reason in the *Answer Analysis* box explaining why it is correct or incorrect.

1. The word inadvertently in paragraph 2 is closest in meaning to

○ suddenly. [A]

○ partially. [B]

○ accidentally. [C]

○ harmlessly. [D]

ANSWER ANALYSIS ▶

Question Type: **Vocabulary**

_____ ✗ While "suddenly" works in the sentence, it doesn't fit the general idea of the passage.

_____ ✗ The poison causes heart attacks in some animals, so eating the poison is not harmless.

_____ ✗ This answer option is illogical because there is no reason that the predator would eat only some of the poison.

_____ ✓ **An animal attacking the rat doesn't know that it is poisonous. Thus, it eats the poison by accident.**

2. Based on the information in paragraph 3, what can be inferred about poison sequestration?

○ A small animal is more likely to sequester poison from plants than animals. [A]

○ Poison sequestration is a common defense strategy among large animals. [B]

○ Poison that is sequestered by animals is usually stored in special pouches. [C]

○ Small animals are typically able to produce their own poisons. [D]

ANSWER ANALYSIS ▶

Question Type: **Inference**

_____ ✗ There is nothing in the passage that suggests that poison sequestration is more common among larger animals.

_____ ✗ The author describes several small animals that sequester poison because they cannot produce their own.

_____ ✗ The author mentions only one animal that stores poison in special pouches.

_____ ✓ **The author states that larger animals are able to hunt other animals, which makes them more likely to get poison from other organisms. This suggests that smaller animals are more likely to get poison from plants.**

3. The word slather in paragraph 3 is closest in meaning to

○ gather. [A]

○ toss. [B]

○ drop. [C]

○ spread. [D]

ANSWER ANALYSIS ▶

Question Type: **Vocabulary**

_____ ✗ While "slather" and "gather" look similar, they do not have the same meaning.

_____ ✗ "Toss" means to throw into the air. There are no clues that this is the action that the author is referring to in the passage.

_____ ✓ **"Slather" means to spread a thick substance over something. This is the correct answer option.**

_____ ✗ This answer option is illogical because it's unlikely that the animals would be able to drop the remains on themselves.

4. Based on the information in paragraph 4, what can be inferred about toxins?

○ Most toxins that are sequestered by animals are produced by plants. [A]

○ Toxins used by snakes are typically sequestered from frogs. [B]

○ Predators that do not eat plants may sequester toxins originally made by plants. [C]

○ Toxins produced by insects are the main source of poisons used by plants. [D]

ANSWER ANALYSIS ▶

Question Type: **Inference**

_____ ✗ There is no information given to support the idea that most snakes sequester poison from frogs.

_____ ✓ **The author says that predators often eat animals that have sequestered poison from sources like plants. This means that even if the predator does not eat plants, it might sequester poison from a plant source.**

_____ ✗ The author does not give any information to support this inference.

_____ ✗ The author says that many insects get their poison from plants, not that plants get poison from insects.

PROGRESSIVE PRACTICE: Go for the TOEFL Test

Read the passage about a topic in astronomy.

TOEFL Reading

VIEW TEXT REVIEW VOLUME HELP BACK NEXT

Question 1 of 12

HIDE TIME 00:17:20

Origins of the Moon

1 Throughout the nineteenth and twentieth centuries, several astronomers advanced competing theories about how the moon formed. For example, in 1878, astronomer George Howard Darwin proposed the fission theory, which claimed that early in Earth's formation, the planet began spinning extremely fast. Darwin believed that the rapid spinning motion caused a large chunk of Earth to break off and launch into space. This chunk then began orbiting Earth and became the moon. Another explanation, called the condensation theory, stated that while the solar system was still forming, a star exploded and left behind mass amounts of debris. According to the condensation theory, Earth and the moon formed from this debris at roughly the same time and through the same processes.

2 These theories were accepted to various degrees among the scientific community, and there was much debate among scientists about which one provided the most complete account of how the moon formed. Ultimately, the validity of both was undermined in the second half of the twentieth century. At this time, newly available data from lunar missions revealed several inconsistencies between the assumptions of the theories and facts about the moon. For one, data collected on the moon showed that, at some point, the moon was subjected to intense heat. However, neither the fission theory nor the condensation theory involved processes that would result in intense heat. Furthermore, there is no evidence that Earth experienced similarly intense heat. Thus, both theories were deemed invalid.

3 Data from lunar explorations also revealed another discrepancy with the condensation theory. According to the theory, the moon and Earth formed through the same process at the same time. Scientists pointed out that if Earth and the moon actually formed this way, they should have the same chemical composition. But when scientists obtained samples from the surface of the moon, they found that the chemical composition of the moon was different from that of Earth, which severely discredited the condensation theory.

4 Information from lunar explorations played a large role in dispelling previous theories of lunar formation. However, it also helped astronomers formulate a theory that better explains how the moon was formed. Today, the most current and widely accepted explanation is called the giant impactor theory. According to this theory, all of the planets in the solar system formed at the same time. In addition to the planets that are currently in our solar system, scientists believe that a planet called Theia also developed at this time. Theia was likely about 4,000 miles in diameter, roughly the size of Mars. During Earth's formation, Theia crashed into Earth and disintegrated. Scientists believe that the collision between Earth and Theia caused at least two large chunks of Earth to break off. The larger of these chunks is thought to have become the moon. Meanwhile, scientists believe that the smaller chunk, which was probably about one-third the size of our moon, also orbited Earth for some time. These two pieces orbited Earth together for a period of time that lasted between 10 million and 100 million years. Then, the smaller moon was eventually destroyed when it collided into the larger one.

5 Unlike previous theories, the giant impactor theory adequately explains most of the data collected on the moon. For example, the theory accounts for why there is evidence that the moon was subjected to strong heat while there is no such evidence on Earth. Scientists speculate that when Theia collided with Earth, intense heat was produced at the point of impact. Moreover, the material that was directly hit by Theia was likely the chunk of Earth that broke off and formed the moon. This also explains why the chemical composition of Earth and the moon is different—the ejected material that formed the moon was primarily from Earth's outer surface. Thus, the chunk that became the moon represents only a portion of the composition of Earth.

Glossary:

⊜ POWERED BY COBUILD

discrepancy: a noticeable difference between two things

dispel: to stop someone from having an idea or feeling

Now answer the questions.

1. Based on the information in paragraph 1, what can be inferred about Darwin's theory of moon formation?
   ○ It was the first theory of moon formation to gain wide acceptance.
   ○ It assumed that Earth and the moon were made of the same material.
   ○ It was inspired by other scientists' work on the condensation theory.
   ○ It explained why Earth and the moon developed at different times.

2. The word undermined in paragraph 2 is closest in meaning to
   ○ dismissed.
   ○ weakened.
   ○ proven.
   ○ expanded.

3. In paragraph 2, the author implies that
   ○ the majority of scientists favored the condensation theory over the fission theory.
   ○ lunar exploration provided evidence to support the fission theory.
   ○ data from lunar missions was not available to the entire scientific community.
   ○ the chemical composition of the moon was unknown until after the 1950s.

4. The word disintegrated in paragraph 4 is closest in meaning to
   ○ became larger.
   ○ softened.
   ○ broke apart.
   ○ disappeared.

5. Based on the information in paragraph 4, what is implied about the giant impactor theory?
   ○ Its accuracy is still disputed by many astronomers.
   ○ It cannot explain what became of the planet Theia.
   ○ It describes the creation of multiple moons.
   ○ It is closely based on the condensation theory.

6. The word speculate in paragraph 5 is closest in meaning to
   ○ theorize.
   ○ confirm.
   ○ overlook.
   ○ reveal.

Sentence Summary Questions

A sentence summary question asks you to choose the answer option that provides the best summary of a highlighted sentence from a passage. Expect to see no more than one sentence summary question per reading passage.

Sentence summary questions may be worded as follows:

» *Which of the following best expresses the essential information in the highlighted sentence? Incorrect answer options change the meaning in important ways or leave out essential information.*

QUICK GUIDE: Sentence Summary Questions

Definition	A sentence summary question asks you to choose the answer option that has the same meaning as the highlighted sentence in the passage. The highlighted sentence that the question is based on is typically two to four lines long.
Targeted Skills	In order to correctly answer a sentence summary question, you must be able to: • understand the main ideas and main supporting details in the reading passage. • identify how the ideas in the highlighted sentence fit in with the rest of the paragraph that it appears in. • recognize the answer option that accurately paraphrases the information from the passage.
The Correct Answer	The correct answer for a sentence summary question correctly rewords and simplifies the information from the highlighted sentence. It will contain all the essential, or important, information from the original sentence.
Wrong Answer Options	Watch out for answer options that: • leave out important ideas from the highlighted sentence. • contradict the main ideas and facts from the passage by changing cause and effect relationships or misstating the frequency of an event. • include the exact wording and sentence constructions from the original highlighted sentence. The correct answer will typically use synonyms and change the construction of the original sentence.

WALK THROUGH: Sentence Summary Questions

A Quickly read the sample sentence summary question below. Underline any key words in the answer options that will help you determine the correct answer.

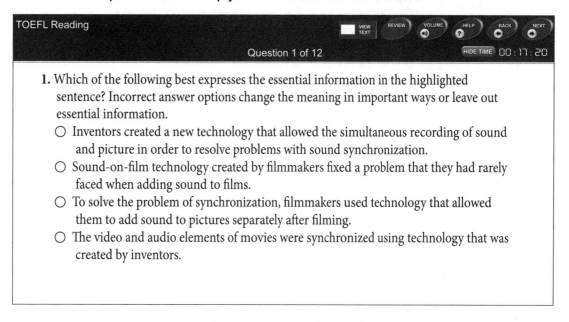

TOEFL Reading

Question 1 of 12

HIDE TIME 00:17:20

1. Which of the following best expresses the essential information in the highlighted sentence? Incorrect answer options change the meaning in important ways or leave out essential information.

○ Inventors created a new technology that allowed the simultaneous recording of sound and picture in order to resolve problems with sound synchronization.

○ Sound-on-film technology created by filmmakers fixed a problem that they had rarely faced when adding sound to films.

○ To solve the problem of synchronization, filmmakers used technology that allowed them to add sound to pictures separately after filming.

○ The video and audio elements of movies were synchronized using technology that was created by inventors.

B Now read the short passage about sound in film. While you read, underline key ideas in the highlighted sentence that should be included in the correct answer. When you are done, mark the correct answer for the question above.

Sound in Early Film

[1] In the late nineteenth century, technological innovations led to the birth of a new art form: the motion picture. The first motion pictures could be viewed by only one person at a time. Further innovation made it possible to show films to larger audiences, and the first motion picture appeared before a live audience in Paris in 1895. These early films were silent, although they were sometimes accompanied by live orchestras or narrators in the theater. Silent films were a popular form of entertainment in the United States, Great Britain, Japan, and India in the early twentieth century, but they were soon replaced by "talking pictures," films that incorporated sound as well as images. The rising popularity of talking pictures was made possible by two important advances in technology.

[2] One of the most significant barriers to producing films with sound was the synchronization, or simultaneous playing, of sound and pictures. In many early films, the sound was played separately from the film. This system was unreliable, however, as skips or other minor problems with the sound disc could cause the sound recording and the video to play at different times or speeds. To solve this problem, inventors created sound-on-film technology that allowed filmmakers to record the sound and the pictures together, making it impossible for the video and audio elements to become separated.

[3] But even when the sound was precisely synchronized with the images onscreen, it was often difficult for audiences to hear the recordings. Advancements in amplification technology, or processes for increasing sound volume, were essential to the popularization of films with sound and dialogue. Improvements in microphones made the recording process more effective, and the development of more powerful speakers made it possible to play sound capable of filling larger and larger spaces.

Glossary:

⊜ POWERED BY COBUILD

synchronization: two activities, processes, or movements happening at the same time

amplification: ability to increase the strength or intensity or something, usually sound

GET IT RIGHT: Tips and Tasks for Answering Correctly

» **TIP 1: Create your own paraphrase of the highlighted sentence.** After reviewing the highlighted sentence, quickly paraphrase it, being sure to include all of the key ideas from the original sentence. Then, look at the answer options and check if any of them are close to your rephrasing.

TASK 1: Paraphrase the highlighted sentence from the passage on page 53. Underline one answer option for the question on page 53 that is similar to your paraphrase.

» **TIP 2: Eliminate answer options that leave out important information from the highlighted sentence.** Remember, the correct answer option will include all of the important information from the highlighted sentence. An answer option that includes factual information from the passage but leaves out important information is incorrect and should be eliminated.

TASK 2: Draw a line through an answer option on page 53 that leaves out important information from the highlighted sentence. What information was left out?

» **TIP 3: Watch out for answers that contradict the facts and main ideas from the passage.** For sentence summary questions, the correct answers will always support the facts and main ideas of the passage. Incorrect answer options may contradict the facts of the passage by switching the cause and effect relationship of an event. In other words, an event that was described as the cause of something else in the passage may be described as the effect in an incorrect answer option. Also, watch out for answer options that contain frequency adverbs, as these may change the meaning of the sentence so that they contradict facts from the passage.

Common Frequency Adverbs	
always	occasionally
frequently	seldom
usually	rarely
often	hardly ever
sometimes	never

TASK 3: Draw a line through one answer option on page 53 that includes one of the frequency adverbs from the table above. How does this frequency adverb change the meaning of the sentence?

» **TIP 4: Check for rewording of language from the passage.** The correct answer option usually contains synonyms and a variation of the original sentence construction. If you see an answer option that has similar wording and / or a similar structure as the highlighted sentence, be sure to read it carefully before choosing it.

TASK 4: Draw a line through one answer option on page 53 that has similar wording as the original sentence. Why is this answer option incorrect?

Passage Summary Questions

A passage summary question (referred to as a prose summary question in ETS preparation materials) presents you with an introductory statement that provides a brief overview of the main idea of the passage. It will also give you six answer options. You will have to choose the three answer options that best summarize the main ideas of the passage. There is typically no more than one passage summary question per reading passage. See the *Walk Through* on page 56 for an example of how passage summary questions are presented on the test.

TEST TIP!

For passage summary questions, you cannot earn partial credit. That means you must choose all three correct answers—if you include even one incorrect answer, you will not get any credit for the question.

QUICK GUIDE: Passage Summary Questions

Definition	A passage summary question provides you with: • an introductory sentence that summarizes the main idea of the passage. • six sentences that are related to the passage. You must choose three of the six sentences that best summarize the entire passage. To choose a sentence, click on it with your mouse and drag it to the gray box.
Targeted Skills	In order to correctly answer a passage summary question, you must be able to: • recognize the main ideas of the passage. • understand the basic organization of the passage. • identify the points that the author uses to support the main topic.
The Correct Answer	The correct answer for a passage summary question will reflect the main ideas of the passage. By reading the introductory sentence and the three correct sentences, a reader who is unfamiliar with the passage should be able to understand what the passage is about.
Wrong Answer Options	Watch out for answer options that include: • information that is mentioned in the passage but is not one of the main ideas of the passage. • ideas that are not mentioned in the passage at all. • information that contradicts the facts presented in the passage.

WALK THROUGH: Passage Summary Questions

A Quickly read the sample passage summary question below. For each answer option, underline key words that will help you while you scan the passage.

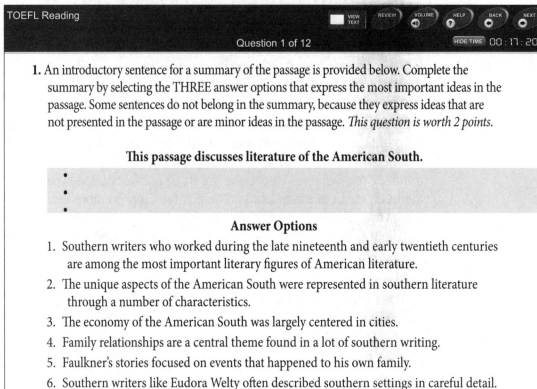

TOEFL Reading

VIEW TEXT | REVIEW | VOLUME | HELP | BACK | NEXT

Question 1 of 12

HIDE TIME 00:17:20

1. An introductory sentence for a summary of the passage is provided below. Complete the summary by selecting the THREE answer options that express the most important ideas in the passage. Some sentences do not belong in the summary, because they express ideas that are not presented in the passage or are minor ideas in the passage. *This question is worth 2 points.*

This passage discusses literature of the American South.

-
-
-

Answer Options

1. Southern writers who worked during the late nineteenth and early twentieth centuries are among the most important literary figures of American literature.
2. The unique aspects of the American South were represented in southern literature through a number of characteristics.
3. The economy of the American South was largely centered in cities.
4. Family relationships are a central theme found in a lot of southern writing.
5. Faulkner's stories focused on events that happened to his own family.
6. Southern writers like Eudora Welty often described southern settings in careful detail.

B Now read the short passage about literature. While you read, underline information that you think will help you answer the questions in Part A. When you are done reading, circle the three correct answers for the question above.

Literature of the American South

[1] The American South has developed a culture that is distinctive in many ways. While the literature of the American South is diverse, southern writers—especially those who worked in the late nineteenth and early twentieth centuries—often employed similar strategies to explore the distinct character of the region.

[2] Family relationships are a central theme found often in southern writing. Many stories describe the events that affect a family for several generations. For example, William Faulkner, a key writer in the southern literary tradition, wrote novels that focused on family structure and familial bonds. Perhaps because the economy of the American South is traditionally agricultural, Faulkner's novels are especially concerned with how land ownership is passed from generation to generation.

[3] In addition to writing about subjects that reflect the values of southern culture, southern writers also created similar settings or locations in their works. Eudora Welty, a southern novelist and short story writer, describes the southern landscape in careful detail. The settings of her stories and novels are filled with plants and animals that are specific to the American South, and her writing often makes a place, like a particular river or a certain town, central to the story she tells. While some stories may seem like they could take place anywhere, many of the stories in southern literature are rooted in a specifically southern environment.

Glossary:

⊏ POWERED BY COBUILD

distinct: different or separate from something of the same type

rooted: strongly influenced by something

GET IT RIGHT: Tips and Tasks for Answering Correctly

» **TIP 1: Look for topic sentences for each paragraph in the passage.** A topic sentence is one that introduces the main topic of the paragraph. For the first paragraph of the passage, the topic sentence will probably appear toward the end of the paragraph. For the paragraphs that follow, expect to find the topic sentence toward the beginning of the paragraph. By locating and rereading the topic sentences in the passage, you will be able to quickly pick out the answer options that are similar in content.

TASK 1: Draw a box around the topic sentence for each paragraph in the passage on page 56. Note the location of these sentences in the passage.

» **TIP 2: Eliminate answer options that include only minor details.** Some answer options may include information that appears in the passage but is nonetheless unimportant. Minor details are those that aren't important when describing the main ideas of the passage. If you are unsure if a detail is minor or not, imagine whether someone who is unfamiliar with the passage would understand the main idea of the passage if you left that detail out.

TASK 2: Draw a line through one answer option on page 56 that contains minor details.

» **TIP 3: Watch out for answer options that include information that wasn't mentioned in the passage.** The correct answers for passage summary questions will always be mentioned in the passage. In some cases, the information in an answer option may seem familiar or appear to relate in some way to the ideas from the passage. However, unless you can find direct references for that information in the passage, it cannot be the correct answer.

TASK 3: Draw a line through one answer option on page 56 that includes information that wasn't mentioned in the passage.

» **TIP 4: Be careful with answers that contradict the facts from the passage.** Because the correct answers for this question type represent the main ideas of the passage, they have to be factual according to the reading. To avoid choosing incorrect answer options, be sure to review the passage and see if you can find information to support each answer option. If you cannot, you should eliminate that answer option.

TASK 4: Draw a line through one answer option on page 56 that contradicts facts from the passage.

TEST TIP!

After you make your choices for passage summary questions, read all three answers again. Would someone who is unfamiliar with the subject of the passage understand what it is about based on your choices? If there is some doubt, consider reviewing your answers and trying to identify better choices.

PROGRESSIVE PRACTICE: Get Ready

A Scan the short passage about silversmithing. Underline the main idea of each paragraph.

Navajo Silversmithing

[1] The Navajo are an indigenous group that has lived for centuries in the southwestern part of what is now the United States. The traditional artwork of the Navajo, which includes rugs, baskets, and pottery, is popular around the globe. However, perhaps no Navajo artwork has attracted as much attention as the group's silverwork. In fact, silver jewelry made by Navajo designers is admired among art collectors all over the world. Interestingly, silversmithing is a relatively recent art form in the Navajo culture, but it is one that craftspeople have transformed into a uniquely Navajo creation that is an important part of modern Navajo culture and commerce.

[2] The origins of Navajo silversmithing can be traced back to a man named Atsidi Chon, who is widely regarded as the father of Navajo silversmithing. In the late 1860s, Chon learned silversmithing techniques from a Mexican craftsman. He brought his knowledge, as well as tools for working silver, back to his hometown and taught silversmithing to his sons. Within a few decades, many people in the Navajo community had learned the craft, though they faced several obstacles. For example, it was often difficult to obtain the materials required in order to work silver. In the early years of Navajo silverwork, craftspeople frequently melted coins or the silver hardware used in wagons and harnesses in order to obtain the silver for their work. Furthermore, it was equally hard to get the tools for crafting silver, and early silversmiths often resorted to using very basic techniques. Despite these early limitations, craftspeople were able to develop the characteristic style for which Navajo silver items are now known.

[3] Today, the work of Navajo silversmiths clearly reflects designs that are culturally important to the group. Characteristic Navajo silver jewelry often uses the traditional squash blossom bead, a hollow, rounded bead with petal-like carvings that, for some Navajo people, represents strength and vitality. Navajo silverwork also frequently incorporates turquoise, a semiprecious green or blue stone found in abundance in the American Southwest.

[4] Some elements of Navajo silverwork are clearly influenced by other cultures. In the late nineteenth and early twentieth centuries, the Navajo traded with Mexicans and Spaniards, whose ornate silver belts, spurs, and saddle decorations inspired early Navajo silversmiths. For instance, early Navajo silver often incorporated designs that resembled pomegranate blossoms, which were very popular among the Spanish who traveled to the American Southwest. The Navajo also traded with other Native American groups. The silverwork they acquired from these groups often copied British colonial styles, which further influenced Navajo silversmiths and inspired their craft.

Glossary:

≡ POWERED BY COBUILD

indigenous: people who belong to the country in which they are found

vitality: having great energy and liveliness

B Read the questions carefully. What type of questions are they? Underline any key words in the questions and answer options that you will look for while you review the passage. Then, answer the questions. Note the correct answers and read why the answer options are correct or incorrect.

1. Which of the following best expresses the essential information in the highlighted sentence in paragraph 3? Incorrect answer options change the meaning in important ways or leave out essential information.

   ○ Typical Navajo jewelry made out of silver uses a squash blossom bead that looks like a hollow bead with petals.

   ○ Navajo silversmiths use traditional squash blossoms and rounded, hollow beads to represent strength and vitality.

   ○ The characteristic Navajo silver jewelry often employs traditional squash blossom beads, a design that symbolizes strength and energy.

   ○ Hollow, rounded beads called squash blossom beads are often used in traditional Navajo jewelry.

ANSWER ANALYSIS ▶

Question Type: **Sentence Summary**

✗ This answer option leaves out the information about what the beads symbolize to the Navajo.

✗ This answer option contains incorrect information. Squash blossoms are the type of bead often used in the jewelry, not something used in addition to the beads.

✓ **This answer option contains all the essential information from the original sentence about squash blossom beads, including the significance of the beads.**

✗ This answer option doesn't include information about the significance of the beads to some Navajo people.

2. An introductory sentence for a brief summary of the passage is provided below. Complete the summary by selecting the THREE answer options that express the most important ideas in the passage. Some sentences do not belong in the summary because they express ideas that are not presented in the passage or are minor ideas in the passage. *This question is worth 2 points.*

This passage discusses the history of Navajo silversmithing.

-
-
-

Answer Options

1. The Navajo are famous for their rugs, baskets, and silver jewelry.

2. Although it was introduced to the group fairly recently, silversmithing is an important part of Navajo culture.

3. Atsidi Chon is credited as the father of Navajo silversmithing because he created new tools for working silver.

4. Though they often lacked the tools for silversmithing, Navajo artists created a distinctive style soon after the art form was introduced to the community.

5. Navajo silverwork employs designs inspired by other cultures but also features styles that are distinctly Navajo.

6. The design of the squash blossom bead and the use of turquoise are two styles that were borrowed from the Spanish.

ANSWER ANALYSIS ▶

Question Type: **Passage Summary**

✗ 1. While this fact was mentioned in the passage, it is minor and does not describe a major point from the passage.

✓ **2. At the end of the first paragraph, the author says that Navajo silversmithing was introduced to the community somewhat recently and that it is an important part of Navajo culture and commerce.**

✗ 3. The passage says that Atsidi Chon introduced silversmithing techniques to Navajo communities, not that he created new tools for working silver.

✓ **4. The author says that Navajo silversmiths created their characteristic style soon after Atsidi Chon first introduced the craft to the culture.**

✓ **5. Paragraph 4 discusses the influence of other cultures, while paragraph 3 discusses the features of Navajo silverwork that are distinctly Navajo.**

✗ 6. The author describes the squash blossom bead and the use of turquoise as Navajo innovations.

PROGRESSIVE PRACTICE: Get Set

A Scan the short passage about history. Write the main idea of each paragraph.

1. _____

2. _____

3. _____

Ancient Trade Routes

[1] In the first millennium, a number of civilizations lived throughout the Eurasian continent. In many cases, there was limited contact between these civilizations, in part because oceans, mountain ranges, and deserts discouraged travel between the east and west. Despite these difficulties, many traders traveled over land and sea in search of new customers and of new items to bring back to their homelands. Historians now refer to these routes, which spanned up to 4,300 miles and connected cultures on the eastern coasts of Asia to North Africa and the Mediterranean, as the Silk Road. Vital to trade from around the first century until about 1400, these routes were important because they allowed the exchange of both goods and ideas.

[2] The Silk Road was first developed by Chinese merchants who sought to trade silk and other goods within the Chinese Empire. Soon, the routes expanded as merchants from places like Persia, India, and Egypt sought out rare commodities that they could sell in their home countries. This kind of trade was very profitable because goods that were common in one place were priceless and exotic in another. For example, the Romans were greatly interested in Chinese silk, and the Chinese often bought horses from their western neighbors. Furthermore, traders from the east often carried items like gunpowder, porcelain, and paper, while traders from the west brought ivory, amber, and cosmetics. People from all over the Eurasian continent exchanged a wide variety of goods, which brought wealth to the merchants who sold the items, to the craftspeople who copied and sold domestic versions of foreign products, and even to people who lived along the trade routes and provided services to travelers.

[3] The trade routes brought many different cultures together, and they often exchanged ideas as well as material goods. Commerce encouraged cultural contact that significantly influenced the development of nations that were very different from one another. For instance, because of trade along the Silk Road, Chinese cities often housed visitors from many different places. Records show that in 754, one Chinese city was home to at least 5,000 foreigners. These visitors often brought new ideas and ways of thinking with them. Chinese thinkers adopted and adapted some of these new ideas, and they were particularly influenced by Indian philosophies. Many merchants also carried artwork with them on the trade routes. This promoted creative exchanges between cultures, and the similarities between some styles of Greek, Iranian, and Indian sculpture and painting are the result of those exchanges. Additionally, some records suggest that performance art forms, such as music, dance, and storytelling, were transformed by the connections the Silk Road permitted between civilizations.

Glossary:

ⓒ POWERED BY COBUILD

commodity: something that is sold for money

priceless: worth a very large amount of money

B Read the questions carefully and note whether they are sentence summary or passage summary questions. Then, answer the questions. Write the letter of each answer option next to the reason in the *Answer Analysis* box explaining why it is correct or incorrect.

1. Which of the following best expresses the essential information in the highlighted sentence in paragraph 2? Incorrect answer options change the meaning in important ways or leave out essential information.

○ People throughout Eurasia traded goods, bringing wealth to merchants and craftspeople and to people who provided services for the residents who lived along the trade routes. [A]

○ Merchants and craftspeople provided services, as did people who lived along the trade routes, and all three groups grew wealthy as a result. [B]

○ Merchants became rich largely because of the trading activities of craftspeople and people who lived along the trade routes in Eurasia. [C]

○ The trading activities throughout Eurasia led to the rise of wealth for merchants, craftspeople, and people who provided services to travelers along the routes. [D]

ANSWER ANALYSIS ▶

Question Type: **Sentence Summary**

_____ ✗ Craftspeople grew rich from selling replicas of foreign products, and people who lived along the routes earned money by providing services to travelers. The passage does not say that these groups were involved in trading.

_____ ✗ In the passage, the author says that services were provided by the people who lived along the trade routes, not by the merchants and craftspeople.

_____ ✓ **The highlighted sentence says that trade on the Eurasian continent brought wealth to merchants, craftspeople, and people who lived along the routes.**

_____ ✗ The passage does not mention a group that provided services to residents who lived along the trade routes.

---

2. An introductory sentence for a brief summary of the passage is provided below. Complete the summary by selecting the THREE answer options that express the most important ideas in the passage. Some sentences do not belong in the summary because they express ideas that are not presented in the passage or are minor ideas in the passage. *This question is worth 2 points.*

This passage discusses the history of trade on the Silk Road.

-
-
-

Answer Options

1. The trade routes known as the Silk Road connected cultures, allowing the exchange of merchandise and ideas. [A]

2. The cultures that lived throughout Eurasia during the first millennium didn't have much contact due to obstacles like oceans, mountains, and deserts. [B]

3. The Silk Road developed when Chinese merchants expanded their trade routes in order to obtain precious goods from Persia, India, and Egypt. [C]

4. While silk originally drove trade along the Silk Road, merchants from a number of cultures eventually began exchanging a variety of goods. [D]

5. In addition to promoting the exchange of goods, the Silk Road also helped people learn about the philosophies and art forms of different cultures. [E]

6. The Silk Road helped people from different cultures exchange ideas and philosophies, which is evident in the art forms produced along the Silk Road. [F]

ANSWER ANALYSIS ▶

Question Type: **Passage Summary**

_____ ✗ In the first paragraph, the author says that the cultures of Eurasia had contact with one another despite the obstacles.

_____ ✗ The author does not describe the art forms produced along the Silk Road.

_____ ✓ **This sentence summarizes the main idea of the entire passage, which is stated in the first paragraph.**

_____ ✓ **In paragraph 3, the author describes the exchange of ideas and art forms via the Silk Road.**

_____ ✗ In paragraph 2, the author states that the Silk Road was expanded when merchants from places like Persia, India, and Egypt sought goods from China, not the other way around.

_____ ✓ **The author says that the route was originally developed by Chinese merchants selling silk but that it later expanded as merchants from different places traded other items.**

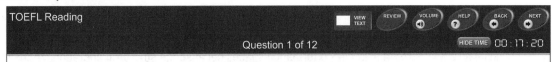

PROGRESSIVE PRACTICE: Go for the TOEFL Test

Read the passage about a topic in music.

TOEFL Reading

VIEW TEXT · REVIEW · VOLUME · HELP · BACK · NEXT

Question 1 of 12

HIDE TIME 00:17:20

Stradivarius Violins

[1] Antonio Stradivari was a famous luthier, or maker of stringed instruments, who lived in Italy during the early sixteenth century. Stradivari began his career at the young age of 12, when he began working under another famous luthier named Nicolò Amati. Stradivari learned the basic skills of violin making from Amati, but he eventually developed his own style, for which he is still known today. During his lifetime, Stradivari created an estimated 1,000 violins, 450 of which still survive. The violins of Antonio Stradivari are commonly regarded as the finest stringed instruments in the world, surpassing nearly all others in terms of sound quality as well as in visual appeal. Yet, despite the universal recognition of their exceptional quality, there is much debate over what makes Stradivarius violins so extraordinary.

[2] Some experts contend that the violins' superior quality derives from their structure. Though his early violins bore a strong resemblance to Amati instruments, the brilliant luthier eventually altered the standard violin structure by experimenting with the shape of the sound hole. Additionally, he varied the width of the purfling, which is the inlaid border located on the violin's back and front end. These structural alterations resulted in violins that produced louder sounds, which, in turn, allowed violinists to perform in larger concert halls because the sound could carry to the very back of the venue.

[3] While changes to the violins' structure allowed players to play more loudly, professional violinists argue that these changes do not sufficiently explain the instruments' superiority to other violins. They explain that the excellence of Stradivarius violins is based not only on the volumes that they are able to achieve, but also on their ability to produce loud sound without a loss of quality.

[4] One factor that may contribute directly to the superior sound quality is the type of varnish Stradivari used on the instruments. Stradivari stained each of his creations using the same process. First, he applied a coat of oil similar to that used on canvas paintings. Then, he added a layer of oil resin, a glaze-like substance. Finally, he applied a coat of red dye that gave the instruments the classic color of the Stradivarius violin. Some experts believe that the simple oil varnish preserves the wood's ability to vibrate, a quality that allows the instrument to produce sound. This hypothesis is supported by studies in which researchers tested the effects of different types of varnishes on sound quality. They found that violins that are stained with oil-based varnishes, like the Stradivarius violin, produce the most brilliant sound.

[5] It is also possible that the wood used to make Stradivarius violins may explain their unique qualities. Analyses have shown that the violins are made out of dense wood, a characteristic that has important implications for sound quality. This is because the particles in dense wood are closer together, resulting in clear, longer-lasting vibrations. As a result, a violin made with dense wood can carry sound over long distances with no loss in quality.

[6] For some time, many people believed that Stradivari acquired this dense wood from ancient cathedrals and castles. However, modern research suggests that, in actuality, it probably originated in the spruce forests that grew near Stradivari's home. Today, the wood from these forests is not very dense, but there are indications that it was denser during a period known as the Maunder Minimum. This period, which lasted from 1645 to 1715, was characterized by unusually cold temperatures in Europe, the coldest that the continent had experienced in 500 years. The cold temperatures, which probably resulted from a decrease in solar activity, are thought to have slowed tree growth, leading to denser wood than what would have resulted from warmer growing conditions. One researcher determined not only that the colder temperatures of the period caused the trees in the forests near the home of Stradivari to grow slower, but that the violin maker used the spruce wood from these forests in constructing his instruments.

Glossary:

ⓒ POWERED BY COBUILD

universal: something that relates to everyone or everything in the world or in a group

venue: the place where an event occurs

Now answer the questions.

1. Which of the following best expresses the essential information in the highlighted sentence in paragraph 2? Incorrect answer options change the meaning in important ways or leave out essential information.

   ○ The changes to the violins' structure increased the instruments' top volume, allowing violinists to perform in larger places because the sound would be heard.

   ○ Violinists could perform in larger performance spaces because the structural alterations to the violins allowed players to perform with greater ease.

   ○ Prior to the structural changes to the basic design of the violins, there were few large performance spaces for violinists.

   ○ Structural changes to the violins resulted in louder sound but a slight decrease in the quality of the sound.

2. Which of the following best expresses the essential information in the highlighted sentence in paragraph 6? Incorrect answer options change the meaning in important ways or leave out essential information.

   ○ Dense wood can grow in warm areas, though it is more common in places that have reduced solar activity and lower-than-usual temperatures.

   ○ Dense wood, which is associated with slow tree growth, resulted from cold temperatures during a period of lowered solar activity.

   ○ A decrease in solar activity led to slower tree growth because growth is affected by cold temperatures and wood density.

   ○ The cold temperatures during the period of decreased solar activity resulted in slow tree growth, which led to less dense wood than what would have grown in warmer temperatures.

3. An introductory sentence for a brief summary of the passage is provided below. Complete the summary by selecting the THREE answer options that express the most important ideas in the passage. Some sentences do not belong in the summary, because they express ideas that are not presented in the passage or are minor ideas in the passage. *This question is worth 2 points.*

This passage discusses the features that contribute to the exceptional sound of Stradivarius violins.

-
-
-

Answer Options

1. With only 450 of these instruments remaining today, Stradivarius violins are among the most valuable musical instruments in the world.

2. Stradivari adjusted the structure of the violins in ways that improved their ability to create loud and clear sounds.

3. Violinists who played Stradivarius violins were able to perform in large venues because the instruments were loud enough to be heard over long distances.

4. Researchers determined that Stradivarius violins had exceptional vibrational quality due to the process in which the varnish was applied.

5. The oil-based finish on all Stradivarius violins likely contributes to their sound quality because it preserves the wood's vibrational ability.

6. The dense wood used to create Stradivarius violins, which likely came from a forest near Stradivari's home, is a factor in the superior sound of the instruments.

Add Text Questions

An add text question (referred to as an insert text question in ETS preparation materials) asks you to determine where a given sentence will best fit in a passage. You will have a choice of four places to insert the sentence in the passage. The spots in the passage where you can insert the sentence will be marked with black squares [■]. Expect to see no more than one add text question per reading passage.

Add text questions may be worded as follows:

» *Look at the four squares [■] in paragraph 1 that indicate where the following sentence could be added to the passage.*
     As a result, scientists disagree about the origins of X.
Where would the sentence best fit?

QUICK GUIDE: Add Text Questions

Definition	An add text question presents you with a sentence. You must determine where in the passage the sentence best fits. The possible places where the sentence can be inserted will be marked with a black square [■]. To place the sentence, click on the appropriate black square in the passage and the sentence will appear in place of the black square. The black squares will typically appear in the same paragraph. However, they will not always appear in consecutive sentences.
Targeted Skills	In order to correctly answer an add text question, you must be able to: • understand the content and meaning of the given sentence. • identify the main idea of the paragraph(s) where the inserted sentence will appear. • recognize context clues, like grammatical agreement, that will help you decide where the sentence fits best. • identify transition words and know what they mean in the context of the passage.
The Correct Answer	The correct answer for an add text question will make sense in the context of the paragraph. The ideas will flow logically between the sentences that precede and follow the given sentence.
Wrong Answer Options	Watch out for answer options that: • don't agree with the grammatical forms in the sentences that come before and after the given sentence. • don't follow the logical progression of ideas in the paragraph.

WALK THROUGH: Add Text Questions

A Quickly read the sample add text question below. Underline the key words that help you understand the given sentence.

TOEFL Reading

VIEW TEXT | REVIEW | VOLUME | HELP | BACK | NEXT

Question 1 of 12

HIDE TIME 00:17:20

1. Look at the four squares [■] in paragraph 2 that indicate where the following sentence could be added to the passage.

   As a result, the agricultural productivity in these areas has declined by 20 percent.

   Where would the sentence best fit?

   ○ a
   ○ b
   ○ c
   ○ d

B Now read the short passage about environmental science. While you read, note the four places where the sentence from Part A can go. When you are done reading, mark the correct answer for the question above. *Note*: the lowercase letters next to the black squares do not appear on the actual test.

Environmental Impacts of Irrigation Systems

[1] Over the last 35 years, agricultural production has increased significantly around the world. It's estimated that half of that increase can be attributed to the advancement and spread of irrigation technology. However, recent research shows that the environmental consequences of this technique may be more serious than previously thought.

[2] Waterlogging, a state in which the ground becomes oversaturated with water, is a particularly harmful effect of irrigation. When waterlogging occurs, the soil, heavy under the weight of the water, begins to become tightly packed. [a] ■ Thus, it is difficult for oxygen to enter the soil, and without it, plant roots essentially suffocate. [b] ■ According to experts, approximately 10 percent of the world's arable land is waterlogged. [c] ■ Additionally, it's difficult to prevent waterlogging from occurring because tests that determine whether a field has a high possibility of becoming waterlogged are very expensive. [d] ■

[3] Another consequence of irrigation is salinization, or the accumulation of salt crystals on the surface of a field. Excessive irrigation causes water to collect on the surface of a field. Eventually, this water begins to evaporate, drawing salt and minerals from underground rocks to the surface in the process. Once it reaches the surface of the soil, the salt forms into crystals, which reduce plants' ability to absorb water from the soil. Thus, even if there is plenty of water, salinization makes it difficult for plants to absorb the water they need to survive. When salinization occurs, plants begin to wither and agricultural productivity suffers.

Glossary:

⋐ POWERED BY COBUILD

arable: land that is used for growing crops, such as wheat and barley

wither: to dry up and die

GET IT RIGHT: Tips and Tasks for Answering Correctly

» **TIP 1: Review the given sentence and the paragraph(s) in which the black squares appear.** When you read the sentence that you are supposed to insert into the passage, make sure you understand it completely. Also, while you read the paragraph in question, pay attention to the main idea in that paragraph and how the author builds the argument. Also, be sure to think about how the given sentence may fit into the paragraph.

TASK 1: Draw a box around the given sentence in the question on page 66. Then, draw a box around the main idea of paragraph 2 in the passage on page 66.

» **TIP 2: Pay attention to any transition words and know what they mean.** Transition words are expressions that writers use to make their writing clear and easy to understand. By learning and recognizing transition words, you will be able to determine the logic of the paragraph, making it easier for you to identify areas where there is a shift in flow or a lack of logical progression. See the table below for examples of transition language.

Function	Transition Language		Examples
Indicating Sequence	first second third eventually	since then until prior to	**First**, the volcano erupts, emptying the chamber beneath it. **Eventually**, the land around the empty chamber collapses.
Continuing in the Same Line of Thinking	again additionally furthermore	and equally likewise	Fleas have extremely long legs relative to their body size. **Likewise**, grasshoppers also have very long legs.
Shift in Focus	although despite regardless	instead even so however	The Atacama Desert is one of the driest places on Earth. **Even so**, it is home to several communities.
Indicating Cause and Effect	**Cause** when as long as in order to because of due to	**Effect** for this reason as a result thus accordingly consequently	**Due to** the speed of the water, the rock becomes eroded quickly. **Consequently**, the channel becomes deep over a short amount of time.

TASK 2: Underline three transition words in paragraph 2 of the passage on page 66.

» **TIP 3: Try inserting the sentence in all of the available spots.** Remember, you are allowed to change the answer as many times as you want, so feel free to try all of the spots. When you do this, read the paragraph and pay attention to how the information flows depending on where you place the sentence. Does it fit with the sentences that come before and after? The correct answer will have the most logical flow.

TASK 3: Try inserting the sentence in each place and reread it for sense. Then, circle the one answer option on page 66 that is the best option when the sentence is set at that place in the passage.

Table Completion Questions

A table completion question (referred to as a fill-in-a-table question in ETS preparation materials) presents you with a list of statements that are related to a passage. You must correctly categorize the statements in the table according to the directions. The table will categorize information presented in the passage. There is typically no more than one table completion question per reading passage. Please see the *Walk Through* on page 69 for an example of how table completion questions are presented.

QUICK GUIDE: Table Completion Questions

Definition	Table completion questions provide you with a table that reflects two or three categories or criteria from the passage. You are also presented with seven or nine statements related to the passage, and you need to select which categories the statements belong in, if any. Here is a summary of the table types that may appear on the test:

Columns/Rows	Statements	Correct Answers	Points
2 columns	7 statements	5 correct answers	3 points
3 columns	7 statements	5 correct answers	3 points
2 columns	9 statements	7 correct answers	4 points
3 columns	9 statements	7 correct answers	4 points

In order to answer the question, you must click on the statements and drag them to the correct categories in the table.

Targeted Skills	In order to correctly answer a table completion question, you must: • be able to recognize the main ideas of the passage. • know the organizational styles that are commonly associated with the question type. • be able to identify the points that the author uses to support the main topic.
The Correct Answer	The correct answers for table completion questions will fit the categories in which they are classified. The correct statements will usually contain reworded information from the passage. Also, the correct statements are usually major ideas from the passage. For this question type, it is possible to earn partial credit depending on how many of the statements you correctly categorize.
Wrong Answer Options	Out of the seven or nine answer options, there are usually two that do not fit into the table. Watch out for answer options that: • do not fit into the general categories described in the chart. • include information that is not mentioned in the passage. • contradict the facts from the passage. • are minor details that are mentioned only briefly in the passage.

WALK THROUGH: Table Completion Questions

A Quickly read the sample table completion question below. Underline key words in the statements that will help you classify them.

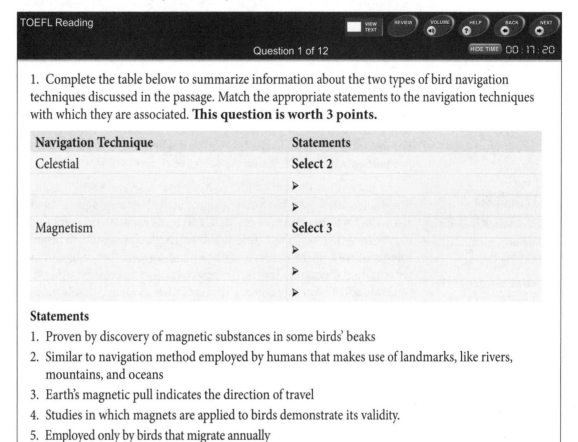

TOEFL Reading

Question 1 of 12

1. Complete the table below to summarize information about the two types of bird navigation techniques discussed in the passage. Match the appropriate statements to the navigation techniques with which they are associated. **This question is worth 3 points.**

Navigation Technique	Statements
Celestial	**Select 2**
	➢
	➢
Magnetism	**Select 3**
	➢
	➢
	➢

Statements

1. Proven by discovery of magnetic substances in some birds' beaks
2. Similar to navigation method employed by humans that makes use of landmarks, like rivers, mountains, and oceans
3. Earth's magnetic pull indicates the direction of travel
4. Studies in which magnets are applied to birds demonstrate its validity.
5. Employed only by birds that migrate annually
6. Allows birds to use the position of the sun or stars to navigate
7. Supported by observations that birds that don't have a clear view of the sky can't navigate effectively

B Now read the sample passage on the next page. While you read, underline information that you think will help you categorize the statements in Part A. When you are done reading, write the number of the statements in the correct boxes in the table. Note that you will use only five of the seven statements.

Bird Navigation Techniques

[1] Many species of birds migrate, flying up to 20,000 miles to temporary habitats in response to seasonal changes in temperature and precipitation. In many cases, migratory birds return to the same lake or particular piece of coastline year after year, which demonstrates their ability to find their way with surprising accuracy. Research suggests that birds have at least two primary methods of navigation.

[2] Some biologists have shown that birds probably use the location of celestial bodies, such as the sun and the stars, to orient themselves. Humans often use landmarks like rivers, mountains, and oceans, to determine their direction. In contrast, birds seem to ignore geographical features and depend on a kind of internal clock that tells them their location based on the time of day and the position of the sun or, if they are flying at night, the stars. For instance, scientists have observed that when the stars are obscured by clouds, birds cannot navigate as accurately as when the stars are clearly visible.

[3] In addition to the sun and stars, birds may also use Earth itself as a kind of compass. Some scientists argue that birds navigate using Earth's magnetic field. Certain metals cause Earth's poles to have a magnetic pull, and birds may use this pull to determine what direction they're traveling in. To test this, one scientist glued magnets to migratory birds. The magnets interfered with the birds' navigation, which suggests that magnetic pull is important for determining direction. Recently, researchers also discovered iron oxide, a magnetic material, in the beaks of homing pigeons. This is further evidence that birds may be sensitive to Earth's magnetic field and use that sense to navigate.

Glossary:

⬠ POWERED BY COBUILD

seasonal: a particular time of year

celestial: relating to the sky or heaven

TEST TIP!

For table completion questions, it's possible to earn partial credit. See the summary below for possible scores.

Five Answers	
# Correct	Points Awarded
5	3
4	2
3	1
0–2	0

Seven Answers	
7	4
6	3
5	2
4	1
0–3	0

GET IT RIGHT: Tips and Tasks for Answering Correctly

» **TIP 1: Learn the organizational styles that are associated with table completion questions.**
Table completion questions often appear with passages that present information that can be
categorized. Learning which types of passages often have table completion questions will help you
pay close attention to the categories as they are presented in the reading and make it easier for you to
quickly find the information you need in order to answer the question. The table below describes the
organizational styles of passages that are often followed by table completion questions.

Organizational Styles Associated With Table Completion Questions	
Pros and Cons	Presents the advantages and disadvantages of a topic
Compare and Contrast	Discusses the similarities and differences between two subjects
Cause and Effect	Describes the causes and effects of something
Theory-Support	Presents multiple theories about a subject and support for each theory
Classification	Discusses different types of something

Regardless of the organizational style, you should read the topic sentences for the paragraphs in order
to get a sense of the focus of each one. Then, you can pinpoint the information you need in order to
categorize the statements correctly.

TASK 1: Underline two sentences in the passage on page 70 that summarize the categories mentioned
in the table on the same page.

» **TIP 2: Watch out for answer options that contain the exact wording from the reading.** Typically,
the correct statements for table completion questions will contain paraphrased information from the
reading. If you see a statement that has the same wording from the passage, be sure to read it carefully
before choosing it.

TASK 2: Draw a line through one incorrect answer option on page 69 that contains the same wording
from the reading.

» **TIP 3: Eliminate answer options that represent minor points or contradict information from the
passage.** A statement that mentions only a minor point or that is not factual according to the passage
will not fit into the categories in the table.

TASK 3: Draw a line through one incorrect answer option on page 69 that contains information that is
not true according to the passage.

PROGRESSIVE PRACTICE: Get Ready

A Scan the short passage about biology. Underline the main idea of each paragraph.

Control of Malaria

[1] Malaria is a disease caused by a parasite in the blood. It has existed since at least 2700 BC, when its symptoms, including headache, fever, and nausea, were described in Chinese medical writings. However, unlike many other ancient diseases, malaria persists today, with approximately 225 million cases reported in 2009. Advances in medical sciences have made it possible to control the disease, but malaria is difficult to eradicate entirely for several reasons.

[2] Though early doctors developed some treatments for malaria using plants and herbs, it was not until the true nature of the disease was discovered that it was possible to formulate a more effective treatment. [a] ■ In 1880, a French surgeon discovered that malaria was not caused by a virus, but by a parasite living in the blood of infected people. [b] ■ The discovery that malaria was not a viral infection led to developments in medicine that focused on destroying the parasite. [c] ■ In 1897, a British doctor stationed in India discovered that malaria parasites were passed from person to person by mosquitoes. [d] ■

[3] Today, medical researchers have made several developments in controlling the spread of malaria. For one, doctors now have access to a wide array of effective medicines for treating malaria, and many of these can be taken to prevent the disease or even build up a partial immunity to it. Furthermore, scientists have developed pesticides to kill mosquitoes and thus prevent the spread of malaria. Additionally, in some places, controlling malaria is achieved through non-medicinal methods, such as the use of mosquito nets that are constructed from fine mesh cloth. The nets are typically placed over beds in order to protect people from mosquito bites while they sleep.

[4] Despite these advancements in treating and preventing malaria, the disease is still a worldwide problem. Because mosquitoes and the malaria parasite are living beings, they can develop resistance to the medicines and pesticides used to kill them. [a] ■ Medical scientists must create new medicines and pesticides to fight these resistant parasites and mosquitoes. [b] ■ Automobiles, airplanes, and other kinds of transportation make it easy for infected people to carry malaria to new locations. [c] ■ Despite these obstacles, malaria cases continue to decline worldwide. [d] ■

Glossary:

◐ POWERED BY COBUILD

nausea: the condition of feeling sick and that you are going to vomit

eradicate: to get rid of something completely

B Read the questions carefully. What types of questions are they? Underline any key words in the questions and answer options that you will look for while you review the passage. Then, answer the questions. Note the correct answers and read why the answer options are correct or incorrect.

1. Look at the four squares [■] in paragraph 2 that indicate where the following sentence could be added to the passage.

   This information led to malaria prevention efforts that involved destroying or avoiding the mosquitoes that carried it.

   Where would the sentence best fit?

   ○ a

   ○ b

   ○ c

   ○ d

ANSWER ANALYSIS ▶

Question Type: **Add Text**

✗ **a:** The sentence before this marker is about how discovering the true nature of the disease led to more effective treatments. Thus, the next sentence after the marker should include information about the discovery that the disease is caused by a parasite.

✗ **b:** The sentence cannot go here because the author has not mentioned the discovery that mosquitoes transmit the disease.

✗ **c:** Grammatically, the sentence does not flow here, as there is no logical referent for the demonstrative pronoun "this."

✓ **d: This is the most logical place for the given sentence. The sentence mentions mosquitoes, and the paragraph brings up mosquitoes only in the sentence that precedes this marker. In addition, the ideas flow most logically when the given sentence is placed in this spot.**

2. Look at the four squares [■] in paragraph 4 that indicate where the following sentence could be added to the passage.

> **Another challenge in eradicating malaria is the increased mobility of human beings.**

Where would the sentence best fit?

○ a

○ b

○ c

○ d

ANSWER ANALYSIS ▶

Question Type: **Add Text**

✗ **a:** The given sentence does not make sense in this position because the sentence after the marker continues discussing ideas about using medicines and pesticides to kill the parasite and mosquitoes.

✓ **b: This is the most logical place for the sentence. The given sentence mentions that increased mobility poses a problem for efforts to eradicate malaria, and the sentence after this marker supports this idea by describing the types of transportation that contribute to increased mobility.**

✗ **c:** The given sentence introduces a second challenge in eradicating malaria. Placing the sentence in this position disrupts the flow of ideas in the paragraph.

✗ **d:** The author has already discussed the role of mobility in the spread of malaria. It does not make sense to add the given sentence after a statement that describes the decline of malaria.

3. Complete the table below to summarize the information about malaria discussed in the passage. Match the appropriate statements to the facts with which they are associated. **This question is worth 4 points.**

Facts About Malaria	Statements
Causes of Malaria	**Select 2** ➤ ➤
Methods for Controlling Spread of Malaria	**Select 3** ➤ ➤ ➤
Obstacles in Controlling Malaria	**Select 2** ➤ ➤

Statements

1. Use of mosquito nets
2. Ease of travel in the modern world
3. Plants and herbs
4. Parasites spread through mosquito bites
5. Immunity to medicines and pesticides
6. Antiparasitic medications
7. Discovered by a French physician
8. Medications that treat the symptoms of the disease
9. Based on a discovery by a British doctor

ANSWER ANALYSIS ▶

Question Type: Table Completion

Facts About Malaria	Statements
Causes of Malaria	**Select 2** ➢ 4. Parasites spread through mosquito bites ➢ 7. Discovered by a French physician
Methods for Controlling Spread of Malaria	**Select 3** ➢ 1. Use of mosquito nets ➢ 6. Antiparasitic medications ➢ 9. Based on a discovery by a British doctor
Obstacles in Controlling Malaria	**Select 2** ➢ 2. Ease of travel in the modern world ➢ 5. Immunity to medicines and pesticides

✓ **1:** In paragraph 3, the author states that mosquito nets control the spread of malaria by preventing mosquito bites.

✓ **2:** In paragraph 4, the author says that the increased mobility of humans contributes to malaria.

✗ **3:** In paragraph 2, the author says that plants and herbs were used to treat malaria. This does not fall under any of the categories in the table.

✓ **4:** In paragraph 1, the author says that malaria is caused by a parasite. In paragraph 2, the author mentions that mosquitoes spread the disease.

✓ **5:** In paragraph 4, the author says that, as living organisms, the parasite that causes malaria and the mosquitoes that transmit it acquire immunity to pesticides and medicines.

✓ **6:** In paragraph 3, the author says that doctors have developed medications for treating malaria. Because malaria is caused by a parasite, these medicines are antiparasitic.

✓ **7:** In paragraph 2, the author says that a French surgeon discovered that malaria is caused by a parasite.

✗ **8:** In paragraph 2, the author mentions that medications were formulated to treat the cause of the disease (i.e., the parasite), not the symptoms. This cannot be classified in the provided categories.

✓ **9:** In paragraph 2, the author says that a British doctor discovered that the malaria parasite is transmitted through mosquito bites.

PROGRESSIVE PRACTICE: Get Set

A Scan the short passage about geology. Write the main idea of each paragraph.

1. _____

2. _____

3. _____

4. _____

History of the Mediterranean Sea

[1] The Mediterranean Sea spans 2.5 million square kilometers and is almost entirely surrounded by Europe, Africa, and northwestern Asia. Despite its size, a number of geological discoveries suggest that the Mediterranean may have entirely dried up about five million to 12 million years ago. For one, during the 1970s, geologists discovered reflective materials at the bottom of the sea by using a specially designed ship and drilling system to take core samples of the Mediterranean's seabed that were about 30 feet long. [a] ■ These samples revealed that the reflective layer was composed of minerals left behind by evaporated seawater. [b] ■ Geologists also found other materials that were unlikely to exist at the bottom of a sea. [c] ■ For example, they found a layer of anhydrite, a mineral that undergoes a chemical transformation when it comes into contact with water. [d] ■

[2] Based on the depth of the layers of non-oceanic materials at the bottom of the sea, many scientists argue that evaporation was caused by the Mediterranean becoming separated from the Atlantic Ocean. Currently, the Mediterranean is connected to the Atlantic at a narrow point, about 8.9 miles wide, called the Strait of Gibraltar. The connection between the two bodies of water is important because the Mediterranean Sea has a negative moisture balance. [a] ■ Because of its negative moisture balance, it's likely that the Mediterranean Sea would dry up in about 1,500 years without extra water from the Atlantic Ocean pouring in through the strait. [b] ■ Researchers speculate that several million years ago, a geological event caused the Strait of Gibraltar to close, cutting off the Mediterranean from its water source. [c] ■ Completely separated from the Atlantic, geologists claim that the Mediterranean dried up in as little as 1,000 years. [d] ■

[3] The evaporation of the Mediterranean had significant effects locally and globally. Emptied of water, the region became a vast desert. It's believed that when the Mediterranean Sea dried up, the water level of the oceans around the world increased by up to 32 feet. Furthermore, a large part of the salt from the world's oceans was stored in the dry seabed. This led not only to decreased salinity in the world's oceans, but also to a hypersaline, or extremely salty, environment in the Mediterranean desert. Because many animals cannot survive in hypersaline conditions, it's likely that many of the species that once lived in the area probably died, resulting in a severe decline in the biodiversity of the area.

[4] However, this desert eventually became a sea again. About five million years ago, geologists theorize that a major geological event opened the dam between the Atlantic and the Mediterranean, causing an enormous waterfall to flood the Mediterranean basin, refilling it in only 100 years. Such a sudden influx of water would wash away any life growing in the Mediterranean desert and affect the climate of the surrounding regions.

Glossary:

ⒸⒺ POWERED BY COBUILD

evaporate: to change from a liquid state to a gas

salinity: the amount of salt in something

B Read the questions carefully and note whether they are add text or table completion questions. Then, answer the questions. Write the letter of each answer option next to the reason in the *Answer Analysis* box explaining why it is correct or incorrect.

1. Look at the four squares [■] in paragraph 1 that indicate where the following sentence could be added to the passage.
   The presence of anhydrite, then, suggests that at some point in the past, there was an absence of water in the region that is now the Mediterranean Sea.
   Where would the sentence best fit?

   ○ a **[A]**

   ○ b **[B]**

   ○ c **[C]**

   ○ d **[D]**

ANSWER ANALYSIS ▶

Question Type: **Add Text**

_____ ✗ The sentence after this marker introduces the topic of other materials that are unlikely to be found on a seabed, like anhydrite. Placing the given sentence here would disrupt the flow of ideas in the paragraph.

_____ ✗ The sentence after this marker continues the discussion of the reflective materials at the sea bottom, so this is not a logical place to insert the given sentence.

_____ ✓ **The sentence before this marker mentions anhydrite for the first time. This is the most logical location for the given sentence because it gives more details about the discovery of anhydrite and how that supports the theory that the Mediterranean once dried up.**

_____ ✗ The sentence after this marker describes anhydrite for the first time, so it's unlikely that the given sentence goes here.

---

2. Look at the four squares [■] in paragraph 2 that indicate where the following sentence could be added to the passage.
   This means that every year, more water evaporates from the sea than is added to it by rivers and rainfall.
   Where would the sentence best fit?

   ○ a **[A]**

   ○ b **[B]**

   ○ c **[C]**

   ○ d **[D]**

ANSWER ANALYSIS ▶

Question Type: **Add Text**

_____ ✗ The sentence before this marker describes how long scientists believe it took the sea to dry up after being cut off from the Atlantic. This is not a good place to add the definition of negative moisture balance.

_____ ✓ **The given sentence provides a definition for negative moisture balance. Thus, it most likely belongs after the sentence in which negative moisture balance is first mentioned.**

_____ ✗ The sentence before this marker discusses the event that probably caused the Mediterranean to become closed off from the Atlantic Ocean. Placing the given sentence here would disrupt the flow of the paragraph.

_____ ✗ The sentence before this marker mentions the effect that negative moisture balance could have on the Mediterranean. It's unlikely that a definition would be introduced at this point.

3. Complete the table below to summarize information about the causes and effects of the evaporation of the Mediterranean Sea. Match the appropriate statements to the methods with which they are associated. **This question is worth 3 points.**

Causes and Effects	Statements
Factors Leading to the Evaporation of the Mediterranean Sea	**Select 2** ➤ ➤
Consequences of the Evaporation of the Mediterranean Sea	**Select 3** ➤ ➤ ➤

Statements

1. The world's oceans became less salty. [A]

2. The Mediterranean Sea became a large desert. [B]

3. The main water source for the Mediterranean was closed off. [C]

4. Many of the animals that once lived around the Mediterranean died off. [D]

5. Hypersaline conditions led to the temporary closing of the Strait of Gibraltar. [E]

6. The sea level of the Atlantic Ocean decreased due to a geological event. [F]

7. The Mediterranean Sea received too little moisture to replenish the water that evaporated from it every year. [G]

ANSWER ANALYSIS ▶

Question Type: **Table Completion**

_____ ✓ **In paragraph 3, the author says the region turned into a vast desert.**

_____ ✗ The author does not mention a connection between hypersalinity and the closing of the Strait of Gibraltar. This choice cannot be classified under either category.

_____ ✓ **In paragraph 2, the author says that the Atlantic supplies the Mediterranean with water. Later, the author says that a geological event caused the Strait of Gibraltar to close.**

_____ ✗ In paragraph 2, the author says that a geological event caused the closing of the Strait of Gibraltar, not a lowering of the Atlantic's sea level.

_____ ✓ **In paragraph 2, the author discusses negative moisture balance and its role in the drying of the Mediterranean.**

_____ ✓ **In paragraph 3, the author says that the drying of the Mediterranean led to decreased salinity in the world's oceans.**

_____ ✓ **In paragraph 3, the author says that biodiversity, or the number of distinct species of animals, in the area declined because of the hypersaline conditions.**

PROGRESSIVE PRACTICE: Go for the TOEFL Test

Read the passage about a topic in astronomy.

TOEFL Reading

VIEW TEXT   REVIEW   VOLUME   HELP   BACK   NEXT

Question 1 of 12

HIDE TIME 00:17:20

Detection of Extrasolar Planets

[1] An extrasolar planet is a planet that is located outside of Earth's solar system. [a] ■ Like the planets in our solar system, which orbit around the sun, extrasolar planets follow the path around stars in the galaxy. [b] ■ In addition, these planets may be able to provide information about astronomical processes like star formation, which could help scientists understand the beginnings of our own solar system. [c] ■ However, because they are located outside of the solar system, extrasolar planets are very difficult to detect. The task of discovering extrasolar planets is further complicated by the fact that, as mature planets, they do not have their own light source, and the intense light from the stars that they orbit usually obscures them. [d] ■ Despite these difficulties, scientists have devised several methods for detecting extrasolar planets.

[2] The primary methods for locating extrasolar planets are indirect, meaning that they involve taking measurements from objects other than extrasolar planets themselves. For example, the radial velocity method involves calculating changes in a star's movement in response to the extrasolar planets orbiting around it. When an extrasolar planet orbits a star, it changes the star's velocity, or the speed at which the star travels. Instruments on Earth that measure the movement of starlight through space can detect changes in a star's velocity from billions of light-years away. [a] ■ By calculating these changes for faraway stars, scientists can determine if there are any extrasolar planets orbiting around them. [b] ■ Furthermore, this method provides researchers with information about the mass of the extrasolar planets that are causing the velocity changes. [c] ■ Typically, extrasolar planets that are discovered using this method are very large. [d] ■ However, researchers are in the process of refining this method in order to be able to detect smaller planets as well.

[3] The radial velocity method provides information about the mass of an extrasolar planet, but by using another indirect detection technique called the transit method, scientists can gather other kinds of information about an extrasolar planet's size. [a] ■ Most importantly, the transit method helps observers to determine an extrasolar planet's radius, which is the distance from the center of a planet to its surface. [b] ■ When a planet comes between a star and the instruments used to observe it, the star's light is momentarily dimmed. [c] ■ Thus, by measuring the star's light output, scientists can determine if an extrasolar planet has traveled between that star and their telescopes. [d] ■ Scientists using this method pay attention not only to the intensity of the star's light output, but to the frequency of any changes in output as well. By using this information, along with the size of the shadow that an extrasolar planet casts as it passes in front of a star, scientists are able to figure out a planet's size. Planets with a larger radius cause the light of a star to dim more significantly than it would with smaller planets.

[4] In addition to these indirect methods, researchers are developing new technology intended to make it easier to obtain images of extrasolar planets directly. They are making advancements toward creating instruments that are capable of filtering out the glare of a star's light and producing extremely clear images that allow scientists to distinguish extrasolar planets from the stars they orbit. Some scientists are researching the possibility of adapting the coronagraph, which is a telescope originally used to block out our sun's light in order to study the fainter light surrounding it. [a] ■ With some modifications, the coronagraph's ability to block out large amounts of light may make it useful for detecting extrasolar planets. [b] ■ Unlike ordinary telescopes, an interferometer uses a system of several mirrors and gathers images from many different angles. [c] ■ By combining the multiple images, the relatively dim light of extrasolar planets is intensified and is therefore more apparent to scientists. [d] ■

Glossary:

⬡ POWERED BY COBUILD

light-year: the distance that light travels in a year

orbit: to move around a sun or moon in a continuous curving path

Now answer the questions.

1. Look at the four squares [■] in paragraph 1 that indicate where the following sentence could be added to the passage.

   Research on extrasolar planets is driven primarily by the possibility that other solar systems may contain planets similar to Earth in that they are capable of supporting life.

   Where would the sentence best fit?

   ○ a

   ○ b

   ○ c

   ○ d

2. Look at the four squares [■] in paragraph 2 that indicate where the following sentence could be added to the passage.

   This is because planets with a larger mass cause more noticeable changes in the speed of a star's movement.

   Where would the sentence best fit?

   ○ a

   ○ b

   ○ c

   ○ d

3. Look at the four squares [■] in paragraph 3 that indicate where the following sentence could be added to the passage.

   Researchers measure the size of extrasolar planets by observing the light a star produces.

   Where would the sentence best fit?

   ○ a

   ○ b

   ○ c

   ○ d

4. Look at the four squares [■] in paragraph 4 that indicate where the following sentence could be added to the passage.

   Other researchers are concentrating on interferometry technology.

   Where would the sentence best fit?

   ○ a

   ○ b

   ○ c

   ○ d

5. Complete the table below to summarize information about the methods for detecting extrasolar planets discussed in the passage. Match the appropriate statements to the methods with which they are associated. **This question is worth 4 points.**

Methods for Detecting Extrasolar Planets	Statements
Indirect Methods	**Select 4** ➤ ➤ ➤ ➤
Direct Methods	**Select 3** ➤ ➤ ➤

Statements

1. Allows researchers to determine the distance between an extrasolar planet and the star it orbits
2. Involves measuring how fast a star moves as a result of the planets orbiting around it
3. Uses technology that makes light from extrasolar planets appear brighter to observers on Earth
4. Uses a star's light output to indicate the size of an extrasolar planet
5. Involves using the light emitted from surrounding planets to detect extrasolar planets
6. Employs technology that allows scientists to create clear images of extrasolar planets
7. Provides researchers with information about the mass of extrasolar planets
8. Involves blocking light from stars that may be located near the extrasolar planet
9. Currently, one of these methods is not effective for locating small extrasolar planets.

Reading Review Test

The following section will test the skills that you've learned so far. In the *Reading Review Test*, you will read three passages. After each passage, you will answer a set of 12–14 questions. The difficulty of the reading passages and the questions is the same as those that appear on the TOEFL® test.

You will have 60 minutes to read all of the passages and answer 39 questions in this section. See the timing guide below for details on how much time you will have to answer the questions.

Reading Section Timing Guide		
Passage	**Number of Questions**	**Time to Complete Section**
Passage 1	13	
Passage 2	12	60 minutes
Passage 3	14	

When you start the review test, be sure to follow the directions exactly as they appear on the page. Use a clock to time yourself while you answer the questions, and make sure that you don't take more than 60 minutes for the entire section. After you complete the review test, check the answer key to see if your answers are correct. Look at the questions you got wrong and determine what type of questions they are. Did you have trouble with a particular question type? If so, make sure to review that question type before you take the TOEFL test.

PASSAGE 1

Read the passage about a topic in economics.

The Decline of the English Cloth Trade

[1] After 45 years of the queen's rule, James I succeeded Elizabeth I to the English throne in 1603, at which point the English economy was struggling. The population of England was swelling, food production was insufficient, and prices were high. Despite its instability, a few industries brought reliable income to the English economy. In particular, many merchants relied on the export of cloth to continental Europe. For the first decade of James I's reign, the cloth trade prospered and was an important source of revenue for the English. However, the king was to make a serious mistake that would eventually lead to the fall of the English cloth trade.

[2] In 1614, William Cockayne, an English merchant and politician, proposed that James I make a dramatic change to the way the English exported cloth. At the time, the English produced primarily unfinished cloth. This meant that they sold cloth that had not been dyed, bleached, or otherwise processed. Most often, companies in the Netherlands bought the plain cloth from England and finished it themselves. The Dutch were experts in the complex procedures and technologies required to finish cloth, and these processes added significant value to the unfinished cloth they had purchased from England. As a result, Dutch cloth companies could sell their goods at much higher prices than the English could. Hoping to transfer these profits to English companies, Cockayne proposed that the English finish the cloth themselves to increase the value of their cloth exports. He also asked James I to establish a company, which was to function under Cockayne's leadership, that would control and monopolize the export of finished cloth to continental Europe. The king was in need of money, and the prospect of increased revenue appealed to him. Thus, he agreed to Cockayne's plan and, per Cockayne's request, founded the King's Merchant Adventurers, a company with a primary purpose of exporting finished cloth.

[3] However, Cockayne's plan disrupted the previously steady English cloth trade and was ultimately ineffective for a number of reasons. First, James I's support of Cockayne's company created a rift between the king and many powerful English merchants, particularly the members of the unfinished cloth company called the Merchant Adventurers, which had been cast aside in favor of Cockayne's group. Furthermore, the Dutch, who had previously been Europe's main supplier of finished cloth, responded to English competition by refusing to purchase any English cloth products, and many other European nations did the same. In addition, merchants in other countries refused to ship English cloth or charged English businesspeople inflated fees for shipping. The resistance from abroad was particularly damaging to the King's Merchant Adventurers because it could not afford the ships that were necessary to transport its goods to European markets.

[4] In addition to the difficulties caused by its widespread unpopularity, Cockayne's company was unable to produce quality goods. For one, Cockayne did not have the funds to acquire the machines needed to finish cloth. [a] ■ Moreover, English cloth makers were not experts in the finishing process and could not match the high-quality finished cloth produced by their competitors in the Netherlands. [b] ■ By 1617, just three years after the company was established, James I had dissolved the King's Merchant Adventurers. [c] ■

Glossary:

⊜ POWERED BY COBUILD

monopoly: a company, person, or state that has complete control over something so that others cannot become involved in it

rift: a quarrel or disagreement

[5] The failure of the King's Merchant Adventurers did more than bankrupt those who had supported its efforts. [d] ■ The damage Cockayne's plan inflicted on the cloth trade had disastrous economic effects on other industries as well. Under the King's Merchant Adventurers, more than 500 families had begun producing finished cloth. However, because they could not sell it, their ventures failed. This caused unemployment to rise and even resulted in riots in London and elsewhere. Furthermore, formerly beneficial trade relationships had been destroyed, and sellers of unfinished cloth had to attempt to reestablish contacts with European buyers who were willing to purchase their goods. Though James I had returned power to the members of the Merchant Adventurers, the group resented the damage that had been done to its business. Business relations were strained both internationally and domestically as the English cloth trade made a slow recovery from Cockayne's experiment.

Now answer the questions.

1. The word succeeded in paragraph 1 is closest in meaning to
   ○ did away with.
   ○ came after.
   ○ turned aside.
   ○ kept back.

2. The word its in paragraph 1 refers to
   ○ population.
   ○ food production.
   ○ income.
   ○ the English economy.

3. In paragraph 1, the author describes insufficient food production as an indication of the
   ○ need for the expansion of the English cloth trade.
   ○ consequences of heavily emphasizing the cloth trade.
   ○ poor state of the English economy in 1603.
   ○ king's mismanagement of the country.

4. Based on the information in paragraphs 1 and 2, what can be inferred about the English cloth trade prior to the establishment of the King's Merchant Adventurers?
   ○ It was neglected in favor of the shipping and agriculture industries.
   ○ It was the only profitable sector of the English economy.
   ○ It was responsible for driving up prices for necessary items in England.
   ○ It consisted of multiple companies working with international partners.

5. According to paragraph 2, William Cockayne proposed all of the following changes to the English cloth trade EXCEPT:
   ○ The establishment of a company that would exclusively handle the cloth trade
   ○ A focus on increasing the value of cloth created in England
   ○ The interruption of cloth supply to merchants in the Netherlands
   ○ A shift in the primary activities of the English cloth industry

6. Which of the following best expresses the essential information in the highlighted sentence in paragraph 2? Incorrect answer options change the meaning in important ways or leave out essential information.

- ○ The procedures and technologies used to create finished cloth, which were often very complex, were primarily used by Dutch workers.
- ○ Unfinished cloth from England was typically finished by the Dutch, who were experts in the complicated procedures that resulted in more valuable cloth.
- ○ Finished cloth from England was often more valuable than Dutch cloth due to the complicated processes used to treat the cloth.
- ○ Unfinished cloth from England lost its value because the Dutch were able to create finished cloth by using expert techniques.

7. Based on the information in paragraph 2, why did the king agree to Cockayne's proposals?

- ○ He was desperate to improve the English economy quickly.
- ○ He believed that the changes would allow England to expand the cloth industry.
- ○ He worried about England's overreliance on trade partnerships with the Netherlands.
- ○ He wanted to encourage technological advancement in English industries.

8. According to paragraph 3, what is true about the Merchant Adventurers?

- ○ It continued to sell cloth to the Dutch after the execution of Cockayne's plan.
- ○ Its members objected to the changes proposed by Cockayne.
- ○ It was forced to focus primarily on shipping instead of the cloth trade.
- ○ It became the top English trader due to the unpopularity of Cockayne's plan.

9. The word inflated in paragraph 3 is closest in meaning to

- ○ unfair.
- ○ special.
- ○ secret.
- ○ increased.

10. According to paragraph 4, which of the following was a factor in the King's Merchant Adventurer's inability to create quality goods?

- ○ It did not have financial support from the king.
- ○ It couldn't afford to pay cloth-finishing experts.
- ○ Its employees didn't have the necessary knowledge about finishing cloth.
- ○ It had an inadequate supply of unfinished cloth.

11. According to paragraph 5, people in London rioted in response to

- ○ the restoration of the Merchant Adventurers.
- ○ the high rate of joblessness.
- ○ the unavailability of jobs in the cloth industry.
- ○ the bankruptcy of the King's Merchant Adventurers.

12. Look at the four squares [■] in paragraphs 4 and 5 that indicate where the following sentence could be added to the passage.

He also reinstated the previous cloth export company, the Merchant Adventurers.

Where would the sentence best fit?

○ a

○ b

○ c

○ d

13. **Directions:** Complete the table below to summarize information about the causes and effects of the decline of the English cloth trade. Match the appropriate statements to the methods with which they are associated. **This question is worth 3 points.**

Causes and Effects	Statements
Factors Leading to the Decline of the English Cloth Trade	**Select 2** ➤ ➤
Consequences of the Fall of the English Cloth Trade	**Select 3** ➤ ➤ ➤

Statements

1. With approval from James I, the English competed with their international partners by attempting to finish their own cloth.

2. The Dutch sold finished cloth from England at high prices.

3. English cloth makers were unable to match the quality of cloth products created in other countries.

4. People who supported the King's Merchant Adventurers lost a lot of money.

5. Companies in other countries were unwilling to purchase goods from England.

6. The king created the Merchant Adventurers and made William Cockayne responsible for managing it.

7. English makers of unfinished cloth had a strained relationship with the king.

PASSAGE 2

Read the passage about a topic in natural history.

Did Birds Evolve from Dinosaurs?

[1] In the mid-1800s, scientists discovered the complete skeleton of a dinosaur called *Archaeopteryx lithographica*. The creature, which might have grown to a maximum size of about one and a half feet, was thought to have lived approximately 150 million years ago and, curiously, had features that resembled not only dinosaurs, but modern birds as well. For instance, while it had sharp teeth and a bony tail like the dinosaurs of its time, it also had wings and feathers like modern birds. Despite these similarities to birds, the general consensus within the scientific community was that the closest living relatives of dinosaurs were reptiles, like lizards and alligators. It wasn't until 1969, when paleontologists discovered the fossils of a dinosaur called *Deinonychus antirrhopus*, that the debate about whether or not birds evolved from dinosaurs was reopened.

[2] The main problem with the theory linking dinosaurs to modern birds—which was also the main support for arguments that reptiles were, in fact, the closest living ancestors of dinosaurs—was the belief that dinosaurs did not have furculae, or wishbones. The main function of this fork-shaped bone, which is located at the base of the neck on birds, is to reinforce the skeleton against the many stresses of flight. However, fossil evidence found in recent years has revealed that many dinosaurs did indeed have furculae. For example, the dinosaurs in the Dromaeosauridae family, a group of bird-like dinosaurs, are all believed to have had furculae. This discovery contradicts the theory that the bones are unique to birds.

[3] [a] ■ In addition to the observation of furculae in dinosaur fossils, paleontologists have identified a number of other structural similarities between birds and dinosaurs. [b] ■ For example, comparisons between the skeletons of birds and those of dinosaurs like *Velociraptor mongoliensis* and *Deinonychus* reveal that birds and dinosaurs share many unique skeletal features. [c] ■ For instance, *Velociraptor* fossils show that the creature's front limbs, the construction of which would have presumably allowed for great flexibility, are similar to those of modern birds. [d] ■ On the other hand, no such likenesses exist between dinosaurs and early reptiles.

[4] Such evidence of structural similarities is only one of many reasons that paleontologists now generally agree that birds evolved from dinosaurs. Another compelling piece of evidence is the presence of feathers in both organisms. Fossils of *Archaeopteryx*, which many experts now consider to be both a dinosaur and a bird, feature imprints of feathers that closely resemble those found on modern birds. Since the discovery of *Archaeopteryx*, paleontologists have discovered fossils demonstrating that a number of other dinosaurs that were likely related to *Archaeopteryx* also had feathers. Furthermore, even the fossils of dinosaurs that were not related to *Archaeopteryx*, such as *Tyrannosaurus rex*, have been found to have long, feather-like structures that are commonly referred to as protofeathers. According to many paleontologists, the main function of protofeathers was to insulate dinosaurs from cold temperatures, not to assist with flight, which accounts for why many flightless dinosaurs may have had them. Because no other animals besides dinosaurs and birds have been found to have feathers, scientists believe that the existence of feathers is a strong indication that the two animals are directly related.

[5] Paleontologists have also found evidence that the lungs of dinosaurs were shaped similarly to birds' lungs. Most animals, including primates, lizards, and frogs, have lungs with two compartments. However, birds have extra air sacs in front of and behind their lungs that allow them to keep their lungs inflated constantly. Studies of dinosaur skeletons indicate that some dinosaurs also had lungs with extra chambers. Like the similarities in skeletal structures and the existence of feathers in both groups, the fact that only birds and dinosaurs have these extra lung chambers reveals that birds probably evolved from dinosaurs and are thus their closest living relatives.

Glossary:

Ⓔ POWERED BY COBUILD

stresses: strong physical pressures

compartment: a separate part or space

Now answer the questions.

14. In paragraph 1, the author mentions wings and feathers in order to

○ point out features shared by *Archaeopteryx* and modern birds.

○ explain the small size of *Archaeopteryx* fossils.

○ argue that *Archaeopteryx* was most likely a bird and not a dinosaur.

○ describe what *Archaeopteryx* probably looked like.

15. The word consensus in paragraph 1 is closest in meaning to

○ question.

○ debate.

○ evidence.

○ agreement.

16. Which of the following best expresses the essential information in the highlighted sentence in paragraph 2? Incorrect answer options change the meaning in important ways or leave out essential information.

○ The idea that dinosaurs did not have wishbones was the chief difficulty in proving that modern birds were related to dinosaurs.

○ Many people believed that reptiles were the closest living ancestors of dinosaurs because, like dinosaurs, they do not have furculae.

○ The main reason that scientists couldn't link modern birds and dinosaurs was because they could not find furculae in most modern bird species.

○ Dinosaurs' presumed lack of wishbones made people think that birds, not reptiles, were their closest living ancestors.

17. The word reinforce in paragraph 2 is closest in meaning to

○ prepare.

○ strengthen.

○ protect.

○ extend.

18. The discovery of dinosaur fossils with furculae was important because it

○ indicated that several bird species had already evolved during the time of dinosaurs.

○ proved that many reptilian animals, including dinosaurs, had furculae.

○ cast doubt on the theory that reptiles were the closest living relatives of dinosaurs.

○ helped scientists determine the purpose of furculae in non-bird species.

19. What can be inferred about dinosaurs in the Dromaeosauridae family?

○ They were closely related to *Archaeopteryx*.

○ They were able to fly.

○ They were the only dinosaurs that had furculae.

○ They were small compared to other dinosaurs.

20. The word those in paragraph 3 refers to

○ *Velociraptor* fossils.

○ front limbs.

○ likenesses.

○ early reptiles.

21. The word compelling in paragraph 4 is closest in meaning to

   ○ persuasive.

   ○ conflicting.

   ○ recent.

   ○ sufficient.

22. According to paragraph 4, what is true about protofeathers?

   ○ They were likely the type of feathers that *Archaeopteryx* had.

   ○ Only bird-like dinosaurs had them.

   ○ They probably helped dinosaurs stay warm.

   ○ Some modern birds have been found to have them.

23. According to paragraph 5, what do primates and lizards have in common?

   ○ They have a more elaborate lung structure than dinosaurs did.

   ○ They are able to keep their lungs full of air constantly.

   ○ Their lungs have a similar structure.

   ○ They have other organs in addition to lungs to help them breathe.

24. Look at the four squares [■] in paragraph 3 that indicate where the following sentence could be added to the passage.

   Scientists have also observed structural similarities in the skulls and necks of some dinosaurs and birds.

   Where would the sentence best fit?

   ○ a

   ○ b

   ○ c

   ○ d

25. An introductory sentence for a brief summary of the passage is provided below. Complete the summary by selecting the THREE answer options that express the most important ideas in the passage. Some sentences do not belong in the summary, because they express ideas that are not presented in the passage or are minor ideas in the passage. *This question is worth 2 points.*

   Today, there is evidence showing that modern birds, not reptiles, are probably the closest living relatives of dinosaurs.

   -
   -
   -

   Answer Options

   1. The shape of the forelimb in many dinosaurs would have allowed for great flexibility and movement.

   2. Many dinosaurs had feathers or protofeathers, making them the only other creatures besides birds known to have any type of feather.

   3. Dinosaur skeletons have revealed that dinosaurs probably had multiple-chambered lungs, as do birds.

   4. Dinosaurs and birds have several structural similarities, including the presence of furculae.

   5. Like modern birds, not all feathered dinosaurs could fly.

   6. Scientists have believed that modern reptiles evolved from dinosaurs since the discovery of *Archaeopteryx lithographica* fossils in the mid-1800s.

PASSAGE 3

Read the passage about a topic in marketing.

Pricing Approaches in Marketing

[1] An important part of marketing is determining what price to charge consumers for goods and services. Companies aspire to set prices that are high enough to allow them to make a profit but low enough to encourage people to purchase their products. To determine these prices, marketing specialists must consider a variety of factors and use a number of different pricing approaches.

[2] Cost-based approaches determine the price of a product based on how much it costs to make. This is the simplest method because manufacturers can easily determine how much it will cost them to produce their goods. After they calculate the price of materials and labor, they add a set percentage to that cost, called a standard markup, which covers advertising, marketing, and other administrative costs, as well as profit. For instance, rather than determining the exact price of a new building before they start to build it, construction companies will often give estimates about prices based on the cost of materials, equipment, and labor, plus a markup of 20 percent. The final price is not calculated until after the building is completed, when the company adds the markup amount to its total building costs.

[3] The main advantage to the cost-based approach to pricing is its simplicity. By using this method, businesses do not need to adjust their prices constantly based on changes in the market for their goods. However, the inability to account for important factors relating to the market is also the weakness of the cost-based approach. This is why many businesses also use more complex approaches to determine their prices.

[4] In many industries, producers often pay less attention to their own costs and set prices based on those of their leading competitors instead. This is called competition-based pricing. Competition-based pricing often relies on the going rate, or the average price that consumers expect to pay for a good or service. If five companies are selling plastic tubing for two dollars per foot, a sixth company is unlikely to be successful selling that same kind of tubing for three dollars per foot. Thus, even if the sixth company's production costs are higher, they cannot afford to set their prices higher than their competitors' prices.

[5] Competition-based pricing sometimes puts small businesses at a disadvantage. Because they can buy their materials or production machinery in bulk, very large companies often have lower production costs than smaller companies do. In order to compete, smaller companies cannot depend on cost-based pricing. They often set their prices lower than those of their larger competitors, even though their production costs may be higher, in order to make their products attractive to consumers and build or maintain their customer base. These sellers will also combine cost-based and competition-based pricing in order to find the most competitive price that will yield the highest profit after costs are subtracted.

[6] While cost-based and competition-based pricing are largely based on objective mathematical factors, like production costs and average prices, buyer-based approaches are based on individual perspective. [a] ■ Perceived value is how much consumers feel an item is worth, as opposed to its actual monetary value. [b] ■ For example, a product like a pet rock, which is simply an ordinary rock marketed as a pet, has very little actual monetary value. [c] ■ Marketers will not use production costs to set their price, because this would make the price too low. [d] ■ Instead, they must determine how much consumers feel their product is worth.

Glossary:

ⓒ POWERED BY COBUILD

in bulk: in large quantities

monetary: relating to money

⁷ Because perceived value is subjective, it is difficult to calculate. One common strategy for determining the perceived value of a product is to interview people in focus groups, small groups of people who share their feelings about a product with market experts. The responses of focus groups often change according to the group being interviewed, so experts try to interview a large enough sample to get useful information. Along with focus groups and market experts, some businesses may even employ psychologists to help them understand the minds and emotions of consumers so that they can create products that people will see as valuable. The more perceived value an item has, the more a company can charge for that item, regardless of its production costs or the prices set by competitors.

Now answer the questions.

26. The word aspire in paragraph 1 is closest in meaning to
   ○ decide.
   ○ hurry.
   ○ aim.
   ○ attempt.

27. The phrase account for in paragraph 3 is closest in meaning to
   ○ summarize.
   ○ take into consideration.
   ○ formulate.
   ○ make clear.

28. In paragraph 4, the author implies that a company with higher production costs couldn't afford to charge more than its competitors because the company would
   ○ lose money because customers would choose its competitors' products.
   ○ be expected to lower its production costs to match its competitors' costs.
   ○ have to buy equipment that would lower its production costs.
   ○ be forced to use the same pricing strategies as its top competitors.

29. According to paragraph 5, all of the following are ways that small businesses are disadvantaged by competition-based pricing approaches EXCEPT:
   ○ It provides benefits for companies that buy materials in bulk.
   ○ It favors companies with low production costs.
   ○ It promotes the use of a single pricing strategy.
   ○ It encourages sellers to set prices lower than their costs will allow.

30. The word yield in paragraph 5 is closest in meaning to
   ○ balance.
   ○ result in.
   ○ withhold.
   ○ make larger.

31. According to paragraph 5, what can be inferred about large businesses?

   ○ They are more likely to use only one pricing approach.

   ○ Their prices are influenced by the pricing strategies of small businesses.

   ○ They spend less money on marketing than small businesses do.

   ○ They tend to have higher production costs when using competition-based pricing.

32. The word objective in paragraph 6 is closest in meaning to

   ○ accessible.

   ○ improper.

   ○ impartial.

   ○ precise.

33. According to paragraph 6, what do cost-based and competition-based approaches have in common?

   ○ They are based on the value of a product or service.

   ○ They depend on measurable information.

   ○ They rely equally on personalized information and averages.

   ○ They focus on the costs to the customer.

34. Why does the author mention a pet rock in paragraph 6?

   ○ To give an example of a product with a low perceived value

   ○ To illustrate why using perceived value is appropriate for certain products

   ○ To contrast the actual and perceived value of a specific item

   ○ To explain how buyer-based and competition-based pricing can be used together

35. Which of the following best expresses the essential information in the highlighted sentence in paragraph 7? Incorrect answer options change the meaning in important ways or leave out essential information.

   ○ In order to determine the perceived value of a product, some focus groups interview experts about their feelings on a product.

   ○ Interviewing people in focus groups is one way that market experts determine the perceived value of a product.

   ○ Focus groups allow market experts to interview people about how they form their ideas about the value of an item.

   ○ One strategy for interviewing small groups of people about perceived value involves asking them how they feel about a product.

36. The word they in paragraph 7 refers to

   ○ market experts.

   ○ businesses.

   ○ psychologists.

   ○ consumers.

37. According to paragraph 7, what is NOT true about an item's perceived value?

○ It allows companies to set prices without concern for other marketing factors.

○ It may vary from group to group.

○ It reflects the psychology of the consumer.

○ It is often higher than the actual value.

38. Look at the four squares [■] in paragraph 6 that indicate where the following sentence could be added to the passage.

In buyer-based pricing, companies set prices based on the perceived value of a commodity. Where would the sentence best fit?

○ a

○ b

○ c

○ d

39. **Directions:** Complete the table below to summarize information about the approaches to pricing discussed in the passage. Match the appropriate statements to the methods with which they are associated. **This question is worth 4 points.**

Pricing Approach	Statements
Cost-based	**Select 2** ➤ ➤
Competition-based	**Select 2** ➤ ➤
Buyer-based	**Select 3** ➤ ➤ ➤

Statements

1. Helps companies set prices for items that have little actual value

2. Forces some companies to set lower prices than they can afford in order to be able to compete

3. The simplest way of determining the price of a product

4. Rarely used in combination with other pricing strategies

5. Often involves the use of focus groups or psychologists in order to understand how much a customer might think a product is worth

6. Not suitable for products that have little actual value

7. The price of a product depends on the cost of making the product, including labor and, in some cases, a standard markup.

8. Prices are based on how consumers feel about the price of a product.

9. Companies set prices based on how much other businesses charge for the same product.

Overview of the Writing Section

The writing section is the fourth and final part of the TOEFL® test. It tests your ability to create written responses based on two different types of prompts. For the first prompt, you will read a short passage, listen to an academic lecture on the same topic, then write an essay which combines information from both sources. For the second prompt, you will read a short question about a familiar topic and write an essay in response to that question.

QUICK GUIDE: TOEFL® Test Writing Section

Definition	The writing section tests your ability to understand written and spoken English and respond to prompts in writing. For each question, you will be required to understand the task, know how to write a well-organized essay, and incorporate main ideas and details to answer the question.
Targeted Skills	In order to do well on the writing section you must be able to: • understand prompts that appear in writing. • take notes on material you hear and read, then combine them to create a well-organized essay. • summarize and paraphrase ideas from a listening and/or reading passage. • express your ideas or the ideas of other people about a subject. • create a well-organized essay in a limited time.
The Questions	The writing section includes two questions. The first question is an integrated task and the second question is an independent task (for more information about question types, see page 107–136).
Timing	The time that you have to prepare and respond to each question varies by question type.

Question 1: Integrated Task		Question 2: Independent Task	
Reading*	3 minutes	n / a	
Listening	3–5 minutes	n / a	
Writing Time	20 minutes	Writing Time	30 minutes

The entire section takes approximately **60 minutes** to complete.

*Remember, you will be able to see the reading on the screen while you write your essay but you will not be able to replay the listening passage.

Writing Section: What You'll See and Hear

On-screen Tools

When you work on the writing section, you will have a number of on-screen tools to help you with the writing process. Familiarize yourself with the tools shown below and how to use them.

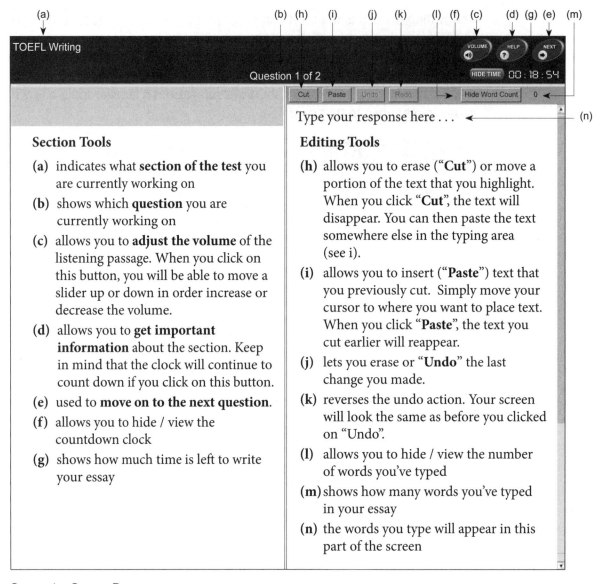

Section Tools

(a) indicates what **section of the test** you are currently working on

(b) shows which **question** you are currently working on

(c) allows you to **adjust the volume** of the listening passage. When you click on this button, you will be able to move a slider up or down in order increase or decrease the volume.

(d) allows you to **get important information** about the section. Keep in mind that the clock will continue to count down if you click on this button.

(e) used to **move on to the next question**.

(f) allows you to hide / view the countdown clock

(g) shows how much time is left to write your essay

Editing Tools

(h) allows you to erase ("**Cut**") or move a portion of the text that you highlight. When you click "**Cut**", the text will disappear. You can then paste the text somewhere else in the typing area (see i).

(i) allows you to insert ("**Paste**") text that you previously cut. Simply move your cursor to where you want to place text. When you click "**Paste**", the text you cut earlier will reappear.

(j) lets you erase or "**Undo**" the last change you made.

(k) reverses the undo action. Your screen will look the same as before you clicked on "Undo".

(l) allows you to hide / view the number of words you've typed

(m) shows how many words you've typed in your essay

(n) the words you type will appear in this part of the screen

Screen-by-Screen Process

You will see a number of screens in the writing section. Review the screens shown below in order to familiarize yourself with the different screens that you will encounter on the day of the test.

1. Instructions: First, you will see a screen that gives you general information about the section. This screen will include general information about the two tasks in the section and how much time you'll have to write your essays for each question. In addition to reading the information on the screen, the narrator will read the instructions. You must wait until the narrator has finished reading the instructions before you are allowed to move on to the next screen.

2. Question 1 Directions: The next screen gives you directions for the integrated reading / lecture synthesis task. It describes the task, how much time you will have to write, and how many words you should include in your essay.

3. Reading screen: Next, you will see the reading passage on left side of the screen. The clock on the upper right part of the screen counts down three minutes. When the three minutes are over, the narrator says: *"Now listen to part of a lecture on the topic you just read about."*

4. Listening screen: When the screen changes, the reading will disappear and you will see a picture of a university setting. The lecture will start immediately after the screen changes. The progress of the passage is marked by a blue bar in the center bottom of the screen. For example, if half of the bar is blue, the listening is half over. Use this bar to gauge how much time is left in the listening passage.

5. Prompt screen: On the next screen, you will see the directions for the task under the on-screen tools. You will see the question under the directions. The reading passage will reappear on the left side of the screen. You will have space to type your essay on the right half of the screen.

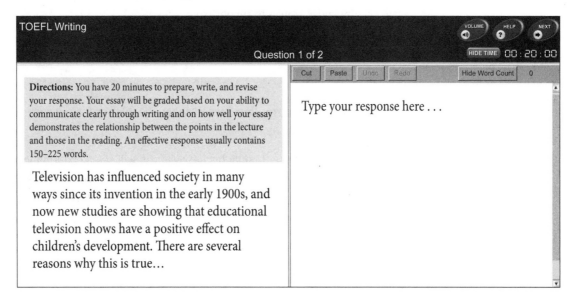

6. End of Task 1 Screen / Confirmation Screen: When the 20 minutes are over, you will see a screen alerting you that the time is up and that you will now move on to the next task.

If you click on "Next" before the 20 minutes are over, you will see a confirmation screen that informs you that you still have time to work on your essay. It also reminds you that if you choose to continue, you will not be able to return to it at a later time. Consider carefully whether you want to proceed or return to your essay.

7. Question 2 Directions: The next screen gives you directions for the personal experiences task. It describes what you will have to do for the task, how much time you will have to write, and how many words you should include in your response.

8. Prompt Screen: Next, you will see the prompt screen. On the left side, you will see a box that has the directions for the task. Under that box, you will see the prompt. On the right side of the screen, you will see the editing tools and the text entry area.

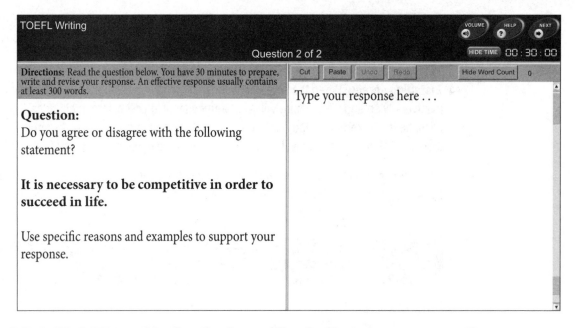

9. End of Task 2 Screen / Confirmation Screen: When the 30 minutes are over, you will see a screen alerting you that the time is done.

If you click on "Next" before the 30 minutes are over, you will see a confirmation screen that informs you that you still have time to work on your essay. It also reminds you that if you choose to continue, you will <u>not</u> be able to return to it at a later time. Consider carefully whether you want to proceed or return to your essay.

10. End of section screen: This screen tells you that you have finished the writing section.

Writing Section: Task Types

In the writing section, there are two types of tasks: integrated questions and independent questions. The main difference between the types of tasks is the skills involved in answering them.

Integrated Task	Independent Task
The first task in the writing section (Reading / Lecture Synthesis Essay) is an integrated task. This task requires you to use a combination of reading, listening, and writing skills.	The second question (Personal Experience Essay) is an independent task. For this question, you will write an essay about a general topic.

Writing Section: Scoring

The essays that you type for the writing section are saved and sent to ETS, where they are scored by human raters. Two raters will review your response and give it a rating of 1 to 5. The scores are then added and converted to a score that falls on the 0–30 score range.

When scoring your responses, the raters will read the entire essay and assign you a rating based on your overall skill. This means that it's possible to make a few mistakes and still receive a top score as long as your overall response fulfills the general scoring criteria described below:

Scoring Category	What Raters Will Be Looking For in the Responses to Question 1	What Raters Will Be Looking For in the Responses to Question 2
Topic Development	<ul><li>You connected information from both the reading passage and the lecture.</li><li>You explained the professor's position by providing specific details from the lecture</li><li>You wrote between 125 and 225 words.</li></ul>	<ul><li>Your introduction clearly stated whether you agreed or disagreed with the statement.</li><li>You explained each of your key points by using specific personal examples and details</li><li>You wrote at least 300 words</li></ul>
Organization and Clarity	<ul><li>You wrote a five-paragraph essay that included an introduction, three body paragraphs, and a conclusion.</li><li>Each body paragraph addresses a key point from the reading as well as the professor's position on that point.</li><li>You used transition words throughout your essay.</li></ul>	<ul><li>You wrote a five paragraph essay that included an introduction, three body paragraphs and a conclusion.</li><li>You used transitions to improve the flow of your essay.</li><li>Each body paragraph introduced a distinct key point which you supported with personal details and examples.</li></ul>
Language Usage	<ul><li>You used correct grammar and punctuation.</li><li>You made few, if any, spelling errors.</li><li>You used a variety of sentence structures and displayed a broad vocabulary</li></ul>	

Challenges and Solutions

» **CHALLENGE 1: "I don't have time to write a complete essay."**

SOLUTION: Know the template for fully answering each question. That way you know what information you must include in your essay in order to get a high score. Then you can spend the majority of your time organizing your essay and thinking of good supporting details.

Template for Task 1	Template for Task 2
Paragraph 1: Main topic from reading; Main topic from the lecture	**Paragraph 1:** Topic sentence; Summary of Key Points
Paragraph 2: Key Point 1 from reading; Key Point 1 from lecture; Support from lecture	**Paragraph 2:** Key Point 1; Personal details
Paragraph 3: Key Point 2 from reading; Key Point 2 from lecture; Support from lecture	**Paragraph 3:** Key Point 2; Personal details
Paragraph 4: Key Point 3 from reading; Key Point 3 from lecture; Support from lecture	**Paragraph 4:** Key Point 3; Personal details
Paragraph 5: Conclusion	**Paragraph 5:** Conclusion

SOLUTION: Be aware of how much time you have. On the day of the test, you will see how much time is remaining on the on-screen clock that appears on the upper right side of the screen. While you work, be sure to check the clock. Use the following timing guide while you write:

Timing for Task 1 Total time: 20 minutes		Timing for Task 2 Total time: 30 minutes	
Time on the Clock	**What you should be doing**	**Time on the Clock**	**What you should be doing**
20:00–18:00	Review notes and write a quick outline. Just write a few words to help you remember what you will write down	30:00–25:00	Read the prompt carefully and brainstorm the topic. Try to come up with as many points as you can for each side. Choose the side with the most supporting points.
18:00–4:00	Write your essay. Be sure that your essay has five paragraphs and that you include specific details from the professor's lecture in your essay.	25:00–4:00	Write your essay. Be sure that your essay has five paragraphs and that you include personal details to support your key points.
4:00–0:00	Review and edit your essay. Be sure to look for misspelled words and ungrammatical sentences.	4:00–0:00	Review and edit your essay. Be sure to look for misspelled words and ungrammatical sentences.

SOLUTION: Practice typing as much as possible before the test. On the day of the test, you will have to type your essay on the computer. If you do not type fast, you will not be able to write your essay within the given time. So you should make sure to practice typing before the test in order to improve your typing speed.

» CHALLENGE 2: "I'm afraid that the raters will not understand the ideas in my essay."

SOLUTION: Use transition words. Transition words are expressions that connect two sentences together by indicating a shift in focus, continuing in the same line of thinking, drawing a conclusion, clarifying a point, indicating sequence, etc. If you use transition words throughout your essay, you will be able to improve the flow of your response and make it easier to understand. Use the following table as a reference of transition language and their uses:

Function	Transition Language	
Shift in focus	but	nonetheless
	conversely	on the contrary
	despite	on the other hand
	however,	still
	in contrast	though
	nevertheless	yet
Continuing in the same line of thinking	additionally	furthermore
	also	in addition
	and	likewise
	besides that	moreover
Drawing a conclusion	accordingly	hence
	as a result	indeed
	consequently	therefore
	for that reason	thus
Clarifying a point	in other words	that is to say
	specifically	namely
Indicating Sequence	after	later
	as soon as	meanwhile
	before	next
	finally	soon
	in the first place	then
Giving Examples	For example,…	
	Take X, for instance.	
	One example of X is…	

SOLUTION: Work on improving your spelling. Remember, the word processing tool on the test does <u>not</u> include a spell checker. While a few misspelled words won't affect your score, if you spell a lot of words incorrectly, it may keep the raters from understanding your meaning. One way to improve your spelling is to read a lot. This is because the more you see words in English, the more you will understand how common words are spelled. Another way to help your spelling is to practice writing. When you check your writing, circle all the misspelled words and make sure you learn how to spell them correctly.

SOLUTION: Don't use an idiomatic expression unless you are <u>sure</u> you know what it means. When the raters score your essay, they will look at how well you can use idiomatic expressions. However, if you use an idiomatic expression incorrectly, it will only harm your score.

» **CHALLENGE 3: "I have trouble talking about opinions."**

SOLUTION: Know when you will be required to express opinions. Question 1 asks you to describe the opinions of the professor while Question 2 requires you to give your opinion. Knowing this information will help you prepare before you take the test. Use the table below to help you know when and how to use opinion language.

Question	Whose Opinion Will You Give?	Expressions You Can Use in Your Response
Question 1: Academic Reading / Listening Synthesis Task	State the opinion of professor. The professor will clearly express agreement or disagreement with the main topic and provide three reasons to support this position. Do not give your own opinion for this task!	• The professor feels that . . . • In the lecture, the professor says that X is a good / bad idea. • The professor says she supports / opposes . . . • In the professor's opinion, X is good / bad . . . • The professor's view is that X is positive / negative . . . • The professor agrees / disagrees with the claim that . . .
Question 2: Personal Experience Task	Give your own opinion about whether you agree or disagree with the statement.	• While some people think that X, I personally believe that . . . • I know that some people feel differently, but it's my opinion that . . . • It's my opinion that . . . • I agree/disagree with the idea that . . . • Other people might disagree, but my view is that . . .

SOLUTION: Learn basic citation skills. On the **academic reading / lecture synthesis task**, you have to talk about attitudes that come from either a reading passage or an audio passage. Use the following citation expressions to indicate whether the information came from the reading or the lecture.

Expressions for Citing the Source
The author / professor thinks / feels that . . . The author / professor agrees / disagrees / opposes / supports . . . According to the passage / professor, . . . In the conversation, the professor says / argues / points out / makes the point that . . . In the reading / lecture, the author / professor says . . .. The author / professor supports X by saying / pointing out / arguing / giving an example of . . .

» **CHALLENGE 4: "For the academic reading / lecture synthesis task, I'm supposed to reword the information from the passage and the lecture, but this is very difficult for me."**

SOLUTION: Make sure you completely understand the meaning of what you are trying to paraphrase. When you paraphrase, you put the information from a source in your own words. But you can't do this effectively if you don't fully understand the meaning. Remember, the reading will appear on the screen, so you will be able to refer to the passage and review parts that you want to paraphrase to make sure you understand them. For the lecture, you should review your notes to make sure that you fully understand the main points made by the professor.

SOLUTION: Learn synonyms for common words that appear on the test. After all, part of paraphrasing involves using synonyms of key terms and phrases. So, by learning synonyms of words that commonly appear on the test, you will be able to paraphrase with ease. To practice, reread one of the reading passages for the integrated writing task in this book. Choose 10–15 key words that appear in the passage. Then look in a thesaurus for synonyms of these words and make a list to study and learn. You can then use these synonyms in your paraphrased sentence. See below for examples of how to use synonyms in your paraphrases.

Original Wording	Paraphrased Version Using Synonyms
A Lazarus taxon is a species[1] that was once believed[2] to have been extinct, but is later found to be alive[3].	Types of organisms[1] that were thought[2] be extinct and are later found to still exist[3] are called a Lazarus taxon.
One advantage of using surveys[1] for data collection[2] is that it allows[3] researchers[4] to ask[5] consumers[6] questions about their attitudes and shopping behavior.	Conducting surveys[1] in order to collect data[2] is advantageous because it gives scientists[3] the opportunity[4] to question[5] customers[6] about their attitudes and shopping behavior.

SOLUTION: Don't copy the words and ideas exactly as they appear in a source. Paraphrasing is putting the ideas from a source into your own words. If you simply copy words and sentences from the reading passage, you will receive a zero for your essay. To avoid copying, check the original source after you create a paraphrase. Is the sentence structure and vocabulary different? If your paraphrase is too similar to the original, be sure to change it by using different types of sentence structures and synonyms of key words. Also, if you write down exactly what the professor says in your notes, be sure to put those words in quotation marks. That way, you will remember to paraphrase in your essay and not pass those words off as your own.

SOLUTION: Practice paraphrasing. The best way to improve your paraphrasing skills is to practice. Find a reading passage from the reading section of this book. Then choose a paragraph to paraphrase. Put the passage away and try paraphrasing. When you are done, compare your paraphrase with the source. Did you change key words by using synonyms? Also, did you change the sentence structures? Practice paraphrasing one paragraph a day until you feel confident about your paraphrasing skills.

» **CHALLENGE 5: "There's too much information to remember on the academic reading / lecture synthesis task."**

SOLUTION: During the integrated task, you will read a passage, then listen to the lecture about the same topic. You don't have to worry about taking notes on the reading passage because you will see it on your screen while you write your essay. However, you will need to take notes on the lecture. The lectures may include a lot of information, but remember that you are allowed to take notes during this portion of the test. Because of this, it's important to develop your note-taking skills. Use the following note-taking strategies to help you write down the most important information:

- Use abbreviations. You won't have enough time to write everything out, so be sure to use shorter forms whenever possible. Also, use abbreviations that make sense to you—it won't matter if you write something down if you don't remember what it means. See the table below for tips for abbreviations. Then, practice writing down things you hear using abbreviations, but remember to be sure you understand what they mean!

Abbreviation Tip	Examples	
Use numerals instead of writing out numbers	one, two, three, etc.→1, 2, 3, etc.	
Leave the vowels out of a word	conversation, forest, novel → cnvrstn, frst, nvl	
Use symbols instead of words	Jane and Jack → Jane+Jack Jane or Jack → Jane / Jack Everyone except Jack → Everyone -Jack The numbers increased → The #s ↑ eight hundred dollars → $800 fifty percent→ 50% at → @	
Other common abbreviations	without → w/o within → w/in approximately → approx. et cetera → etc.	because → b/c before → b4 example → ex regarding → re

- Study the table below for the basic information you should be writing down during the academic lecture:

What you should write down
• Whether the professor agrees or disagrees with the main topic from the reading • Three reasons that the professor gives for either agreeing or disagreeing • Details such as studies or discoveries that support each of the professor's key points

- Organize your notes as you write. It can be very helpful to write headings for all of the information you need to write down (Main Idea, Key Point 1, Support, etc.) Then, if you leave room beneath each of the above points, you can write down supporting details under them later.

» CHALLENGE 6: "I have a hard time choosing what to write about on the Personal Experience Task."

SOLUTION: Practice brainstorming techniques. Brainstorming involves thinking about the topic and trying to come up with major supporting details quickly. One technique you might find useful is to spend a minute or two writing down all of the points you can think of for both sides of the argument. Don't worry about whether the points you're writing down are good or not—sometimes, writing down a weak point will help you think of a better one. Try this technique for the topics in this book. When you are done, review your notes from brainstorming. Can you think of a way to adjust the technique so it works better for you?

SOLUTION: Don't waste time considering which point to support. When you are writing your personal experience essay, you should choose the position that is easiest for you to support. You can determine this by looking at the notes you've created when you brainstormed. Which side has more points? Also, remember that there are no right or wrong opinions on the TOEFL test. In other words, you are <u>not</u> being graded based on your opinions themselves. What's really important is how well you support your opinion in your essay.

SOLUTION: Don't be afraid of making up personal examples to include in your essay. For the personal experience task, you are required to support all key points with relevant personal examples. However, nobody is going to check whether your personal examples are true or not. If you have to change the details of one of your examples so that it supports your key point better, go ahead and do it. It will make your essay even stronger.

SOLUTION: Make a list of familiar topics and practice coming up with key points for them. Give yourself about two to three minutes to think of key points for each topic. That way, you'll get used to thinking of supporting points in timed conditions like you'll have to on the day of the test. Use the topics from the list below or try to come up with your own topics:

- Some people think it is important to get a degree from a top school in order to get a good job. Others feel that real-world experience is more helpful for getting a good job. Which do you think is more important and why? Use reasons and specific examples to support your answer.
- Do you agree or disagree with the following statement?
    Teachers are the most influential people in a child's life.
  Use specific reasons and examples to support your answer.
- Some people think that having a good diet is the most important factor for physical health. Others think that exercise plays a larger role in health. Which do you think is true and why? Use reasons and specific examples to support your answer.
- Do you agree or disagree with the following statement?
    It is best to travel before starting a career.
  Use specific reasons and examples to support your answer.

Overview of Question Types on the Writing Section

Question Type	Skills	Description
1. Integrated Task: Academic Reading / Lecture Synthesis Essay	Reading Listening Writing	• First you will read a passage about an academic subject. • Then, you will listen to a professor's lecture on the same topic. • The question will ask you to combine information from the reading passage and the lecture. **Response Time:** 20 minutes
2. Independent Task: Personal Experience Essay	Writing	• The question will ask you whether you agree or disagree with a statement, usually related to a familiar topic. You need to answer the question and use your experiences to support your answer. **Response Time:** 30 minutes

Academic Reading / Lecture Synthesis

For writing task 1, you will first read a passage on an academic topic, and then you will listen to an audio passage on the same topic. Next, you will see a prompt that asks you to combine information from the reading passage and the lecture.

The prompt for the academic reading / lecture synthesis task may be worded as follows:

» *Summarize the points made in the lecture you just heard, explaining how they challenge the points made in the reading.*

» *Summarize the points made in the lecture, being sure to explain how they support the points made in the reading.*

» *Summarize the points made in the lecture you just heard, explaining how they cast doubt on the points made in the reading passage.*

First, a short academic reading passage will appear on your computer screen. The reading passage is typically between 250 and 300 words and will remain on the screen for about three minutes. After these three minutes, the reading passage will disappear, but it will reappear after the listening passage is over, and you will be able to see it while you are typing your response. The reading passage for writing task 1 is always about an academic subject that may include the following:

- anthropology
- art history
- astronomy
- biology
- botany
- environmental science
- literature
- psychology
- sociology

The reading passage is typically organized as follows:

Introduction of the topic
Point 1
Supporting details
Point 2
Supporting details
Point 3
Supporting details

The audio passage is an academic lecture given by a university professor. You will hear it after you read the text and before you type your response. You will hear the lecture only once, so take good notes! In the lecture, the professor either casts doubt on or supports the points made in the reading passage. "To cast doubt on" means that the professor disagrees with the main claim of the reading and provides three points that show why the claim is wrong. Please note that in the majority of cases, the professor casts doubt on the points from the reading rather than supporting them. The listening passage is typically organized as follows:

> Statement of agreement or disagreement
> Point 1
> Supporting details
> Point 2
> Supporting details
> Point 3
> Supporting details

You will then be asked to summarize and integrate the information from the reading and the listening passages. In your response, you will need to use only the information provided by the reading passage and lecture. You do <u>not</u> need to have specific knowledge of any academic subject in order to respond effectively.

TEST TIP!

For the writing section, you will have to type your response. Be sure to practice typing as much as possible before the test in order to improve your typing speed and accuracy.

Academic Reading / Lecture
QUICK GUIDE: Synthesis Task

Definition	The academic reading / lecture synthesis task requires you to create a typed response that describes how a lecture either supports or challenges information presented in a reading passage.
The Question	• After you read the passage and listen to the lecture, you will hear the narrator ask a question. • The question asks you how the points in the lecture either support or challenge the points made in the reading. • The question and the reading passage will remain on your screen until you have completed your response. You will hear the lecture only once. • You will have 20 minutes to plan and type your response. A clock on the screen will show how much time you have left to complete the task. • There is no minimum word count for your essay. However, in order to get a top score, you should write between 150 and 225 words for this task.
Targeted Skills	In order to achieve a high score for the academic reading / lecture synthesis task, you must: • identify the major points in the reading and the lecture. • determine whether the professor supports or challenges the points made in the reading. • analyze the writing prompt and understand what information you need to include in your response. • create an outline for your response. • connect information from both sources and correctly cite where the information came from. • organize your response so it is clear and easy to understand.
A Great Response	A top-scoring response will be between 150 and 225 words. It will clearly identify the important points or ideas from the lecture and accurately describe how the lecture either challenges or supports the information from the reading. The response should be well organized, use topic sentences, provide specific details, cite the source of the information, and generally be easy to understand.
Things to Remember	1. Take good notes and make sure that you understand the professor. Organize your notes so you can clearly see each key point from the reading and the corresponding points from the lecture. 2. Begin your typed response by briefly summarizing the main ideas of both the reading and the lecture. Be sure to describe whether the professor supports or casts doubt on the points from the reading. 3. Your essay should have three body paragraphs. Each body paragraph should address one point from the reading and the professor's supporting point or counterpoint from the lecture. Don't forget to include the supporting details from the lecture for each key point! 4. Write a concluding sentence that restates the main point of the reading and the main point of the lecture. In total, you should have five paragraphs: an introduction, three body paragraphs, and a conclusion. 5. Use the time given to plan, write, and proofread your essay.

WALK THROUGH: Academic Reading / Lecture Synthesis Task

A Below is a sample academic reading / lecture synthesis task. Read the passage and then listen to the lecture. While you read and listen, underline the information in the passage and the sample script that you think will be important to include in a response. CD1, Track 2

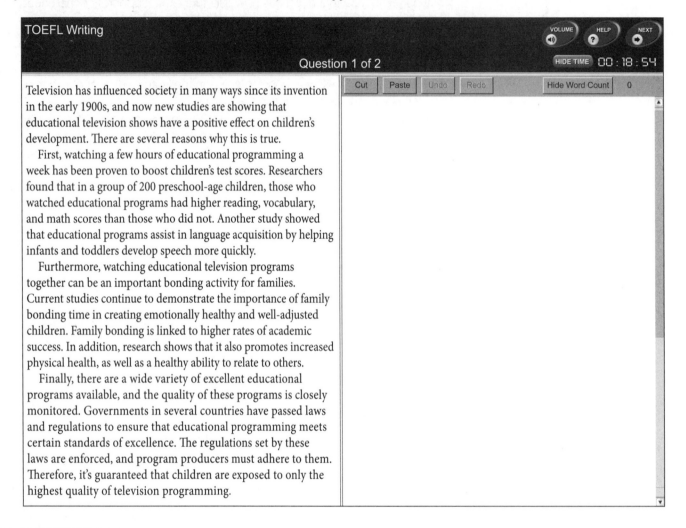

TOEFL Writing

VOLUME   HELP   NEXT

Question 1 of 2

HIDE TIME   00 : 18 : 54

Cut   Paste   Undo   Redo   Hide Word Count   0

Television has influenced society in many ways since its invention in the early 1900s, and now new studies are showing that educational television shows have a positive effect on children's development. There are several reasons why this is true.

First, watching a few hours of educational programming a week has been proven to boost children's test scores. Researchers found that in a group of 200 preschool-age children, those who watched educational programs had higher reading, vocabulary, and math scores than those who did not. Another study showed that educational programs assist in language acquisition by helping infants and toddlers develop speech more quickly.

Furthermore, watching educational television programs together can be an important bonding activity for families. Current studies continue to demonstrate the importance of family bonding time in creating emotionally healthy and well-adjusted children. Family bonding is linked to higher rates of academic success. In addition, research shows that it also promotes increased physical health, as well as a healthy ability to relate to others.

Finally, there are a wide variety of excellent educational programs available, and the quality of these programs is closely monitored. Governments in several countries have passed laws and regulations to ensure that educational programming meets certain standards of excellence. The regulations set by these laws are enforced, and program producers must adhere to them. Therefore, it's guaranteed that children are exposed to only the highest quality of television programming.

Glossary:

POWERED BY COBUILD

boost: to cause something to increase, improve, or be more successful

enforce: to make sure that a rule or law is obeyed

SAMPLE SCRIPT ▶

*for reference only,
not available in test*

Professor: It seems that TV is everywhere these days, especially in the home. There are a lot of contradicting views about the impact of TV on families and especially on young children. Overall, though, evidence indicates that watching educational programs on TV is not particularly beneficial for young toddlers and preschoolers.

Although some studies do indicate that watching educational programming boosts test scores, there are plenty of studies that directly contradict this notion. In fact, one research team found that watching TV of any kind was harmful to brain development in young children. Specifically, children under three years old who were exposed to a well-known educational program showed delayed speech development in comparison to those who watched no TV at all.

Second, it's true that family bonding time is an important part of emotional development for children. Unfortunately, studies show that parents are present with their children during just 32 percent of the time that kids watch TV. In addition, watching TV together simply is not an effective form of bonding. Although family members might be physically present while watching TV, there is no direct interaction between the individuals. Research shows that for bonding to take place, more contact and communication needs to occur between parents and children. Some good examples of this type of bonding are playing a game or eating a meal together.

Finally, although government regulations aim to ensure programming excellence, they often fail to do so. A 2008 study revealed that only one in eight educational programs actually met standards set by the regulations. This means that most of what kids are watching on TV is not very helpful in an educational sense. The regulations are in place, but they just don't work very well.

B Now review the notes that the test taker wrote down. Notice how the test taker organized his notes in two columns so he can easily see how the points from the lecture challenge those made in the reading. Read the passage and lecture again and circle the information that the test taker included in his outline. Compare the information you underlined and the information you circled. Did you notice all of the important points?

SAMPLE NOTES

<u>Reading</u>: Edu TV is good for kids
1. Boost test scores
   - Study w/200 preschoolers: those who watch edu TV had better reading, vocab, math scores
   - Study showed TV helps kids learn language faster
2. Bonding for families
   - Studies show fam time is important for emotional health
   - Fam time = academic success, phys health
3. Quality of edu programs is good b/c monitored by govt

<u>Lecture</u>: TV is bad for kids
1. TV does NOT help test scores
   - Studies show watching any kind of TV not good for brain dev
   - Kids under 3 watched pop TV shows, had slower speech dev
2. TV doesn't help families bond
   - Watching TV isn't a good way to bond: no interaction; need contact and communication (ex. playing games, eating)
3. Govt doesn't monitor quality of edu TV
   - 2008: 1 in 8 edu shows met govt standards = most edu TV is not helpful

C Below is a sample prompt and essay for an academic reading / lecture synthesis task. While you read, notice how the test taker uses his notes from Part B to create his essay.

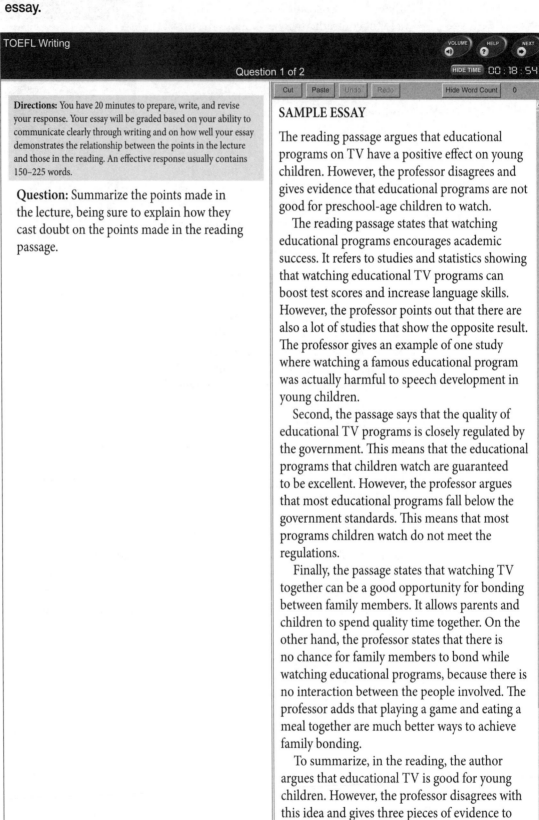

TOEFL Writing

Question 1 of 2

VOLUME   HELP   NEXT

HIDE TIME   00:18:54

Cut   Paste   Undo   Redo   Hide Word Count   0

Directions: You have 20 minutes to prepare, write, and revise your response. Your essay will be graded based on your ability to communicate clearly through writing and on how well your essay demonstrates the relationship between the points in the lecture and those in the reading. An effective response usually contains 150–225 words.

Question: Summarize the points made in the lecture, being sure to explain how they cast doubt on the points made in the reading passage.

SAMPLE ESSAY

The reading passage argues that educational programs on TV have a positive effect on young children. However, the professor disagrees and gives evidence that educational programs are not good for preschool-age children to watch.

The reading passage states that watching educational programs encourages academic success. It refers to studies and statistics showing that watching educational TV programs can boost test scores and increase language skills. However, the professor points out that there are also a lot of studies that show the opposite result. The professor gives an example of one study where watching a famous educational program was actually harmful to speech development in young children.

Second, the passage says that the quality of educational TV programs is closely regulated by the government. This means that the educational programs that children watch are guaranteed to be excellent. However, the professor argues that most educational programs fall below the government standards. This means that most programs children watch do not meet the regulations.

Finally, the passage states that watching TV together can be a good opportunity for bonding between family members. It allows parents and children to spend quality time together. On the other hand, the professor states that there is no chance for family members to bond while watching educational programs, because there is no interaction between the people involved. The professor adds that playing a game and eating a meal together are much better ways to achieve family bonding.

To summarize, in the reading, the author argues that educational TV is good for young children. However, the professor disagrees with this idea and gives three pieces of evidence to show that TV is actually bad for children.

GET IT RIGHT: Tips and Tasks for Answering Correctly

» **TIP 1: Scan the reading for the most important points.** When you read the passage for the first time, immediately look for and write down the author's main claim and the three key points used to support this claim. Remember, you will be able to see the reading passage when you write your essay. Therefore, you don't have to worry about writing down every detail. However, understanding the major points in the reading will help you predict what information will be included in the listening.

TASK 1: Draw a box around the author's claim and three key points presented in **the reading passage** on page 110.

» **TIP 2: Take notes during the listening!** You will hear the academic lecture only once. However, by knowing ahead of time what information to write down, you will have all of the information you need in your notes to write a great essay. When you listen to the lecture, write down the professor's position about the claim made in the reading. Does the professor support or challenge the claim? You should also write down the three key points that the professor uses to support his or her position.

TASK 2: Draw a box around the professor's position and three key points presented in **the lecture** on page 111.

» **TIP 3: Read the prompt carefully.** In most cases, the prompt asks how the professor's lecture either supports or challenges the points made in the reading.

TASK 3: Underline a phrase in **the prompt** on page 112 that tells you if the professor supports or challenges the claim made in the reading.

» **TIP 4: Write a clear introduction and conclusion.** The introduction of your essay should describe the claim made in the reading and whether the professor supports or challenges the claim. You can then reword your introduction to form a concluding sentence at the end of your essay. Use the phrases below to describe the relationship between the reading and the lecture.

Lecture Supports Reading	Lecture Challenges Reading
The reading passage says that [main topic from reading]. The professor supports this by providing examples of . . .	The reading passage argues that [main topic from reading]. However, the professor disagrees and gives evidence that [main topic from lecture].
In the reading passage, the author claims that [main topic from reading]. In the lecture, the professor discusses several studies that show that [main topic from reading] is true.	The reading states that [main topic from reading]. In the lecture, the professor argues the opposite. He gives evidence to support [main topic from lecture].
The author of the passage says that [main topic from reading]. The professor agrees with [main topic from reading] and supports it by mentioning a number of specific studies.	The reading claims that [main topic from reading]. The professor disagrees and says that [main topic from lecture].

TASK 4: Underline four sentences in **the sample essay** on page 112 that describe the relationship between the reading and the lecture. Look for the phrases mentioned in the table above.

» **TIP 5: Mention all three key points from the reading.** The reading passage will always include three key points. Organize your essay by writing an introduction and then writing three paragraphs that each address one of the key points. In addition to describing the key points from the reading, you must write about how the professor either supports or challenges each point.

TASK 5: In **the sample essay** on page 112, double underline the three key points from the reading. Notice the words that the test taker uses to report the key points from the reading and the lecture.

PROGRESSIVE PRACTICE: Get Ready

A Read the passage and underline the points that you feel may be important for responding to the question. Then, listen to the lecture on the same topic. Make notes about the important points. 🎧 CD1, Track 3

Scientists have been testing vegetable oil as a source of fuel for cars since the early 1900s. However, some key factors indicate that vegetable oil is not an ideal source of fuel.

First, using vegetable oil as fuel requires the installation of special equipment in a vehicle, which can be quite costly. A person can expect to pay as much as $1,600 for basic equipment, including a fuel tank, filters, fuel lines, and sensors. Also, when vegetable oil is used as fuel, impurities within the oil can cause the equipment to become clogged over time. These pieces of equipment must be fixed or replaced, which makes regular maintenance more expensive.

Next, using vegetable oil as fuel for cars can be a complicated process. In order for the vehicle to function properly, the special equipment must be turned on when first starting the vehicle and turned off several minutes before stopping. The amount of detail required to use the equipment requires a high level of attention.

Another issue is that using vegetable oil as fuel has the potential to reduce the availability of food crops. Most vegetable oil used for fuel comes from crops that are also used for food, such as corn and sunflowers. In regular production, it takes more than 400 sunflower plants to make just one gallon of sunflower oil. If this vegetable oil were to be used primarily for fuel, then the price of some foods that use the oil, such as french fries or salad dressings, could increase dramatically.

B Why did the test taker write down the information below? Answer the questions about the person's notes. Then, compare the notes to your underlined content in the reading and your notes from the listening. Did you notice the same important information?

Reading: Veg oil not good source of fuel (**A**)
1. Expensive
   - Need to install special equip; costs up to $1,600
   - Veg oil clogs; more $ to fix / replace equip
2. Complicated (**B**)
   - Driver needs to turn on / off equipment at certain times; needs lots of attn
3. Reduce avail of food crops
   - Veg oil comes from corn, sunflowers (food)
   - 400 sf plants for 1 gallon of oil
   - Food prices ↑ (ex. french fries, salad dressing)

Lecture: Veg oil is good (**C**)
1. Equip pays for itself
   - Avg miles / tank is 800–1,000 using veg fuel (500 mi for 1 tank of gas)
   - Price of equip will ↓ as tech becomes more common
2. Not hard to use
   - Becomes automatic
   - Automatic converters in dev
3. Veg fuel is waste product (**D**)
   - From factories and rests: used, no intrrptn to food supply

1. What does item A in the notes tell us?

[　] The main topic presented in the reading

[　] The first point in the reading

2. What is item B?

[　] The first point from the lecture

[　] The second point from the reading

3. What does item C in the notes tell us?

[　] The professor's main topic

[　] The professor's first point

4. What is item D?

[　] The third point from the lecture

[　] The third point from the reading

C Read the prompt. Is it asking if the professor supports or challenges the points made in the reading? Then, read a sample essay. Notice the words and expressions the writer uses to introduce the main topic from the reading and the lecture, introduce and talk about key points, and introduce and talk about supporting details. Then, identify the purpose of each section in the essay. Write the numbers of the phrases from the *Section Purposes* box in front of the correct sections in the sample essay.

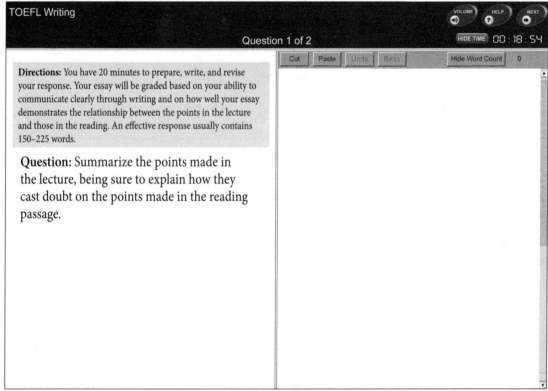

Directions: You have 20 minutes to prepare, write, and revise your response. Your essay will be graded based on your ability to communicate clearly through writing and on how well your essay demonstrates the relationship between the points in the lecture and those in the reading. An effective response usually contains 150–225 words.

Question: Summarize the points made in the lecture, being sure to explain how they cast doubt on the points made in the reading passage.

Section Purposes

1. ~~Main Topic from Reading~~   2. Key Point from Lecture   3. Key Point from Reading

4. Professor's Main Topic   5. Support from Lecture   6. Conclusion

SAMPLE ESSAY ▶ [1] The reading states that vegetable oil is not a good source of fuel for cars. It gives several reasons for this argument.

[　] However, in the lecture, the professor argues the opposite. She gives evidence to support the idea that vegetable oil is an excellent source of fuel for vehicles.

[　] The passage points out that it's expensive to install conversion equipment. There are many different pieces that cost money. Maintenance is also expensive.

[　] However, the professor argues that while it is expensive, the equipment pays for itself quickly by saving money.

[　] Using vegetable oil as fuel is a lot cheaper than gas. This way, drivers save money in the long term.

Continued on next page

[ ] Second, the passage suggests that using the special equipment needed for vegetable oil fuel could be very complicated. It requires a lot of attention.

[ ] The professor disagrees.

[ ] She points out that it's not very hard and that people get used to these motions. Also, she explains that there are new systems that are automatic and don't need a person to turn them on or off.

[ ] Finally, the passage argues that using vegetable oil could affect crops normally used for food, like sunflowers. This could cause the price of certain foods to go up.

[ ] In contrast, the professor says that the oil used for fuel is a waste product from places like food factories.

[ ] It's already been used once, so using it for fuel does not affect food production.

[ ] In conclusion, both the reading and the lecture discuss using vegetable oil as a source of fuel for cars. While the author claims that vegetable oil is not a good source of fuel, the professor disagrees and offers several pieces of evidence to show that vegetable oil is, in fact, a good source of fuel for vehicles.

D Now fill in the template below to create your own sample essay.

[***Introduction:*** *Main Topic from Reading, Main Topic from Lecture*]

In the reading, the author says that _____.

The professor disagrees and shows that vegetable oil is a good source of fuel by _____

_____.

[***Paragraph 2:*** *Key Point 1 from Reading, Key Point 1 from Lecture, Support from Lecture*]

First, the reading says that using vegetable oil as fuel is _____

_____.

The professor rejects this point and says that _____

_____

_____.

[***Paragraph 3:*** *Key Point 2 from Reading, Key Point 2 from Lecture, Support from Lecture*]

Next, the reading claims that _____

_____.

Again, the professor disagrees. According to the professor, _____

_____

_____.

[***Paragraph 4:*** *Key Point 3 from Reading, Key Point 3 from Lecture, Support from Lecture*]

The final point in the reading is that _____

_____.

The professor disproves this point as well. She argues that _____

_____

_____

_____.

[***Conclusion:*** *Restatement of Introduction*]

To summarize, _____

_____

_____.

E Now review your complete sample essay. Then, read the statements below. Did your response meet the scoring requirements for academic reading / lecture synthesis task? Check (✓) *Yes* or *No*. Keep drafting until you can check *Yes* for all of the statements.

Response Checklist: Academic Reading / Lecture Synthesis Task	Yes	No
1. My essay accurately connected information from both the academic reading and the lecture.	☐	☐
2. My essay has five paragraphs, including an introduction, three body paragraphs that discuss the three points from both sources, and a conclusion.	☐	☐
3. I mentioned the three points presented in the reading and described the professor's point of view for each one.	☐	☐
4. I used specific details and examples from both the lecture and the reading.	☐	☐
5. I used correct grammar, vocabulary, and punctuation and had few, if any, typographical errors (typos).	☐	☐
6. I used signposts and transition words to effectively show the relationships between my ideas.	☐	☐

PROGRESSIVE PRACTICE: Get Set

A Read the passage. Then, listen to the lecture on the same topic. ⌾ CD1, Track 4

The runic alphabet is a set of letters made up of forms called runes. This writing system was used by various Germanic groups in central and northern Europe as early as 150 AD until about 1100 AD. The origins of this alphabet have remained unclear, but archaeological evidence shows that runes most likely developed independently of any other alphabet.

First, Germanic groups had little interaction with people from other parts of Europe until around 700 AD, when the Romans conquered many parts of central Europe. Because people in central and northern Europe were culturally isolated from other groups, it is unlikely that the runic alphabet was based on a previous writing system.

Furthermore, according to the legends of some Germanic people, the alphabet was created by a mythological god called Odin. In one mythological text, Odin claims that the runes allow him to bring the dead back to life. The mythology of the Germanic groups was very different from the mythology in other parts of Europe, and the magical significance of the local alphabet within this mythology is also distinct. This implies that Germanic groups connected the runes to their unique mythology and traditions and not to writing systems from other groups.

Finally, many archaeologists note that the runic alphabet lacks similarities to any other alphabet that existed before or at the same time as the runic system. Any similarities between the runic alphabet and other alphabets are most likely random or coincidental. This makes it difficult to verify that the runic alphabet is a variant of an earlier alphabet.

B Read the passage and listen to the lecture again. Complete the notes below using the information from both sources.

Reading: Runic alphabet developed independently
  of other alphabets
1. Cultural isolation of Germanic ppl
  – No contact w/other ❶ _____
    Europeans until 700 (Roman conquest)
2. Germanic ppl thought alphabet came from
  ❷ _____ (Norse god)
  – Myth text: ❸ _____ let Odin bring
    ppl back from dead
3. No ❹ _____ to other alphabets
  – Any sim are coincidental

Lecture: Runes came from ❺ _____
  (script common throughout Europe)
1. Influenced by groups that used O.I., like
  ❻ _____ and Romans
  – Germanic ppl traded with Greeks and Italians
2. No evidence of myth origins
  – Italic groups traveled all over Europe before
    Norse myths became popular.
3. Similarities between O.I. and runes
  – Use same ❼ _____ letters

C Read the prompt and decide if it's asking you to support or challenge the points made in the reading. Then, use the notes on page 118 to complete the sample response template on page 120. Be sure to use citing expressions and transition words like the ones listed below to introduce your topics. Type your response if possible.

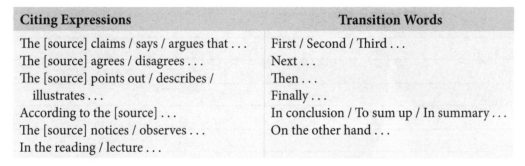

Citing Expressions	Transition Words
The [source] claims / says / argues that . . .	First / Second / Third . . .
The [source] agrees / disagrees . . .	Next . . .
The [source] points out / describes / illustrates . . .	Then . . .
	Finally . . .
According to the [source] . . .	In conclusion / To sum up / In summary . . .
The [source] notices / observes . . .	On the other hand . . .
In the reading / lecture . . .	

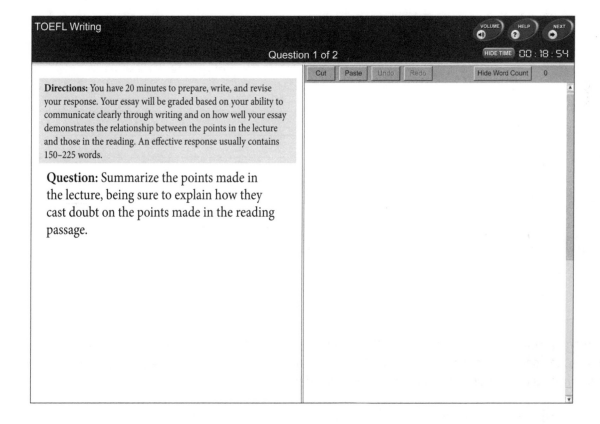

TOEFL Writing

VOLUME HELP NEXT

Question 1 of 2

HIDE TIME 00 : 18 : 54

Cut   Paste   Undo   Redo   Hide Word Count   0

Directions: You have 20 minutes to prepare, write, and revise your response. Your essay will be graded based on your ability to communicate clearly through writing and on how well your essay demonstrates the relationship between the points in the lecture and those in the reading. An effective response usually contains 150–225 words.

Question: Summarize the points made in the lecture, being sure to explain how they cast doubt on the points made in the reading passage.

Main Topic from Reading: _____

_____

Main Topic from Lecture: _____

Key Point 1 from Reading: _____

Key Point 1 from Lecture: _____

Support from Lecture: _____

Key Point 2 from Reading: _____

Key Point 2 from Lecture: _____

Support from Lecture: _____

Key Point 3 from Reading: _____

Key Point 3 from Lecture: _____

Support from Lecture: _____

Conclusion: _____

D Now review and proofread your complete sample essay. Then, read the statements below. Did your response meet the scoring requirements for academic reading / lecture synthesis tasks? Check (✓) *Yes* or *No*. Keep drafting until you can check *Yes* for all of the statements.

Response Checklist: Academic Reading / Lecture Synthesis Task	Yes	No
1. My essay accurately connected information from both the academic reading and the lecture.	☐	☐
2. My essay has five paragraphs, including an introduction, three body paragraphs that discuss the three points from both sources, and a conclusion.	☐	☐
3. I mentioned the three points presented in the reading and described the professor's point of view for each one.	☐	☐
4. I used specific details and examples from both the lecture and the reading.	☐	☐
5. I used correct grammar, vocabulary, and punctuation and had few, if any, typographical errors (typos).	☐	☐
6. I used signposts and transition words to effectively show the relationships between my ideas.	☐	☐

PROGRESSIVE PRACTICE: Go for the TOEFL Test

Read the passage in three minutes. Begin reading now.

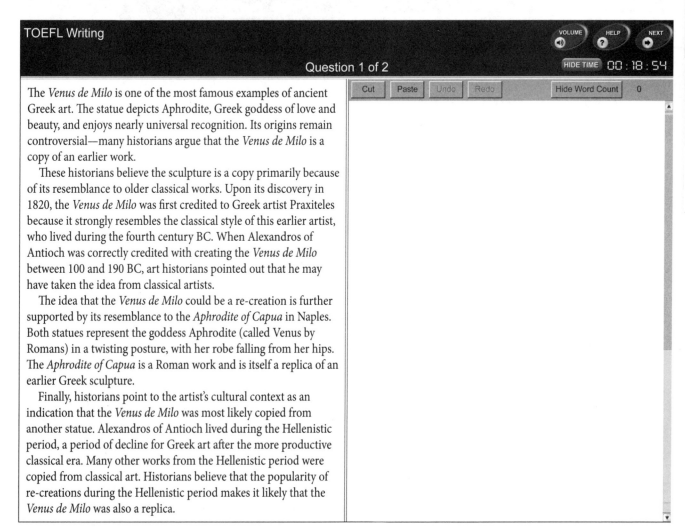

TOEFL Writing

VOLUME   HELP   NEXT

Question 1 of 2

HIDE TIME 00:18:54

Cut | Paste | Undo | Redo | Hide Word Count | 0

The *Venus de Milo* is one of the most famous examples of ancient Greek art. The statue depicts Aphrodite, Greek goddess of love and beauty, and enjoys nearly universal recognition. Its origins remain controversial—many historians argue that the *Venus de Milo* is a copy of an earlier work.

These historians believe the sculpture is a copy primarily because of its resemblance to older classical works. Upon its discovery in 1820, the *Venus de Milo* was first credited to Greek artist Praxiteles because it strongly resembles the classical style of this earlier artist, who lived during the fourth century BC. When Alexandros of Antioch was correctly credited with creating the *Venus de Milo* between 100 and 190 BC, art historians pointed out that he may have taken the idea from classical artists.

The idea that the *Venus de Milo* could be a re-creation is further supported by its resemblance to the *Aphrodite of Capua* in Naples. Both statues represent the goddess Aphrodite (called Venus by Romans) in a twisting posture, with her robe falling from her hips. The *Aphrodite of Capua* is a Roman work and is itself a replica of an earlier Greek sculpture.

Finally, historians point to the artist's cultural context as an indication that the *Venus de Milo* was most likely copied from another statue. Alexandros of Antioch lived during the Hellenistic period, a period of decline for Greek art after the more productive classical era. Many other works from the Hellenistic period were copied from classical art. Historians believe that the popularity of re-creations during the Hellenistic period makes it likely that the *Venus de Milo* was also a replica.

Now listen to part of a lecture in an art history class and take notes. 🎧 CD1, Track 5

Notes:

Read the prompt and write your response.

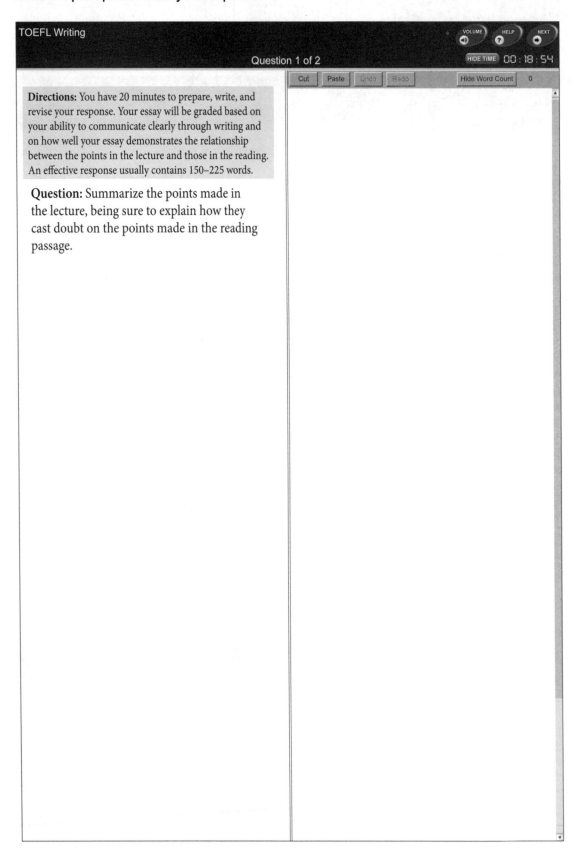

To see sample responses and rater's comments see page 158.

Personal Experience Essay

For writing task 2, you will write an essay that is based on a short question. The question will typically ask whether you agree or disagree with a statement. The statement in the question will relate to a familiar topic, such as school or family.

The prompt for the personal experience essay task may be worded as follows:

» *Do you agree or disagree with the following statement?*
   It is impossible for a town to grow without a good public transportation system.
   Use specific reasons and examples to support your response.

» *Some people like to save extra money. Other people prefer to spend it right away. Which do you prefer to do? Use specific reasons and examples to support your opinion.*

» *Do you agree or disagree with the following statement?*
   It is wrong to judge people before getting to know them.
   Use specific reasons and examples to support your response.

TEST TIP!

On the day of the test, you will type your response using a very basic word processing tool. This tool does <u>not</u> include a spell-checker, so be sure to practice typing responses before the day of the test without the help of a spell-checker.

In your typed essay, you must clearly state if you agree or disagree with the statement and justify your response by describing three reasons why you hold that opinion. Furthermore, you will have to provide personal examples and details to support your justifications.

You will have 30 minutes to prepare and write your essay. There is no limit on how many words you can write, but a strong response will typically include at least 300 words. At the end of the 30 minutes, your essay will automatically be saved. It will then be sent to ETS in order to be scored.

QUICK GUIDE: Personal Experience Essay

Definition	For the personal experience essay task, you will read a prompt that asks whether you agree or disagree with a statement. The statement is always about a general issue related to school, family, or community matters. You will <u>not</u> need to have any in-depth knowledge of a specific academic subject in order to answer the question.
The Question	• You will see the directions and the prompt on the left side of your screen. This information will remain on the screen for the entire time. • The directions instruct you to read the prompt and create your essay in 30 minutes. The directions also inform you that a top-scoring response usually has at least 300 words. • The prompt is a question. In most cases, you will be asked if you agree or disagree with a statement.
Targeted Skills	In order to achieve a high score for the personal experience essay task, you must: • analyze and understand the writing prompt. • consider both sides of the argument and choose the side that you can support with the most details and personal information. • state your opinion based on the prompt. • support your opinion with personal details. • organize your response so it is clear and easy to understand.
A Great Response	A top-scoring essay should be about 300 words or more. It will clearly answer all aspects of the question and use examples and personal details to support and connect the main ideas. The essay should be well organized and thorough, the vocabulary and grammar usage should be correct and varied, and the essay should generally be easy to understand.
Things to Remember	1. First, analyze the prompt. What information do you need in your response? 2. Next, spend a moment or two brainstorming the topic on your notepaper or your computer screen. You should decide which position to support (do you agree or disagree?) and come up with three key points to support your position. Also, it's helpful to write down a few words that you can use as examples. 3. Create a brief introduction. Your introduction should describe the general topic and clearly state your opinion. It should also summarize the three key points that support your opinion. 4. Explain the first reason for your preference and then provide personal details to support this reason. 5. Explain the second reason for your preference and then provide personal details to support this reason. 6. Explain the third reason for your preference and then provide personal details to support this reason. 7. Write a short conclusion that summarizes your essay.

WALK THROUGH: Personal Experience Essay

A Below is a sample prompt for the personal experience essay. Underline two pieces of information that must be included in the response.

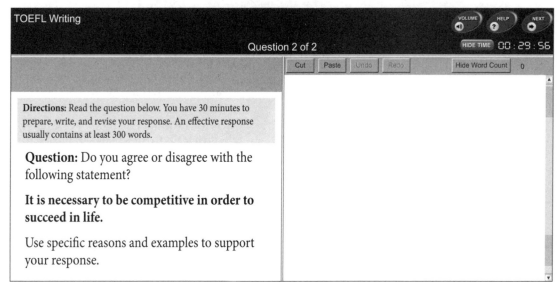

TOEFL Writing   VOLUME   HELP   NEXT

Question 2 of 2   HIDE TIME `00:29:56`

Cut   Paste   Undo   Redo   Hide Word Count   0

Directions: Read the question below. You have 30 minutes to prepare, write, and revise your response. An effective response usually contains at least 300 words.

Question: Do you agree or disagree with the following statement?

It is necessary to be competitive in order to succeed in life.

Use specific reasons and examples to support your response.

B Now review the sample notes that the test taker made while brainstorming. Notice how the test taker writes points for each side of the argument before deciding which side to support. Also note that while you can brainstorm on your notepaper, it might save you some time to brainstorm on the computer. That way, you can just turn your notes into sentences and change the organization using the "cut" and "paste" functions on the screen.

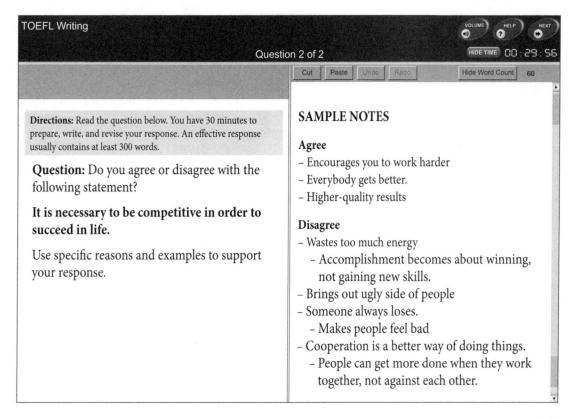

TOEFL Writing   VOLUME   HELP   NEXT

Question 2 of 2   HIDE TIME `00:29:56`

Cut   Paste   Undo   Redo   Hide Word Count   60

Directions: Read the question below. You have 30 minutes to prepare, write, and revise your response. An effective response usually contains at least 300 words.

Question: Do you agree or disagree with the following statement?

It is necessary to be competitive in order to succeed in life.

Use specific reasons and examples to support your response.

SAMPLE NOTES

Agree
– Encourages you to work harder
– Everybody gets better.
– Higher-quality results

Disagree
– Wastes too much energy
  – Accomplishment becomes about winning, not gaining new skills.
– Brings out ugly side of people
– Someone always loses.
  – Makes people feel bad
– Cooperation is a better way of doing things.
  – People can get more done when they work together, not against each other.

C Below is a sample essay for a personal experience essay task. While you read, notice how the test taker turns the notes from Part B into a full essay.

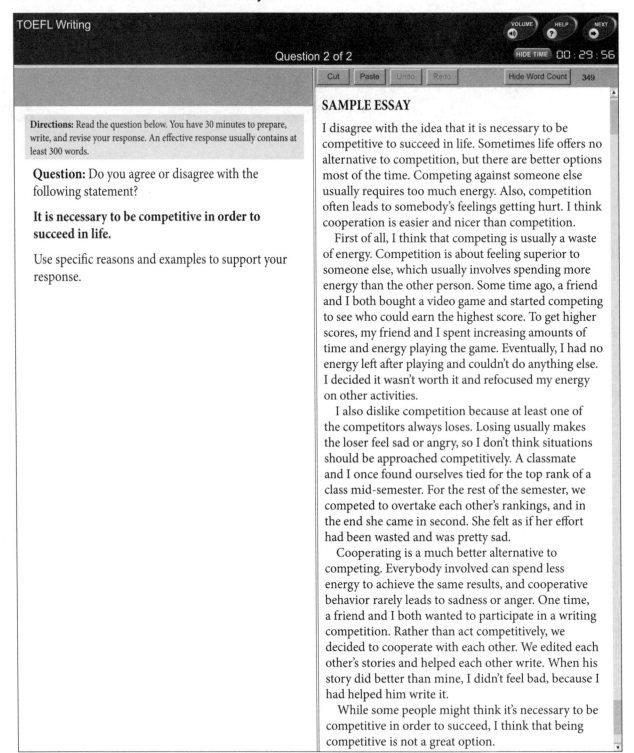

TOEFL Writing

VOLUME   HELP   NEXT

Question 2 of 2

HIDE TIME 00 : 29 : 56

Cut | Paste | Undo | Redo | Hide Word Count | 349

Directions: Read the question below. You have 30 minutes to prepare, write, and revise your response. An effective response usually contains at least 300 words.

Question: Do you agree or disagree with the following statement?

It is necessary to be competitive in order to succeed in life.

Use specific reasons and examples to support your response.

SAMPLE ESSAY

I disagree with the idea that it is necessary to be competitive to succeed in life. Sometimes life offers no alternative to competition, but there are better options most of the time. Competing against someone else usually requires too much energy. Also, competition often leads to somebody's feelings getting hurt. I think cooperation is easier and nicer than competition.

First of all, I think that competing is usually a waste of energy. Competition is about feeling superior to someone else, which usually involves spending more energy than the other person. Some time ago, a friend and I both bought a video game and started competing to see who could earn the highest score. To get higher scores, my friend and I spent increasing amounts of time and energy playing the game. Eventually, I had no energy left after playing and couldn't do anything else. I decided it wasn't worth it and refocused my energy on other activities.

I also dislike competition because at least one of the competitors always loses. Losing usually makes the loser feel sad or angry, so I don't think situations should be approached competitively. A classmate and I once found ourselves tied for the top rank of a class mid-semester. For the rest of the semester, we competed to overtake each other's rankings, and in the end she came in second. She felt as if her effort had been wasted and was pretty sad.

Cooperating is a much better alternative to competing. Everybody involved can spend less energy to achieve the same results, and cooperative behavior rarely leads to sadness or anger. One time, a friend and I both wanted to participate in a writing competition. Rather than act competitively, we decided to cooperate with each other. We edited each other's stories and helped each other write. When his story did better than mine, I didn't feel bad, because I had helped him write it.

While some people might think it's necessary to be competitive in order to succeed, I think that being competitive is not a great option.

Glossary:

⋐ POWERED BY COBUILD

superior: to be better than something or someone

overtake: to pass or move ahead

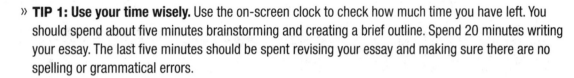

GET IT RIGHT: Tips and Tasks for Answering Correctly

» **TIP 1: Use your time wisely.** Use the on-screen clock to check how much time you have left. You should spend about five minutes brainstorming and creating a brief outline. Spend 20 minutes writing your essay. The last five minutes should be spent revising your essay and making sure there are no spelling or grammatical errors.

TASK 1: Read **the sample notes** on page 125 and **the sample essay** on page 126. Notice how the notes are very short.

» **TIP 2: Brainstorm before you start writing.** Spend two minutes writing as many points that you can think of for each side of the argument. When you are done, notice which side of the argument has more points. Don't worry about choosing a "wrong" answer. Remember, your response is being graded on the basis of how well you support your ideas, not on the opinions you hold.

TASK 2: Look at **the sample notes** on page 125. Which side of the argument did the test taker come up with more support for?

» **TIP 3: Make sure you have three distinct key points to explain your preference.** Once you pick which side to support, make sure you have three points to support your main idea. In order to achieve a strong score, the three points should be completely different from one another. If any of your points are too similar, spend another moment trying to think of a different point. One common way of supporting a position is by pointing out why the other side is bad.

TASK 3: Circle three key points in **the sample essay** on page 126 that the test taker uses to support his opinion.

» **TIP 4: Start your essay by clearly stating your position.** By clearly stating your preference in your introduction, you will show that you understand the prompt. Also, stating upfront whether you agree or disagree helps the organization of your essay because you can spend the rest of the essay justifying your position.

TASK 4: Draw a box around the introductory statement in **the sample essay** on page 126.

» **TIP 5: Provide plenty of personal details.** For the independent writing task, the raters will be looking for personal details to support your key points. Remember, you can make up or exaggerate your personal details in order to create stronger support. The graders will not be concerned with whether or not your personal details are true. They just want to know that you can support your opinions.

TASK 5: Draw a circle around the three personal details in **the sample essay** on page 126.

PROGRESSIVE PRACTICE: Get Ready

A Look at the prompt and circle two pieces of information that must be included in the response.

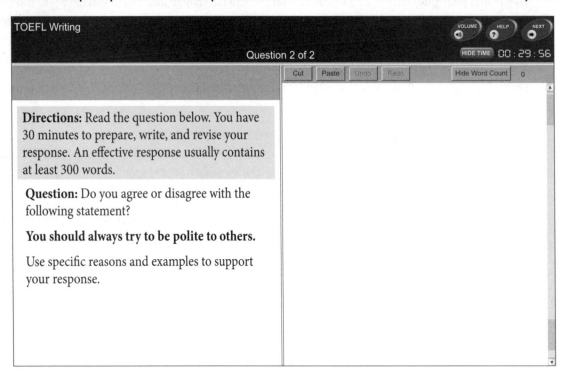

B Based on the notes below, which side do you think the test taker will support in her essay?

☐ Agree

☐ Disagree

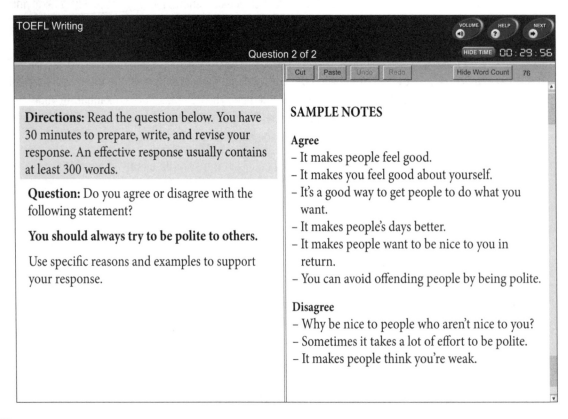

C Read a sample essay in response to the prompt on page 128. Notice the words and expressions the writer uses to state her position, introduce and write about key points, offer personal details, and end her essay. Then, read the essay again. Identify the purpose of each section in the essay. Write the numbers of the phrases from the *Section Purposes* box in front of the correct sections in the sample essay.

Section Purposes		
1. ~~Topic Sentence~~	2. Summary of Key Points	3. Key Point 1
4. Key Point 2	5. Key Point 3	6. Personal Details
7. Conclusion		

SAMPLE ESSAY ▶ [1] I agree with the idea that you should always try to be polite to others.

[ ] I think that being polite makes you feel good. I think it also makes the person who receives your politeness feel good. Moreover, impoliteness can cause people to become angry with you.

[ ] I have found that when I am polite to others, it makes me feel good. Being polite makes me feel like I am a decent and kind person.

[ ] For instance, one time as I was walking into a grocery store, a woman was walking in the opposite direction, and she accidentally spilled her groceries all over the parking lot. I stopped and helped her pick them up. She didn't thank me, but my act of politeness made me feel good anyway.

[ ] The act of being polite also benefits the person who receives the politeness. It often brightens the recipient's day and can positively change the way he or she looks at people.

[ ] For example, I was traveling in a foreign country last summer and wasn't sure what I was going to do one evening. A local spotted me wandering around and asked me if I needed help finding something. He ended up giving me many good suggestions on places to visit. That one act of politeness made me happy the entire rest of my week.

[ ] Another good reason for being polite is that people sometimes become offended when you are impolite, and generally it is not a good idea to offend people.

[ ] For instance, an old friend of mine once introduced me to a woman he had met and was dating. At one point, when I thought she wasn't listening, I made a rude comment about her dress. She heard me and became very offended. My friend stopped spending time with me after that. The woman remains close to my friend, but neither of them has spoken to me since.

[ ] To summarize, it's my opinion that you should always try to be polite to others. Being polite not only makes you feel good, it makes others feel good, too. Also, being polite helps you avoid offending people.

D Now fill in the template with your own experiences and opinions. Use the ideas from the sample notes on page 128 or use your own ideas. Be sure to use personal details to support your key points. Try to type your response.

In my opinion, I _____ you should always be polite to others. I feel this way for a number of

reasons, including that _____

_____.

First, I think that _____. By that, I mean that _____

_____.

For example, _____

_____

_____.

Next, _____

_____.

Frankly, there are times when _____

_____

_____.

Finally, _____.

I know somebody who is _____

_____

_____

_____.

In summary, _____

_____.

E Now review your complete sample essay. Then, read the statements below. Did your response meet the scoring requirements for personal experience essay task? Check (✓) *Yes* or *No*. Keep drafting until you can check *Yes* for all of the statements.

Response Checklist: Personal Experience Essay Task	Yes	No
1. My essay thoroughly addressed the question asked in the prompt.	☐	☐
2. I clearly described in the introduction of my essay whether I agreed or disagreed with the statement.	☐	☐
3. My essay presented three key points to support my topic sentence. My three key points were completely different from one another.	☐	☐
4. I included personal details to support each of my key points.	☐	☐
5. I used correct grammar, vocabulary, and punctuation and had few, if any, typographical errors (typos).	☐	☐
6. My essay was well organized, and I used transition words to help the flow of my essay.	☐	☐

PROGRESSIVE PRACTICE: Get Set

A Look at the prompt and write the two pieces of information that must be included in the essay.

1. _____

2. _____

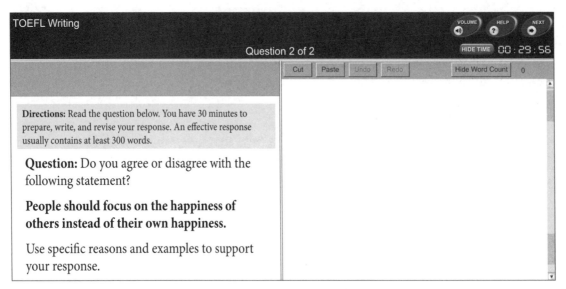

B Read the sample notes. Then, use the phrases from the *Section Purposes* box to label the main points that the test taker has written down. Some items will be used more than once.

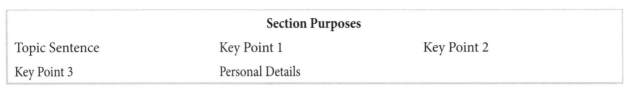

Section Purposes		
Topic Sentence	Key Point 1	Key Point 2
Key Point 3	Personal Details	

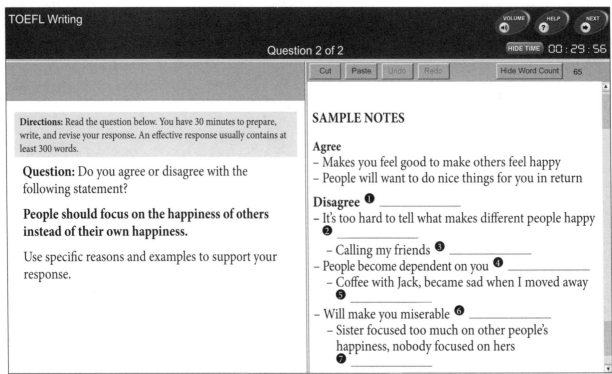

C The information in the sample essay below is out of order. Write the numbers 1–5 to put the paragraphs in the order they should appear.

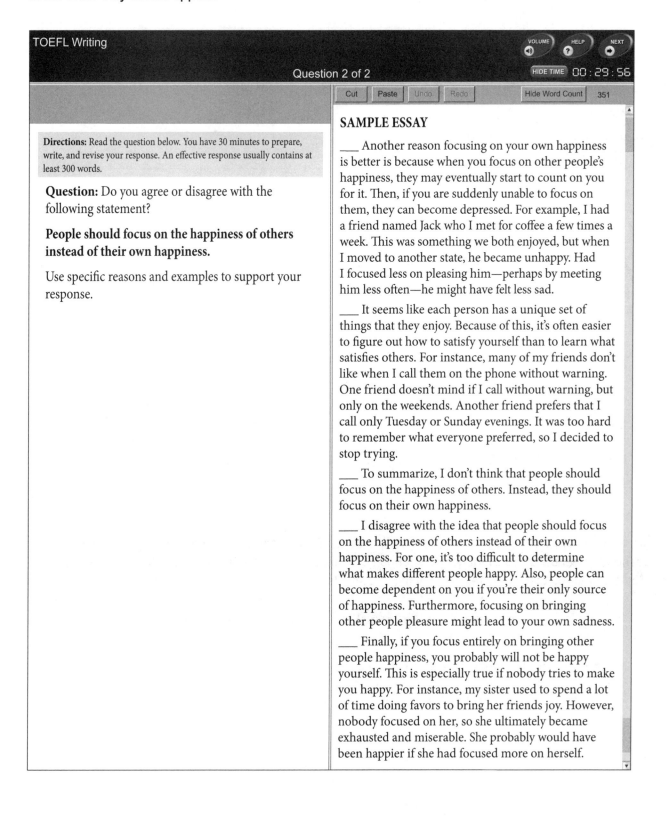

TOEFL Writing

VOLUME   HELP   NEXT

Question 2 of 2

HIDE TIME 00:29:56

Cut   Paste   Undo   Redo   Hide Word Count   351

Directions: Read the question below. You have 30 minutes to prepare, write, and revise your response. An effective response usually contains at least 300 words.

Question: Do you agree or disagree with the following statement?

People should focus on the happiness of others instead of their own happiness.

Use specific reasons and examples to support your response.

SAMPLE ESSAY

____ Another reason focusing on your own happiness is better is because when you focus on other people's happiness, they may eventually start to count on you for it. Then, if you are suddenly unable to focus on them, they can become depressed. For example, I had a friend named Jack who I met for coffee a few times a week. This was something we both enjoyed, but when I moved to another state, he became unhappy. Had I focused less on pleasing him—perhaps by meeting him less often—he might have felt less sad.

____ It seems like each person has a unique set of things that they enjoy. Because of this, it's often easier to figure out how to satisfy yourself than to learn what satisfies others. For instance, many of my friends don't like when I call them on the phone without warning. One friend doesn't mind if I call without warning, but only on the weekends. Another friend prefers that I call only Tuesday or Sunday evenings. It was too hard to remember what everyone preferred, so I decided to stop trying.

____ To summarize, I don't think that people should focus on the happiness of others. Instead, they should focus on their own happiness.

____ I disagree with the idea that people should focus on the happiness of others instead of their own happiness. For one, it's too difficult to determine what makes different people happy. Also, people can become dependent on you if you're their only source of happiness. Furthermore, focusing on bringing other people pleasure might lead to your own sadness.

____ Finally, if you focus entirely on bringing other people happiness, you probably will not be happy yourself. This is especially true if nobody tries to make you happy. For instance, my sister used to spend a lot of time doing favors to bring her friends joy. However, nobody focused on her, so she ultimately became exhausted and miserable. She probably would have been happier if she had focused more on herself.

D Now fill in the template to create your own sample essay. Use the words given or your own ideas. Be sure to use personal details to support your key points. Try to type your response.

I _____ with the statement that people should focus on the happiness of others over their own

happiness. Focusing on the happiness of others _____

_____ and _____.

Also, it often _____.

First, in my experience, I've found that _____.

For the past _____ years, I have _____

_____

_____

_____

Second, I think that focusing on the happiness of others _____

_____

_____

_____

Third, a lot of the time, focusing on the happiness of other people _____

_____

_____

_____

In conclusion, it is best if _____

_____

E Now review and proofread your complete sample essay. Then, read the statements below. Did your response meet the scoring requirements for personal experience essay tasks? Check (✓) *Yes* or *No*. Keep drafting until you can check *Yes* for all of the statements.

Response Checklist: Personal Experience Essay Task	Yes	No
1. My essay thoroughly addressed the question asked in the prompt.	☐	☐
2. I clearly described in the introduction of my essay whether I agreed or disagreed with the statement.	☐	☐
3. My essay presented three key points to support my topic sentence. My three key points were completely different from one another.	☐	☐
4. I included personal details to support each of my key points.	☐	☐
5. I used correct grammar, vocabulary, and punctuation and had few, if any, typographical errors (typos).	☐	☐
6. My essay was well organized, and I used transition words to help the flow of my essay.	☐	☐

PROGRESSIVE PRACTICE: Go for the TOEFL Test

Read the prompt and write your response.

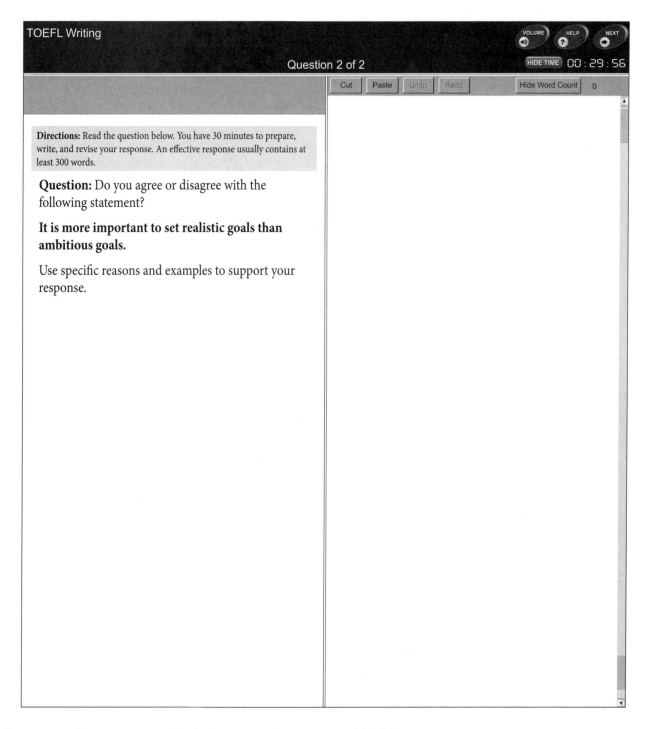

TOEFL Writing

VOLUME HELP NEXT

Question 2 of 2

HIDE TIME 00 : 29 : 56

Cut   Paste   Undo   Redo   Hide Word Count   0

Directions: Read the question below. You have 30 minutes to prepare, write, and revise your response. An effective response usually contains at least 300 words.

Question: Do you agree or disagree with the following statement?

It is more important to set realistic goals than ambitious goals.

Use specific reasons and examples to support your response.

To see sample responses and rater's comments see pages 160–161.

Writing Review Test

The following section is designed to put the skills you have learned to the test. In the *Writing Review Test*, you will encounter both question types as they appear on the writing section. Furthermore, the questions are the same difficulty as those on the TOEFL® test.

In order to make the review test as true to the TOEFL test as possible, please be sure to follow the directions on the page. When you play the CD track that is listed on the page, you will hear instructions that let you know when to start writing your essay. The following timing guide shows how much time you will have to write your essay for each question type on the writing section. Time yourself.

Writing Section Timing Guide			
Question	Reading Time	Lecture Time	Response Time
Question 1: Academic Reading / Lecture Synthesis Task	About 3 minutes (shown on-screen)	About 3–5 minutes	20 minutes
Question 2: Personal Experience Essay Task	n/a	n/a	30 minutes

For the best results, you should use a simple word processor to type your responses for the questions in the *Writing Review Test*. Remember, the word processor on the TOEFL test does not have a spell-checker. In the answer key for the *Writing Review Test*, you will find two model responses for each question. Each model response has been rated and is accompanied by a rater's analysis that explains the good and bad points of the response. Use these evaluations, along with the scoring guides in the writing section on pages 98–99 to determine what score you would have received.

When evaluating your essays, try to identify your weaknesses. Did you provide enough personal details? Is your essay long enough? By understanding your weaknesses, you will know exactly what sections to review in order to improve.

QUESTION 1

Read the passage in three minutes. Begin reading now.

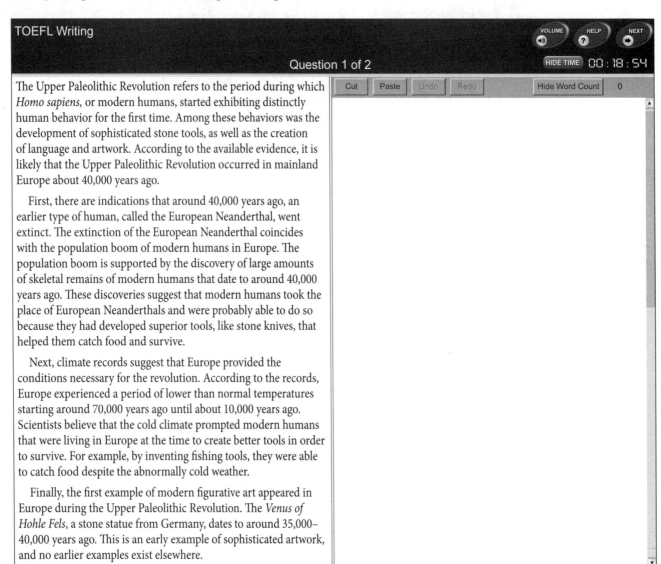

TOEFL Writing

Question 1 of 2

HIDE TIME 00:18:54

The Upper Paleolithic Revolution refers to the period during which *Homo sapiens,* or modern humans, started exhibiting distinctly human behavior for the first time. Among these behaviors was the development of sophisticated stone tools, as well as the creation of language and artwork. According to the available evidence, it is likely that the Upper Paleolithic Revolution occurred in mainland Europe about 40,000 years ago.

First, there are indications that around 40,000 years ago, an earlier type of human, called the European Neanderthal, went extinct. The extinction of the European Neanderthal coincides with the population boom of modern humans in Europe. The population boom is supported by the discovery of large amounts of skeletal remains of modern humans that date to around 40,000 years ago. These discoveries suggest that modern humans took the place of European Neanderthals and were probably able to do so because they had developed superior tools, like stone knives, that helped them catch food and survive.

Next, climate records suggest that Europe provided the conditions necessary for the revolution. According to the records, Europe experienced a period of lower than normal temperatures starting around 70,000 years ago until about 10,000 years ago. Scientists believe that the cold climate prompted modern humans that were living in Europe at the time to create better tools in order to survive. For example, by inventing fishing tools, they were able to catch food despite the abnormally cold weather.

Finally, the first example of modern figurative art appeared in Europe during the Upper Paleolithic Revolution. The *Venus of Hohle Fels*, a stone statue from Germany, dates to around 35,000–40,000 years ago. This is an early example of sophisticated artwork, and no earlier examples exist elsewhere.

Cut | Paste | Undo | Redo | Hide Word Count | 0

Now listen to part of a lecture in a history class and take notes.

🎧 CD1, Track 6

Notes:

Read the prompt and write your response.

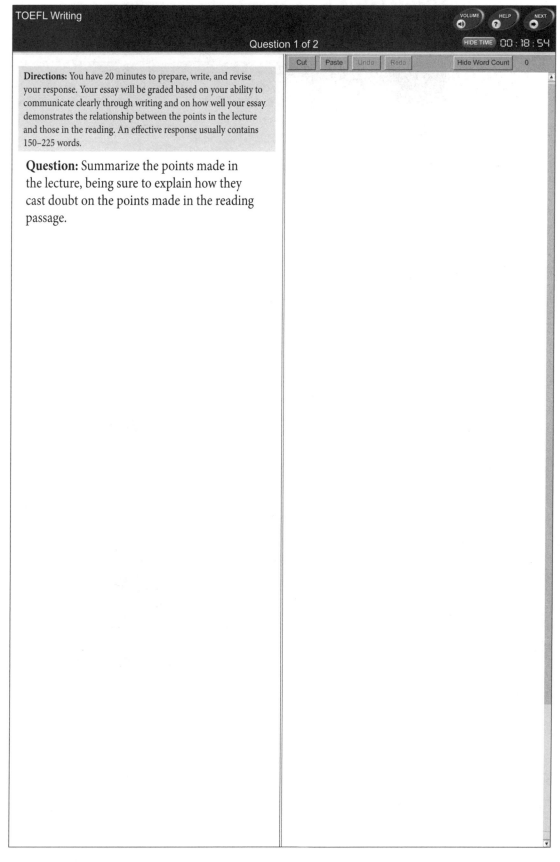

To see sample responses and rater's comments see pages 162–163.

QUESTION 2

Read the prompt and write your response in 30 minutes.

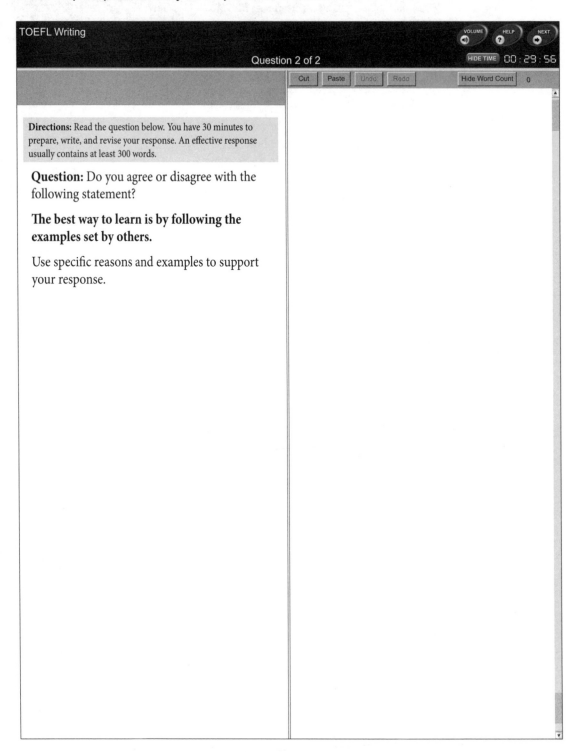

To see sample responses and rater's comments see pages 163–164.

Answer Key

READING

Lesson 1: Detail Questions and Referent Questions

Walk through: Detail Questions

A 1. *Key Words:* repetition strategy used in ancient India; add new details; more complex; memorize sacred texts; remember entire paragraphs   *Correct Answer:* It is more complex than other repetition methods.

B *Key Words / Phrases:* Thus, sentence by sentence, one can learn a complete narrative.; Of course, some forms of repetition are more complicated than the method just described.; For example, in ancient India, people memorized sacred texts by repeating the words in a different order.

Get It Right: Detail Questions

Task 1: paragraph 2; true about the repetition strategy used in ancient India   **Task 2:** some forms of repetition are more complicated; For example, in ancient India, people memorized sacred texts by repeating the words in a different order.   **Task 3:** It was primarily used to memorize sacred texts.   **Task 4:** It allowed users to add new details to narratives.; It required users to remember entire paragraphs at a time.   **Task 5:** One such technique is repetition, which involves saying the words of a story many times.

Walk through: Referent Questions

A 1. *Key Words:* The word it; paragraph 1   *Correct Answer:* Venice, Italy   **2.** *Key Words:* The word they; paragraph 2   *Correct Answer:* printers

B *Answer Options for Question 1:* However, one city in particular emerged as the leader in printing by the end of the fifteenth century: Venice, Italy. Printing nearly a quarter of all books in Europe during the 1490s, it was a top producer of books.   *Answer Options for Question 2:* The city's legacy as a trade hub proved useful for printers in the fifteenth century because it was relatively easy to sell and distribute the books that they produced. According to historians, many printers in Venice created books specifically for export to other countries.

Get It Right: Referent Questions

Task 1: *Paragraph 1:* the fifteenth century; Venice, Italy; Europe; a top producer   *Paragraph 2:* the city's legacy; printers; books; historians   **Task 2:** *Question 1:* Europe   *Question 2:* the city's legacy

Get Ready

A *Paragraph 1:* England offers a clear example—in the early sixteenth century, a new type of theater, called English Renaissance Theater, flourished there. This new theatrical style, which was more for entertainment and less for promoting religious values, developed because of a number of changes in England.   *Paragraph 2:* One major reason for the popularity of English Renaissance Theater was that it reflected the cultural changes that were occurring in England at the time.   *Paragraph 3:* During the same period, English theater companies and performance spaces also underwent a number of changes that helped bolster English Renaissance Theater.

B 1. *Key Words:* best describes popular theater in mainland Europe during the 1500s; based on Greek plays; primary goal was to teach lessons; work of William Shakespeare; developed in churches   **2.** *Key Words:* The word those   **3.** *Key Words:* role did noble families play; growth of English Renaissance Theater; discouraged the production of morality plays; formed traveling companies; provided inspiration; paid to have public theater spaces built   **4.** *Key Words:* The word they

Get Set

A 1. Piazzolla's nuevo tango retains elements of traditional tango, but it is also distinct in several ways. **2.** Piazzolla began to explore traditional Argentine music by learning how to play the *bandoneón*, an accordion-like instrument that is often employed in tango music.   **3.** While there were clear influences of traditional Argentine tango in his work, Piazzolla's nuevo tango also reflected the other types of music he was exposed to as a young man.   **4.** Another unique element of Piazzolla's nuevo tango music is its experimental tendency.

B 1. D, A, C, B   **2.** D, A, B, C   **3.** B, C, D, A   **4.** C, A, B, D

Go for the TOEFL Test

1. The subjects of the paintings   **2.** the Bradshaws   **3.** Chemicals have damaged the paint.   **4.** By testing the age of an object that was covering the painting   **5.** The Bradshaws look similar to paintings created by Australian Aborigines in other parts of the country.   **6.** the artists

Lesson 2: Negative Fact Questions and Function Questions

Walk through: Negative Fact Questions

A 1. *Key Words:* According to paragraph 1; accurately describe dynamic pricing EXCEPT; started to decline at the end of the twentieth century; buyer some control over the price; used by sellers in online auctions; sellers charge different prices according to the situation   *Correct Answer:* Its popularity started to decline at the end of the twentieth century.

Get It Right: Negative Fact Questions

Task 1: popularity; buyer's; online auctions; price   **Task 2:** It gives the buyer some control over the price of an item.; It means that sellers charge different prices according to the situation.   **Task 3:** It is used by sellers in online auctions.

Walk through: Function Questions

A 1. *Key Words:* In paragraph 3; the pyramid in Teotihuacan; the feathered serpent; Mayans inspired; symbolic images; archaeological technique; symbol popular in Teotihuacan   *Correct Answer:* To point out that the symbol was popular in Teotihuacan before the Maya used it   **2.** *Key Words:* Paragraph 1 gives examples; Paragraph 2 describes the background; Paragraph 1 defines a key term; Paragraph 2 provides evidence to support a theory   *Correct Answer:* Paragraph 2 provides evidence to support a theory that is introduced in paragraph 1.

B *Information for Question 1:* Between the years 150 and 200, the Teotihuacanos even built a pyramid that featured the symbol extensively. The same symbol has been found in Mayan texts. However, the Maya didn't use it before the year 1000.   *Information for Question 2:* Evidence suggests that the Maya were greatly influenced by the Teotihuacanos, especially in the areas of architecture and ideology. The Maya used a variety of architectural styles. However, one that was likely inspired by Teotihuacan was a technique called the slope-and-panel style.

Get It Right: Function Questions

Task 1: feathered serpent; religious symbols; symbol; Teotihuacanos   **Task 2:** *Phrase from Passage:* This is particularly apparent in   *Answer Option:* To point out that the symbol was popular in Teotihuacan before the Maya used it   **Task 3:** To give an example of an archaeological technique used by the Teotihuacanos   **Task 4:** *Main Idea for Paragraph 1:* Evidence suggests that the Maya were greatly influenced by the Teotihuacanos, especially in the areas of architecture and ideology. *Main Idea for Paragraph 2:* The Maya used a variety of architectural styles. However, one that was likely inspired by Teotihuacan was a technique called the slope-and-panel style. *Relationship Between Paragraphs:* Paragraph 2 provides support for a theory introduced in paragraph 1.

Get Ready

A *Paragraph 1:* Active design uses a number of techniques to encourage the occupants of a building to be more active.   *Paragraph 2:* One of the most important strategies of active design is inspiring people to make walking part of their routine.   ***Paragraph 3:*** Active design encourages physical activity using not only the interior features of a building, but the relationship between a building and its surroundings as well.

Get Set

A 1. Advances in technology have provided modern archaeologists with several methods that give them the absolute age of an object.   **2.** The most common absolute dating technique is radiocarbon dating.   **3.** For some inorganic remains, like pottery, archaeologists use a technique called thermoluminescence dating.   **4.** Thermoluminescence dating is particularly useful for dating pottery because of the process by which pottery is made.

B 1. C, D, A, B   **2.** A, C, B, D   **3.** D, A, B, C   **4.** D, B, A, C

Go for the TOEFL Test

1. Some cultures use body language more than others.   **2.** give an example of body language that can have multiple interpretations   **3.** Paragraph 2 presents a theory about some body language, and paragraph 3 demonstrates that the theory is not always true.   **4.** Promoting language development   **5.** To recognize members of the same group   **6.** To illustrate how nonverbal communication can have unintended consequences

Lesson 3: Inference Questions and Vocabulary Questions

Walk through: Inference Questions

A 1. ***Key Words:*** paragraph 2; abacuses used in Babylon; earliest calculators; did not have any educational value; not easy to move around; inspired the invention of the wire abacus   ***Correct Answer:*** They were not easy to move around.

B ***Key Words / Phrases:*** The earliest form of calculator; used them to teach mathematics; invented the wire abacus; more portable

Get It Right: Inference Questions

Task 1: abacuses used in Babylon; earliest calculators; did not have any educational value; were not easy to move around; inspired the invention of the wire abacus   **Task 2:** They were the earliest calculators.   **Task 3:** They inspired the invention of the wire abacus.

Walk through: Vocabulary Questions

A 1. ***Definitions:*** *hurried:* in a rush; *continuous:* constant; *slow:* not fast; *graceful:* moving smoothly   ***Correct Answer:*** slow   **2.** ***Definitions:*** *dangerous:* not safe; *insignificant:* not important; *unnoticeable:* not recognized; *impassible:* not able to be passed   ***Correct Answer:*** unnoticeable

B ***Information for Question 1:*** on average, glaciers move a mere 30 centimeters a day; However, in some cases, glaciers move at a much faster rate.   ***Information for Question 2:*** even to someone standing on the glacier as the earthquake occurs; However, some scientists hypothesize that a significant glacial earthquake could cause oceanic disturbances and perhaps even tsunamis.

Get It Right: Vocabulary Questions

Task 1: ***Indirect Definition:*** on average, glaciers move a mere 30 centimeters a day   ***Contrasting Word:*** However   ***Correct Answer:*** slow   **Task 2:** ***Prefix:*** im- ***Definition:*** not   **Task 3:** ***Question 1:*** hurried   ***Question 2:*** dangerous   **Task 4:** (*answers may vary*) *gradual:* proceeding by steps or degrees; *imperceptible:* extremely slight or subtle

Get Ready

A ***Paragraph 1:*** its location plays a large role in the climate of the region   ***Paragraph 2:*** The latitude of the Atlantic Archipelago undoubtedly influences its climate.   ***Paragraph 3:*** The islands enjoy mild temperatures largely because of their proximity to the ocean.

B 1. ***Key Words:*** sunlight; intensity; latitude; north of the equator; near the equator; near the ocean   **2.** ***Key Words:*** The word temperate   **3.** ***Key Words:*** The word proximity   **4.** ***Key Words:*** Gulf Stream; water temperatures; Gulf of Mexico; Atlantic Ocean; summer; Atlantic Archipelago

Get Set

A 1. many animals have developed multiple strategies for obtaining poison through poison sequestration   **2.** One method of poison sequestration involves obtaining toxins from plant sources.   **3.** Another poison sequestration strategy involves obtaining poison from other animals.
4. It is also common for poison sequestration to progress up the food chain, meaning that many predators sequester poison from prey that have also sequestered poison.
B 1. A, D, B, C   **2.** B, D, C, A   **3.** A, B, D, C   **4.** B, C, A, D

Go for the TOEFL Test

1. It assumed that Earth and the moon were made of the same material.   **2.** weakened   **3.** the chemical composition of the moon was unknown until after the 1950s.   **4.** broke apart   **5.** It describes the creation of multiple moons.   **6.** theorize

Lesson 4: Sentence Summary and Passage Summary Questions

Walk through: Sentence Summary Questions

A 1. *Key Words:* simultaneous recording of sound and picture; problems with sound synchronization; Sound-on-film technology; problem that they had rarely faced; problem of synchronization; add sound to pictures separately after filming; video and audio elements of movies were synchronized; created by inventors   *Correct Answer:* Inventors created a new technology that allowed the simultaneous recording of sound and picture in order to resolve problems with sound synchronization.

B *Key Ideas:* inventors created sound-on-film technology; allowed filmmakers to record the sound and the pictures together; impossible for the video and audio elements to become separated

Get It Right: Sentence Summary Questions

Task 1: *Paraphrased Sentence:* Answers will vary but should be most similar to the correct answer option. *Correct Answer Option:* Inventors created a new technology that allowed the simultaneous recording of sound and picture in order to resolve problems with sound synchronization.   **Task 2:** *Answer Option:* The video and audio elements of movies were synchronized using technology that was created by inventors.   *Missing Information:* This answer option does not describe the problem inventors were trying to solve with the new technology.   **Task 3:** *Answer Option:* Sound-on-film technology created by filmmakers fixed a problem that they had rarely faced when adding sound to films.   *Change to Meaning:* The passage says that the problem of synchronization was a constant one, not a rare one.   **Task 4:** *Answer Option:* To solve the problem of synchronization, filmmakers used technology that allowed them to add sound to pictures separately after filming.   *Reason It's Incorrect:* This answer option contains information that contradicts the facts of the passage.

Walk through: Passage Summary Questions

A 1. *Key Words:* Southern writers; late nineteenth and early twentieth centuries; important literary figures; unique aspects of the American South; economy of the American South; centered in cities; Family relationships; Faulkner's stories; Eudora Welty; southern settings   *Correct Answers:* 2. The unique aspects of the American South were represented in southern literature through a number of characteristics.; 4. Family relationships are a central theme found in a lot of southern writing.; 5. Southern writers like Eudora Welty often described southern settings in careful detail.

B *Important Information:* southern writers—especially those who worked in the late nineteenth and early twentieth centuries—often employed similar strategies to explore the distinct character of the region; Family relationships are a central theme found often in southern writing.; southern writers also created similar settings or locations in their works

Get It Right: Passage Summary Questions

Task 1: *Paragraph 1:* While the literature of the American South is diverse, southern writers—especially those who worked in the late nineteenth and early twentieth centuries—often employed similar strategies to explore the distinct character of the region.   *Paragraph 2:* Family relationships are a central theme found often in southern writing.   **Paragraph 3:** In addition to writing about subjects that reflect the values of southern culture, southern writers also created similar settings or locations in their works.   **Task 2:** Southern writers who worked during the late nineteenth and early twentieth centuries are among the most important literary figures of American literature.   **Task 3:** Faulkner's stories focused on events that happened to his own family.   **Task 4:** The economy of the American South was largely centered in cities.

Get Ready

A Paragraph 1: Interestingly, silversmithing is a relatively recent art form in the Navajo culture, but it is one that craftspeople have transformed into a uniquely Navajo creation that is an important part of modern Navajo culture and commerce.   **Paragraph 2:** The origins of Navajo silversmithing can be traced back to a man named Atsidi Chon, who is widely regarded as the father of Navajo silversmithing.   **Paragraph 3:** Today, the work of Navajo silversmiths clearly reflects designs that are culturally important to the group.   **Paragraph 4:** Some elements of Navajo silverwork are clearly influenced by other cultures.
B 1. Key Words: Typical Navajo jewelry; silver; squash blossom bead; hollow bead with petals; Navajo silversmiths; traditional squash blossoms; rounded, hollow beads; represent strength and vitality; characteristic Navajo silver jewelry; traditional squash blossom beads; symbolizes strength and energy
2. Key Words: famous; rugs, baskets, and silver jewelry; fairly recently; important part of Navajo culture; Atsidi Chon; new tools for working silver; lacked the tools; distinctive style; inspired by other cultures; distinctly Navajo; squash blossom bead; use of turquoise; borrowed from the Spanish

Get Set

A 1. these routes were important because they allowed the exchange of both goods and ideas   **2.** This kind of trade was very profitable because goods that were common in one place were priceless and exotic in another.   **3.** The trade routes brought many different cultures together, and they often exchanged ideas as well as material goods.
B 1. C, B, D, A   **2.** B, F, A, E, C, D

Go for the TOEFL Test

1. The changes to the violins' structure increased the instruments' top volume, allowing violinists to perform in larger places because the sound would be heard.   **2.** Dense wood, which is associated with slow tree growth, resulted from cold temperatures during a period of lowered solar activity.   **3.** Stradivari adjusted the structure of the violins in ways that improved their ability to create loud and clear sounds.; The oil-based finish on all Stradivarius violins likely contributes to their sound quality because it preserves the wood's vibrational ability.; The dense wood used to create Stradivarius violins, which likely came from a forest near Stradivari's home, is a factor in the superior sound of the instruments.

Lesson 5: Add Text and Table Completion Questions

Walk through: Add Text Questions
A 1. Key Words: As a result; agricultural productivity; declined by 20 percent   **Correct Answer:** c

Get It Right: Add Text Questions
Task 1: Given Sentence: As a result, the agricultural productivity in these areas has declined by 20 percent.   **Main Idea of Paragraph 2:** Waterlogging, a state in which the ground becomes oversaturated with water, is a particularly harmful effect of irrigation.   **Task 2:** When; Thus; Additionally   **Task 3:** c

Walk through: Table Completion Questions
A 1. Key Words: magnetic substances; beaks; humans; landmarks; magnetic pull; migrate; magnets; sun or stars; view of the sky   **Correct Answers:** *Celestial:* 6. Allows birds to use the position of the sun or stars to navigate; 7. Supported by observations that birds that don't have a clear view of the sky can't navigate effectively *Magnetism: 1.* Proven by discovery of magnetic substances in some birds' beaks; 3. Earth's magnetic pull indicates the direction of travel; 4. Studies in which magnets are applied to birds demonstrate its validity.

B *Important Information:* birds probably use the location of celestial bodies, such as the sun and the stars, to orient themselves; birds seem to ignore geographical features; when the stars are obscured by clouds, birds cannot navigate as accurately as when the stars are clearly visible; birds navigate using Earth's magnetic field; The magnets interfered with the birds' navigation; researchers also discovered iron oxide, a magnetic material, in the beaks of homing pigeons

Get It Right: Table Completion Questions
Task 1: *Celestial:* Some biologists have shown that birds probably use the location of celestial bodies, such as the sun and the stars, to orient themselves. *Magnetism:* In addition to the sun and stars, birds may also use Earth itself as a kind of compass. **Task 2:** Similar to navigation method employed by humans that makes use of landmarks, like rivers, mountains, and oceans **Task 3:** Employed only by birds that migrate annually

Get Ready
A *Paragraph 1:* Advances in medical sciences have made it possible to control the disease, but malaria is difficult to eradicate entirely for several reasons. *Paragraph 2:* Though early doctors developed some treatments for malaria using plants and herbs, it was not until the true nature of the disease was discovered that it was possible to formulate a more effective treatment. *Paragraph 3:* Today, medical researchers have made several developments in controlling the spread of malaria. *Paragraph 4:* Despite these advancements in treating and preventing malaria, the disease is still a worldwide problem.
B **1.** *Key Words:* malaria prevention efforts; destroying or avoiding mosquitoes **2.** *Key Words:* challenge in eradicating malaria; increased mobility of human beings **3.** *Key Words:* mosquito nets; Ease of travel; Plants and herbs; Parasites; mosquito bites; Immunity; medicines and pesticides; Antiparasitic medications; French physician; Medications; symptoms of the disease; British doctor

Get Set
A 1. Despite its size, a number of geological discoveries suggest that the Mediterranean may have entirely dried up about five million to 12 million years ago. **2.** Based on the depth of the layers of non-oceanic materials at the bottom of the sea, many scientists argue that evaporation was caused by the Mediterranean becoming separated from the Atlantic Ocean. **3.** The evaporation of the Mediterranean had significant effects locally and globally. **4.** However, this desert eventually became a sea again.
B 1. B, A, D, C **2.** D, A, C, B **3.** *Factors Leading to the Evaporation of the Mediterranean Sea:* C, G
Consequences of the Evaporation of the Mediterranean Sea: A, B, D *Answer Analysis:* B, E, C, F, G, A, D

Go for the TOEFL Test
1. b **2.** d **3.** c **4.** b **5.** *Indirect Methods:* 2. Involves measuring how fast a star moves as a result of the planets orbiting around it; 4. Uses a star's light output to indicate the size of an extrasolar planet; 7. Provides researchers with information about the mass of extrasolar planets; 9. Currently, one of these methods is not effective for locating small extrasolar planets. *Direct Methods:* 3. Uses technology that makes light from extrasolar planets appear brighter to observers on Earth; 6. Employs technology that allows scientists to create clear images of extrasolar planets; 8. Involves blocking light from stars that may be located near the extrasolar planet

Reading Review Test

Passage 1: The Decline of the English Cloth Trade

1. *Question Type:* Vocabulary
Answer Analysis:

✗ To "do away" with something means to eliminate it. There are no clues that James I eliminated Elizabeth I.

✓ **"Succeed" means to come after. James I came to the throne after Elizabeth I, so this is the correct answer.**

✗ "Turn aside" means to turn away from. This definition does not work in the sentence.

✗ "Keep back" means to keep someone from doing something. The author does not give any indication that James I kept Elizabeth I from the throne.

2. *Question Type:* Referent
Answer Analysis:

✗ The author is not talking about the instability of the population of England, so this option does not work in the sentence.

✗ Because the author is not talking about the instability of food production, this is not the correct answer.

✗ The author is not referring to unstable incomes, so this answer is incorrect.

✓ **The author mentions that a few industries brought reliable income to the English economy, which was struggling and unstable.**

3. *Question Type:* Function
Answer Analysis:

✗ The author says that the cloth trade was one of the reliable sources of income for England's economy. However, there is no indication that the English cloth trade needed to be expanded.

✗ In paragraph 1, the author mentions that the cloth trade was one of the few successful industries in England. There's no indication that the emphasis on the cloth trade led to insufficient food production.

✓ **The author mentions insufficient food production and two other facts as signs that the English economy was struggling.**

✗ There is no mention in the passage of the king's mismanagement of the country.

4. *Question Type:* Inference
Answer Analysis:

✗ In paragraph 1, the author says that the cloth trade was one of the few successful industries in England. It's unlikely that it was neglected in favor of other industries.

✗ The author says that the cloth trade was one of England's few successful industries, but we cannot assume that it was the only successful industry.

✗ The author mentions that prices were high in England, but there is no way of knowing whether the cloth trade was responsible for this based on the passage.

✓ **The author says that the King's Merchant Adventurers were given a monopoly over exports, meaning that prior to the company's creation, there were numerous companies working on exports of English cloth. The author also mentions that England's unfinished cloth was sent to companies in the Netherlands—those companies would be considered international partners.**

5. *Question Type:* Negative Fact
Answer Analysis:

✗ In paragraph 2, the author says that Cockayne asked James I to create a company that would handle all English cloth exports.

✗ In paragraph 2, the author explains that Cockayne proposed that English cloth makers finish cloth themselves, which would allow them to charge more for the cloth.

✓ **While Cockayne hoped that English cloth makers would finish cloth themselves and thus compete with the Dutch, he did not plan for the English to stop selling cloth to Dutch merchants.**

✗ Cockayne wanted the English to finish cloth themselves instead of just sending unfinished cloth to other countries. This represented a shift in the primary activity of the English cloth industry.

6. *Question Type:* Sentence Summary
Answer Analysis:

✗ This answer option leaves out important information about how finished cloth was more valuable than unfinished cloth.

✓ **This sentence includes the two key ideas in the highlighted sentence: the Dutch usually finished the cloth, and finishing it allowed Dutch merchants to charge more for it.**

✗ This answer option contains non-factual information. The highlighted sentence does not talk about finished cloth from England. Rather, it talks about why the Dutch charged more for cloth they originally bought from England.

✗ This answer option contains non-factual information. The cloth from England didn't lose its value. Rather, the cloth from the Netherlands was more valuable due to the finishing process.

7. *Question Type:* Detail
Answer Analysis:

✓ **In the passage, the author says that the English economy was struggling and that the king needed money. These facts demonstrate the king's desperation to improve the economy.**

✗ There is no indication that the king was interested in expanding the cloth trade.

✗ The author does not mention England's reliance on trade partnerships with the Dutch.

✗ The author mentions that the Dutch had the technology to finish cloth but does not say that the king's motivation for approving Cockayne's plan was to encourage technological advancement in England.

8. *Question Type:* Detail
Answer Analysis:

✗ The author says that the Dutch refused to buy English products after the creation of the King's Merchant Adventurers. Thus, it's unlikely that the Merchant Adventurers could have continued selling to the Dutch.

✓ **The author says that there was a rift between the Merchant Adventurers and the king as a result of the plan. This suggests that the Merchant Adventurers did not approve of the plan.**

✗ There is no mention of what the Merchant Adventurers did after the execution of Cockayne's plan.

✗ The author specifically mentions that the King's Merchant Adventurers had trouble transporting their goods to European markets. However, based on this information alone, it's impossible to determine if the Merchant Adventurers became the top English traders.

9. *Question Type:* Vocabulary
Answer Analysis:

✗ While "unfair" works in the sentence, there are no context clues to suggest that this is the correct answer.

✗ "Special" works in the sentence, but this is not the correct meaning of "inflated."

✗ There are no clues that suggest that the fees were secret.

✓ **"Inflated" means increased. Shipping companies increased the fees for English traders.**

10. *Question Type:* Detail
Answer Analysis:

✗ There is no mention of whether the king provided financial support to the company.

✗ The author does not mention how much it would cost to pay cloth-finishing experts or whether the company could afford to pay them.

✓ **The author says that English cloth makers lacked the expertise of their Dutch counterparts. For this reason, they couldn't match the quality of Dutch finished cloth.**

✗ The author says that the English provided unfinished cloth to other countries before the Cockayne plan, so it's unlikely that they wouldn't have sufficient cloth to finish.

11. *Question Type:* Detail

Answer Analysis:

✗ The author says that the Merchant Adventurers were reinstated but does not mention the public response to this.

✓ **The author says that more than 500 families tried to go into business but failed. This led to high unemployment, or joblessness, which, in turn, made people in London riot.**

✗ The author does not mention if people wanted jobs in the cloth industry or speak to those jobs' availability following the failure of the King's Merchant Adventurers.

✗ The author says that the people who supported the King's Merchant Adventurers went bankrupt. We do not know if these were the same people who rioted in London.

12. *Question Type:* Add Text

Answer Analysis:

✗ The sentence that comes before this marker talks about why the King's Merchant Adventurers couldn't produce quality finished cloth. Thus, if placed here, the given sentence would disrupt the flow of ideas.

✗ The sentence that comes after this marker discusses the failure of the King's Merchant Adventurers. If placed here, the given sentence would not make sense.

✓ **The sentence that comes before this marker discusses the failure of the King's Merchant Adventurers. The "also" in the given sentence indicates a continuation of ideas, so this is the best place for it.**

✗ The sentence that comes before this marker mentions the consequences of the failure of Cockayne's plan. Therefore, a sentence about the king's actions does not fit here.

13. *Question Type:* Table Completion

Answer Analysis:

✓ 1. *Decline*: **Part of Cockayne's plan was to compete with the Dutch. The failure of this plan eventually led to the decline of the English cloth trade.**

✗ 2. This statement is incorrect. The Dutch acquired unfinished cloth from England and then finished it themselves before selling it at high prices.

✓ 3. *Decline*: **One of the reasons that Cockayne's plan failed, leading to the decline of the English cloth trade, was that English cloth makers couldn't match the quality of finished cloth products made in the Netherlands.**

✓ 4. *Consequence*: **According to the passage, those who had supported the King's Merchant Adventurers lost money because of the failure of the company. This was one consequence of the fall of the English cloth trade.**

✓ 5. *Consequence*: **The author says that companies in other countries lost confidence in English trade and did not want to do business with English companies anymore. This happened as a result of Cockayne's plan.**

✗ 6. This statement is untrue. The king created the King's Merchant Adventurers, not the Merchant Adventurers.

✓ 7. *Consequence*: **The author says that the Merchant Adventurers remained resentful of the king even after being reinstated.**

Passage 2: Did Birds Evolve from Dinosaurs?

14. *Question Type:* Function

Answer Analysis:

✓ **The author says that *Archaeopteryx* had features similar to those on both dinosaurs and birds. To show the animal's similarities to birds, the author mentions wings and feathers.**

✗ While the author describes the size of *Archaeopteryx*, the mention of wings and feathers does not explain its size.

✗ The author later describes *Archaeopteryx* as a bird-like dinosaur. However, by describing wings and feathers, the author is not saying that it was a bird.

✗ Though the description of these features helps the reader imagine what *Archaeopteryx* looked like, the author doesn't mention them specifically to describe the animal's appearance.

15. *Question Type:* Vocabulary
Answer Analysis:

✗ The sentence in which the highlighted word appears makes it seem as though the entire community agreed on the theory, so "question" does not work.

✗ If "debate" were the correct answer, the sentence would probably mention two sides of the debate. Also, you can eliminate this answer option because it is the antonym of the correct answer.

✗ "Evidence" does not work in the sentence. If this were the correct answer, the passage would probably include examples of such evidence.

✓ **To reach a "consensus" means to come to an agreement. In the context of the sentence, this word best replaces the original word.**

16. *Question Type:* Sentence Summary
Answer Analysis:

✓ **This answer option best summarizes the highlighted sentence because it includes all of the key ideas from the original sentence.**

✗ The sentence mentions that people believed that reptiles were the closest living ancestors of dinosaurs because of dissimilarities between birds and dinosaurs, not similarities between reptiles and dinosaurs.

✗ The sentence says that birds have furculae, so this sentence contains non-factual information.

✗ This sentence is incorrect because it says that the lack of wishbones in dinosaurs made people think that dinosaurs were related to birds, which is untrue.

17. *Question Type:* Vocabulary
Answer Analysis:

✗ "Prepare" does not work in the sentence, as it's unlikely that a bone could prepare the skeleton for the stresses of flight.

✓ **To "reinforce" something means to strengthen it. In the sentence, it means that the bone strengthens the skeleton in order to better handle the stresses of flight.**

✗ While "protect" works in the sentence, it's unlikely that a bone could protect the skeleton from the stresses of flight.

✗ "Extend" does not work in the sentence.

18. *Question Type:* Detail
Answer Analysis:

✗ The author does not mention the existence of any bird species during the time of dinosaurs.

✗ The author says that only dinosaurs and birds have furculae.

✓ **The author says that the idea that dinosaurs and reptiles are relatives was based on the belief that dinosaurs didn't have furculae like birds do. Thus, the discovery of dinosaurs with furculae showed that their closest living ancestors are birds, not reptiles.**

✗ The author doesn't describe the purpose of furculae in dinosaurs, which are the only other animals that have the bones.

19. *Question Type:* Inference
Answer Analysis:

✗ The author doesn't give any clues to suggest that dinosaurs in the Dromaeosauridae family were related to *Archaeopteryx*.

✓ **The author says that the function of the wishbone was to reinforce the skeleton against the stresses of flight. Therefore, if the dinosaurs in the Dromaeosauridae family had wishbones, it's probable that they were able to fly.**

✗ The author gives the Dromaeosauridae family as one example of dinosaurs with furculae. The author says that many dinosaurs had furculae.

✗ The author gives no indication about the size of dinosaurs in the Dromaeosauridae family.

20. *Question Type:* Referent
Answer Analysis:

✗ "*Velociraptor* fossils" does not work in place of the highlighted word.

✓ **The author is referring to the dinosaur's front limbs.**

✗ The author is not referring to the likenesses of modern birds.

✗ "Early reptiles" would not make sense in the sentence.

21. *Question Type:* Vocabulary
Answer Analysis:

✓ **In the sentence, "compelling" means persuasive. The evidence is persuasive because it further supports the theory that birds are the closest living relatives of dinosaurs.**

✗ "Conflicting" would mean that the evidence doesn't support the theory, so this answer option is incorrect.

✗ There are no clues to suggest that "compelling" could be replaced with "recent." If "recent" were the correct answer, the author would have probably mentioned a date or another time marker.

✗ If something is "sufficient," that means there is enough of it. This definition does not work in place of the highlighted word.

22. *Question Type:* Detail
Answer Analysis:

✗ The author says that *Archaeopteryx* had feathers much like those found on modern birds. Furthermore, protofeathers are described as feather-like structures found on dinosaurs not related to *Archaeopteryx*.

✗ The author says that *Tyrannosaurus rex*, which was not a bird-like dinosaur, had protofeathers.

✓ **The author says that protofeathers insulated dinosaurs from cold, or helped keep them warm.**

✗ The author does not mention any modern birds that have protofeathers.

23. *Question Type:* Detail
Answer Analysis:

✗ The author says that dinosaurs had multiple-chambered lungs, while primates and lizards have two-chambered lungs. That means the lungs of dinosaurs were more elaborate.

✗ The author says that the lung structure of birds, not primates and lizards, allows them to keep their lungs full of air at all times.

✓ **The author says that primates and lizards have two-chambered lungs, which means they have a similar structure.**

✗ The author does not mention whether primates and lizards have other organs to help them breathe.

24. *Question Type:* Add Text
Answer Analysis:

✗ The sentence that comes after this marker mentions the last idea from the previous paragraph and introduces a new topic. Thus, this is not the correct place for the given sentence.

✗ The sentence that comes after this marker gives examples of structural similarities between birds and dinosaurs, continuing the ideas from the first sentence of the paragraph. The given sentence does not belong here.

✗ The sentence that comes before this marker discusses the skeletal features shared by birds and two specific types of dinosaurs. The next sentence gives more details about these similarities. Placing the sentence here would disrupt the logical flow of the paragraph.

✓ **The sentence that comes after this marker mentions that there are no similarities between dinosaurs and early reptiles. The first similarity between dinosaurs and birds, regarding the limbs, is discussed earlier in the paragraph. The second similarity, about the skull and neck, is mentioned in the given sentence.**

25. *Question Type:* Passage Summary
Answer Analysis:

✗ 1. While this is true according to the passage, it is not a major point in supporting the idea that modern birds, not reptiles, are probably the closest living relatives of dinosaurs.

✓ **2. The fact that dinosaurs had feathers or protofeathers is mentioned as an important piece of evidence in support of the theory that birds are the closest living ancestors of dinosaurs.**

✓ **3. The author mentions that birds and dinosaurs had similarly shaped lungs and that this is further proof that the two are probably related.**

✓ **4. The author describes the presence of furculae in both birds and dinosaurs, as well as other structural similarities between the two, as proof of their relation.**

✗ 5. This detail is mentioned briefly in the passage but is only a minor point.

✗ 6. This statement is incorrect. The discovery of *Archaeopteryx lithographica* fossils in the mid-1800s led many scientists to believe that birds are the closest living relatives of dinosaurs.

Passage 3: Pricing Approaches in Marketing
26. *Question Type:* Vocabulary
Answer Analysis:

✗ "Decide" does not have the same meaning as "aspire."

✗ If "hurry" were the correct answer, the author would have likely included some information about why a company would want to set prices quickly.

✓ **"Aspire" and "aim" have similar definitions—both words mean to want to achieve something.**

✗ To "attempt" something means to try to do it. This is not the correct meaning of "aspire."

27. *Question Type:* Vocabulary
Answer Analysis:

✗ "Summarize" means to give information in a brief form. This word does not work in the sentence.

✓ **In the sentence, to "account for" something means to take it into consideration. The sentence highlights that cost-based pricing approaches fail to consider market-related factors.**

✗ "Formulate" means to create something. This word does not work in the sentence.

✗ "Make clear" means to fully explain something, which does not work in the sentence.

28. *Question Type:* Inference
Answer Analysis:

✓ **The author explains that a sixth company selling tubing for one dollar more per foot than its competitors would not be successful. This suggests that customers would probably buy the less expensive alternatives.**

✗ The author doesn't mention how a company could lower its production costs or that it would have to in order to compete.

✗ The author does not say that buying new equipment would lower production costs.

✗ The author says that a company with higher production costs would have to match the prices set by its competitors but does not say that the companies' pricing strategies would necessarily be the same.

29. *Question Type:* Negative Fact
Answer Analysis:

✗ The author says that because larger companies can buy materials in bulk, they often have lower production costs and can afford to charge less for products.

✗ The author explains that companies with low production costs can afford to charge less for items.

✓ **In paragraph 5, the author says that small companies often combine competition-based pricing with cost-based pricing to find the best price.**

✗ The author says that smaller companies often have higher production costs and that setting prices to match their competitors' prices puts them at a disadvantage.

30. *Question Type:* Vocabulary
Answer Analysis:

✗ "Balance" means to make something steady. This word does not work in the sentence.

✓ **In the sentence, "yield" means to result in. In other words, small companies look for a pricing strategy that will result in a large profit even after considering costs.**

✗ "Withhold" means to keep away from. This word does not work in the sentence.

✗ In the sentence, "yield the highest profit" means to result in the largest profit. "Make larger" would not make sense in the context of the sentence.

31. *Question Type:* Inference
Answer Analysis:

✓ **The author says that smaller businesses often combine different pricing strategies in order to make profits. Because larger companies don't have to worry as much about how their production costs will affect profits, it's more likely that they will use a single pricing strategy.**

✗ The author explains how the pricing strategies of large companies influence those of smaller companies, not the other way around.

✗ The author does not mention how much large or small businesses spend on marketing.

✗ The author describes why smaller companies have higher production costs than large companies. There is no information about how using a particular pricing method affects production costs.

32. *Question Type:* Vocabulary
Answer Analysis:

✗ "Accessible" means easily reached. This word does not work in the sentence.

✗ "Improper" means not correct. This word does not work in the sentence.

✓ **"Impartial" means not affected by personal opinions or beliefs. If cost-based and competition-based pricing are described in contrast to buyer-based approaches, which are based on individual perspective, then "impartial" must have the opposite meaning of "based on individual perspective."**

✗ "Precise" means extremely exact. This word does not work in the sentence.

33. *Question Type:* Detail
Answer Analysis:

✗ Only cost-based approaches are based on the value of a product or service. Competition-based methods are based on what a company's competitors are charging.

✓ **The author explains that cost-based and competition-based approaches are based on factors like production costs and average prices, both of which can be measured.**

✗ The author mentions that personalized information is used for buyer-based approaches, not for cost-based and competition-based strategies.

✗ The author does not mention a pricing strategy based on the costs to the customer.

34. *Question Type:* Function
Answer Analysis:

✗ The author says that pet rocks have a low actual value but does not describe their perceived value.

✓ **The author mentions the pet rock to demonstrate how some products have a low actual value, meaning sellers need to use perceived value to set prices.**

✗ The author does not mention the perceived value of a pet rock.

✗ The author describes determining the perceived value of pet rocks only as part of a buyer-based strategy.

35. *Question Type:* Sentence Summary
Answer Analysis:

✗ This sentence incorrectly expresses the actions in the original sentence. The experts interview the focus groups, not the other way around.

✓ **This sentence correctly summarizes the important information from the highlighted sentence. It describes why market experts interview focus groups.**

✗ The highlighted sentence says that the point of focus groups is for people to share their feelings about a product with market experts, not to share how they form their ideas about product values.

✗ The highlighted sentence describes one way of determining the perceived value of products, not ways for interviewing people in focus groups.

36. *Question Type:* Referent
Answer Analysis:

✗ Market experts play a role in finding the perceived value of a product, but they do not actually create products.

✓ **Businesses hire psychologists and create products.**

✗ Psychologists are hired by businesses, but psychologists do not create products.

✗ Consumers' opinions about a product are important to companies, but consumers do not create products.

37. *Question Type:* Negative Fact
Answer Analysis:

✗ The author explains that some companies base prices on perceived value and not on other factors.

✗ The author says that the perceived value of an item may change depending on the focus group being interviewed and that experts interview many groups in order to get useful information.

✗ The author says that some companies hire psychologists to understand the emotions of consumers.

✓ **The author does not mention if the perceived value of an item is always higher than its actual value.**

38. *Question Type:* Add Text
Answer Analysis:

✓ **The sentence that comes before this marker describes how cost-based and competition-based pricing work. It makes sense that the author would then define buyer-based pricing to contrast it with the other two pricing strategies.**

✗ In the sentence that comes before this marker, the author defines perceived value. It does not make sense to change the topic to buyer-based pricing.

✗ The sentence that comes before this marker gives an example of an item with a low perceived value. Placing the given sentence here would disrupt the flow of the ideas about perceived value.

✗ The sentence that comes before this marker explains why companies would not use cost-based approaches for certain products. The next sentence, which starts with "instead," provides a better method for determining the price for such products. Placing the given sentence here would disrupt the flow of the ideas in the paragraph.

39. *Question Type:* Table Completion
Answer Analysis:

✓ **1. *Buyer-based*: The author explains that companies use perceived value, which is part of buyer-based pricing, to set prices for items with low actual value.**

✓ **2. *Competition-based*: In paragraph 5, the author describes why some companies have to set lower prices than they can afford or risk losing sales to competitors who offer the same product for less money.**

✓ **3. *Cost-based*: In paragraphs 2 and 3, the author says that cost-based pricing is simple and that it is the easiest way of determining the price of a product.**

✗ **4.** The author doesn't describe any pricing strategies that aren't used in combination with other strategies.

✓ **5.** *Buyer-based*: **In paragraph 7, the author describes the use of focus groups and psychologists in buyer-based pricing.**

✗ **6.** In paragraph 6, the author says that buyer-based pricing works well for items that have little actual value. However, the author never specifically says that competition-based and cost-based strategies are not well suited for items with little actual value.

✓ **7.** *Cost-based*: **In paragraph 2, the author explains that cost-based approaches involve figuring out the production costs and, in some industries, adding a standard markup.**

✓ **8.** *Buyer-based*: **In paragraph 6, the author says that buyer-based pricing is based on how customers feel about the value of a product.**

✓ **9.** *Competition-based*: **In paragraph 4, the author describes competition-based pricing as setting prices based on how much competitors charge for the same item.**

WRITING

WRITING TASK 1: Academic Reading / Lecture Synthesis

Get It Right

Task 1: ***Author's Claim:*** now new studies are showing that educational television shows have a positive effect on children's development ***Key Points:*** First, watching a few hours of educational programming a week has been proven to boost children's test scores.; Furthermore, watching educational television programs together can be an important bonding activity for families.; Finally, there are a wide variety of excellent educational programs available, and the quality of these programs is closely monitored. **Task 2:** ***Professor's Position:*** Overall, though, evidence indicates that watching educational programs on TV is not particularly beneficial for young toddlers and preschoolers. ***Key Points:*** Although some studies do indicate that watching educational programming boosts test scores, there are plenty of studies that directly contradict this notion.; In addition, watching TV together simply is not an effective form of bonding.; Finally, although government regulations aim to ensure programming excellence, they often fail to do so. **Task 3:** explain how they cast doubt on **Task 4:** The reading passage argues that educational programs on TV have a positive effect on young children.; However, the professor disagrees and gives evidence that educational programs are not good for preschool-age children to watch.; To summarize, in the reading, the author argues that educational TV is good for young children. However, the professor disagrees with this idea and gives three pieces of evidence to show that TV is actually bad for children. **Task 5:** The reading passage states that watching educational programs encourages academic success.; Second, the passage says that the quality of educational TV programs is closely regulated by the government.; Finally, the passage states that watching TV together can be a good opportunity for bonding between family members.

Get Ready

A However, some key factors indicate that vegetable oil is not an ideal source of fuel.; First, using vegetable oil as fuel requires the installation of special equipment in a vehicle, which can be quite costly.; Next, using vegetable oil as fuel for cars can be a complicated process.; Another issue is that using vegetable oil as fuel has the potential to reduce the availability of food crops.

B 1. The main topic presented in the reading   **2.** The second point from the reading
    3. The professor's main topic   **4.** The third point from the lecture

C [1] The reading states that vegetable oil is not a good source of fuel for cars. It gives several reasons for this argument. [4] However, in the lecture, the professor argues the opposite. She gives evidence to support the idea that vegetable oil is an excellent source of fuel for vehicles.

[3] The passage points out that it's expensive to install conversion equipment. There are many different pieces that cost money. Maintenance is also expensive. [2] However, the professor argues that while it is expensive, it pays for itself quickly by saving money. [5] Using vegetable oil as fuel is a lot cheaper than gas. This way, drivers save money in the long term.

[3] Second, the passage suggests that using the special equipment needed for vegetable oil fuel could be very complicated. It requires a lot of attention. [2] The professor disagrees. [5] She points out that it's not very hard and that people get used to these motions. Also, she explains that there are new systems that are automatic and don't need a person to turn them on or off.

[3] Finally, the passage argues that using vegetable oil could affect crops normally used for food, like sunflowers. This could cause the price of certain foods to go up. [2] In contrast, the professor says that the oil used for fuel is a waste product from places like food factories. [5] It's already been used once, so using it for fuel does not affect food production.

[6] In conclusion, both the reading and the lecture discuss using vegetable oil as a source of fuel for cars. While the author claims that vegetable oil is not a good source of fuel, the professor disagrees and offers several pieces of evidence to show that vegetable oil is, in fact, a good source of fuel for vehicles.

D **Sample Essay:** In the reading, the author says that vegetable oil isn't a good source of fuel for cars. The professor disagrees and shows that vegetable oil is a good source of fuel by describing some of the advantages of using vegetable oil as fuel in cars.

First, the reading says that using vegetable oil as fuel is too expensive because cars using this type of fuel require special, expensive equipment. The professor rejects this point and says that the equipment pays for itself in the end. That's because cars can travel long distances with vegetable oil.

Next, the reading claims that the equipment is too complicated to use. Again, the professor disagrees. According to the professor, using the converter becomes automatic, so drivers don't have to really think about it. In addition, she says that automatic converters are available, so drivers don't have to worry at all about switching the equipment on and off.

The final point in the reading is that using vegetable oil as fuel will lead to higher food prices. The professor disproves this point as well. She argues that the vegetable oil used as fuel is a waste product that typically comes from restaurants and factories. It's used for cooking before it's used as fuel, so it doesn't affect food prices at all.

To summarize, the author of the reading argues that vegetable oil is not a good source of fuel for cars. The professor disagrees with this idea and discusses three reasons why vegetable oil is a good source of fuel.

Get Set
B 1. Europeans   **2.** Odin   **3.** runes   **4.** similarities   **5.** Old Italic   **6.** Greeks   **7.** angular

C **Sample Response: Main Topic from Reading:** The reading claims that runes most likely developed as an independent writing system. **Main Topic from Lecture:** The professor disagrees and says that there is strong evidence that runes actually originated in an Old Italic alphabet.

Key Point 1 from Reading: First, the reading describes how Germanic groups who used runes could not have based their alphabet on an earlier system, because they were culturally isolated until 700 AD. **Key Point 1 from Lecture:** The professor says that this is not completely true. **Support from Lecture:** He says that Germanic groups interacted with early Romans and traders who used Old Italic scripts long before this.

Key Point 2 from Reading: Next, the passage describes how runes appear in mythology as creations of the god Odin. **Key Point 2 from Lecture:** The professor, however, points out that people from the Italian Peninsula traveled to Germanic regions long before that mythology became popular. **Support from Lecture:** The runes could have been derived from an Old Italic alphabet and added to mythology later on.

Key Point 3 from Reading: Finally, the reading claims that runic symbols are not visibly similar to letters used in Old Italic alphabets. **Key Point 3 from Lecture:** The professor, on the other hand, notices many similarities between the two alphabets. **Support from Lecture:** In particular, he says that the similar shapes of their letters indicate a relationship between the runic and the Old Italic alphabets.

Conclusion: In summary, while the reading says that runes developed independently from other writing systems, the professor disagrees and provides evidence to show that runes probably came from Old Italic scripts.

Go for the TOEFL Test

Sample Essay #1

The reading argues that the *Venus de Milo* is a copy of an earlier Greek or Roman sculpture. The professor, however, disagrees and explains why she thinks the *Venus de Milo* is an original piece of art and not a replica.

First, the reading points out that this Hellenistic sculpture strongly resembles older classical sculptures, particularly those of Greek artist Praxiteles. The professor disagrees with this because she feels that the *Venus de Milo* is very Hellenistic in style and that its similarities to classical works have been exaggerated.

The reading also suggests that the *Venus de Milo* must be a replica because of its similarities to *Aphrodite of Capua*. The professor says that there were so many Aphrodite and Venus sculptures created between the fourth and first centuries BC that of course some of them look similar, but she points out that the similarities between these two statues are not substantial enough to prove that the *Venus de Milo* is a copy.

Finally, the reading claims that because the statue was created during the Hellenistic period, and because so many Hellenistic pieces were replicas of classical works, the *Venus de Milo* must also be a replica. The professor feels that the Hellenistic period is underrated and that it produced many original works.

To summarize, in the reading, the author says that the *Venus de Milo* is a replica of a previous work. The professor disagrees with this.

Sample Essay #2

The lecture is about the *Venus de Milo* and why it's not a copy. The reading is opposite of that. The reading first says that it looks like a sculpture that was first discovered in 1820. That sculpture was by an artist who worked during the classical era. But the professor says it actually looks like something from the Hellenistic period. It took place after the classical period. That's why the *Venus de Milo* looks like that.

Next, the professor says that the *Venus de Milo* doesn't look like the *Aphrodite of Capua* that much. The reading argues that the similarity between these two is proof that the *Venus de Milo* copied the *Aphrodite of Capua*. So if the *Venus de Milo* doesn't look like the *Aphrodite of Capua*, the professor says that means it's not a copy.

Sample Score #1

This essay would likely score very well because the test taker provides an accurate and complete response to the prompt. The essay is organized in such a manner that the relationship between the reading and the lecture is very clear. For example, in the introduction, the test taker writes, "The professor, however, disagrees." This sentence shows that the student understands the professor's stance with respect to the claim made in the reading. Furthermore, the test taker writes about each of the points in the reading and describes how the professor casts doubt on those points. In order to do this, the writer provides plenty of specific details from the lecture. Finally, the language in the response is clear and easy to understand. The essay is well organized, and the ideas flow very well. The writer uses a variety of grammatical structures and makes no spelling errors.

Sample Score #2

This response would likely score poorly because it is difficult to understand and does not completely answer the prompt. After a short introduction, the test taker discusses only two of the points in the reading. At 138 words, the essay is too short. The score would have been higher if the writer had addressed the third point and, in doing so, extended the word count of the essay. Next, the language used in the essay severely limits understanding. In several cases, the writer uses pronouns without making the referent clear, as in the following sentence: "But the professor says it actually looks like something from the Hellenistic period." In this sentence, the referent of "it" is not clear. The writer also provides inaccurate information about the discovery of the *Venus de Milo* (the *Venus de Milo* was discovered in 1820; it did not, as the essay suggests, resemble a different sculpture that was discovered in 1820).

WRITING TASK 2: Personal Experience Essay

Get It Right

Task 2: The test taker disagrees with the statement. **Task 3:** First of all, I think that competing is usually a waste of energy.; I also dislike competition because at least one of the competitors always loses.; Cooperating is a much better alternative to competing. **Task 4:** I disagree with the idea that it is necessary to be competitive to succeed in life. **Task 5:** Some time ago, a friend and I both bought a video game and started competing to see who could earn the highest score. To get higher scores, my friend and I spent increasing amounts of time and energy playing the game. Eventually, I had no energy left after playing and couldn't do anything else. I decided it wasn't worth it and refocused my energy on other activities.; A classmate and I once found ourselves tied for the top rank of a class mid-semester. For the rest of the semester, we competed to overtake each other's rankings, and in the end she came in second. She felt as if her effort had been wasted and was pretty sad.; One time, a friend and I both wanted to participate in a writing competition. Rather than act competitively, we decided to cooperate with each other. We edited each other's stories and helped each other write. When his story did better than mine, I didn't feel bad, because I had helped him write it.

Get Ready

A Do you agree or disagree; Use specific reasons and examples

B Agree

C [1] I agree with the idea that you should always try to be polite to others. [2] I think that being polite makes you feel good. I think it also makes the person who receives your politeness feel good. Moreover, impoliteness can cause people to become angry with you.

[3] I have found that when I am polite to others, it makes me feel good. Being polite makes me feel like I am a decent and kind person. [6] For instance, one time as I was walking into a grocery store, a woman was walking in the opposite direction, and she accidentally spilled her groceries all over the parking lot. I stopped and helped her pick them up. She didn't thank me, but my act of politeness made me feel good anyway.

[4] The act of being polite also benefits the person who receives the politeness. It often brightens the recipient's day and can positively change the way he or she looks at people. [6] For example, I was traveling in a foreign country last summer and wasn't sure what I was going to do one evening. A local spotted me wandering around and asked me if I needed help finding something. He ended up giving me many good suggestions on places to visit. That one act of politeness made me happy the entire rest of my week.

[5] Another good reason for being polite is that people sometimes become offended when you are impolite, and generally it is not a good idea to offend people. [6] For instance, an old friend of mine once introduced me to a woman he had met and was dating. At one point, when I thought she wasn't listening, I made a rude comment about her dress. She heard me and became very offended. My friend stopped spending time with me after that. The woman remains close to my friend, but neither of them has spoken to me since.

[7] To summarize, it's my opinion that you should always try to be polite to others. Being polite not only makes you feel good, it makes others feel good, too. Also, being polite helps you avoid offending people.

D *Sample Essay:* In my opinion, I don't think you should always be polite to others. I feel this way for a number of reasons, including that there's no reason to be nice to someone who is not nice to you first, it takes a lot of work to be nice to others, and politeness makes people think you're weak.

First, I think that politeness should be earned. By that, I mean that I don't think I should have to be nice to someone who hasn't been nice to me first. For example, I work at a grocery store, where I deal with a lot of different people every day. Sometimes the customers there are very rude. I don't treat them badly, but if somebody's been rude to me, I don't try to be nice to them. I just don't think I should have to be polite to people who have treated me badly.

Next, it takes a lot of effort to be polite. You have to listen to the other person and make sure you don't offend them. Frankly, there are times when I just don't have the energy to be polite, like when I'm riding the subway home after a long day at school and work. I just want to sit back and relax until I get home.

Continued on the next page

Finally, there are situations in which being polite makes people think you are weak. I know somebody who is a manager at a busy office. She told me that if she behaves politely by doing things like saying "thank you" or "please," her employees don't take her seriously and won't listen to her. For the people in her office, this polite behavior means that she's weak and can't just say what she means. So my friend doesn't act as politely at work anymore, and people treat her with respect. In her case, it just doesn't make sense to be polite all of the time.

In summary, I disagree with the idea that you should always be polite to others. I think people need to earn my politeness, and in some cases, it's just too much work to be polite. Finally, I don't think you should be polite if it makes people think you are weak.

Get Set

A 1. Do you agree or disagree   **2.** Use specific reasons and examples

B 1. Topic Sentence   **2.** Key Point 1   **3.** Personal Details   **4.** Key Point 2   **5.** Personal Details
   6. Key Point 3   **7.** Personal Details

C 3, 2, 5, 1, 4

D Sample Essay: I agree with the statement that people should focus on the happiness of others over their own happiness. Focusing on the happiness of others helps you understand others and makes you a better person. Also, it often encourages other people to focus on your happiness in return.

First, in my experience, I've found that focusing on the happiness of others broadens the ways in which you see the world, which, in turn, helps you understand others better. For the past two years, I have volunteered at a local school as a tutor. One of my students was obviously very smart, but he was doing badly in school. Through my work with him, I eventually realized that he didn't have time to study because he helped take care of his younger brothers and sisters. By focusing on helping this student, I realized that everybody has a different situation that may affect how he or she does in school.

Second, I think that focusing on the happiness of others helps you be a better person in general. To return to my example of volunteering, I've found that in order to be a good volunteer, I have to be unselfish and think about the happiness of the students before my own happiness. Because of this experience, I try to be unselfish in other parts of my life, too. In my opinion, these qualities are a really important part of being a good person.

Third, a lot of the time, focusing on the happiness of other people encourages them to focus on your happiness in return. My best friend, Sally, is a great example of this. Because she's my friend, I always try to make her happy by spending time with her and doing fun things, like going to the movies or listening to music together. In return, Sally always makes sure that I'm happy, too. There's never a time when she lets me down, and I'm sure that my happiness is as important to her as hers is to me.

In conclusion, it is best if you focus on the happiness of others. In general, it helps you to understand people and to be unselfish. It also encourages others to make you happy.

Go for the TOEFL Test

Sample Essay #1	Sample Essay #2
I agree with the idea that it is more important to create realistic goals than ambitious ones. I think it's easier to get started when you have a realistic goal. Also, it's easier to stay motivated when you're trying to reach a realistic goal. Finally, having realistic goals is a lot less stressful than having ambitious goals.	People have different types of goals. You can make ambitious goals, like climbing Mount Everest or writing a great book, or you can make realistic goals, like learning how to speak a different language. I think it's possible to achieve an ambitious goal, but in my opinion, it's better to have realistic goals.
First of all, realistic goals are better because they're easier to start. For example, my friend wanted to become a rock star, which was a very ambitious goal. When he realized	First, realistic goals are a lot easier to achieve, if you think about it. For example, I had a friend who had dreams of writing best-selling novels. That's a pretty

(Continued)   (Continued)

how much work was involved in reaching that goal, he decided to not even try. He felt that achieving that goal was impossible and that it was useless to even try.

Next, I think it's a lot easier to stay motivated when you have realistic goals. The fact is, achieving an ambitious goal requires a lot of patience and hard work, and you probably have to face a lot of failure before you achieve your dream. This is what happened to my friend Melissa, who wanted to be a photographer for a famous magazine. Eventually, she became discouraged because the magazine kept rejecting her photographs, and she decided to abandon her goal. I think that if she'd had a more realistic goal, like being a photographer for a newspaper, she wouldn't have faced as much rejection and probably would have stuck with her goal.

Finally, it's better to set realistic goals because it's less stressful. That's because there's less at stake when you have a realistic goal, so it doesn't feel like your whole life is ruined if you don't achieve it. For example, I knew a girl who had the realistic goal of dancing in the city ballet. She didn't get the lead part, but that was OK with her. At least she got a smaller part and was able to dance onstage.

To conclude, if you want to reach your goals and feel successful, you should set realistic ones.

ambitious goal, and he'll probably never reach it. It's too much work, I think. Ambitious goals are usually too much work. If he had chosen a realistic goal, I think it would be easier for him to achieve his dream. You don't have to work as hard or commit a lot of time to achieve realistic goals. In that way, you'll be more likely to achieve a realistic goal long before achieving an ambitious goal.

Next, I think that realistic goals are better because they are easier to prepare for. In order to achieve an ambitious goal, you have to prepare a lot. But it's not as hard to prepare for a realistic goal.

Third, I also think that realistic goals are easy to achieve because you have a lot more control. I mean, you can change your expectations if you need to. If it seems like you can't achieve the goal, you should change it and that might also help you.

To create a realistic goal, you should think about what you can accomplish. And it's helpful to think of when you want to accomplish the goal, too. That way, you will have a deadline for when to finish.

Sample Score #1

This essay would probably score very well because the test taker answers the question in the prompt in a clear and well-organized manner. The test taker writes his position at the very beginning of the essay, so it's easy to tell whether he agrees or disagrees with the statement. He also gives a brief summary of the key points that he will use to support his opinion, which makes it easy to understand the organization of the essay from the beginning. Furthermore, the test taker gives three distinct key points, which are supported with relevant personal details. The details help make the key points clear to the reader. Finally, the sentences in the essay are well written and contain no grammatical or spelling errors, and the essay contains more than 300 words.

Sample Score #2

This response would likely score in the mid-level range. While the essay addresses the main topic, the writer doesn't fully develop the points. Adding more personal examples would have improved this aspect of the essay. Next, the body paragraphs show some progression, but the ideas are often unclear. For example, in the third paragraph, the writer mentions that it's easier to prepare for realistic goals but does not give any examples to clarify this idea. At the end of the essay, the focus of the response shifts to a discussion of how to create a realistic goal, which is off topic. Overall, the writer repeats much of the same key language throughout the response and does not show that he has a wide vocabulary.

WRITING REVIEW TEST

Question 1

Sample Essay #1

Both the reading and the lecture are about the Upper Paleolithic Revolution, which was a period during which humans started displaying modern behavior, like making tools and creating artwork. According to the reading, the Upper Paleolithic Revolution took place in Europe about 40,000 years ago. However, the professor disagrees with this and claims that it probably took place in Africa much earlier than that.

The first point in the reading is that a population boom among modern humans in Europe was a sign that modern behavior started there about 40,000 years ago. The author also mentions that European Neanderthals, an earlier type of human, went extinct because of the success of the modern humans. In the lecture, the professor disagrees that modern humans emerged in Europe. He points out that sophisticated tools much older than those found in Europe were found in Africa. According to him, this is an indication that the tools were developed in Africa and brought to Europe when people migrated there.

Next, the reading argues that a period of cold weather in Europe prompted humans there to develop better tools so they could survive. Again, the professor disagrees by saying that sophisticated tools, like projectile points and engraving tools, were found in Africa that date to about 50,000 years ago. He says that this is a sign that the tools were actually developed in Africa and not Europe.

Last, the author says that the earliest piece of art was found in Germany. The stone statue is called the *Venus of Hohle Fels*, and it was probably created between 35,000 and 40,000 years ago. The professor challenges the idea that this is the first piece of art. He describes two rock carvings that were found in a cave in South Africa. He says these carvings were created in 70,000 BC, which makes them much older than the piece found in Germany.

In conclusion, the reading says that the Upper Paleolithic Revolution took place in Europe 40,000 years ago. But the professor disagrees and provides evidence that it actually took place in Africa earlier than that.

Sample Essay #2

The reading and the lecture talk about the Upper Paleolithic Revolution. The reading says that the Upper Paleolithic Revolution happened 40,000 years ago in Europe.

First of all, the reading says that European humans during the Upper Paleolithic Revolution caused Neanderthals to go extinct. The lecturer agrees that the sophistication of human tools was probably the reason for Neanderthal extinction in Europe.

Next, there's the idea that humans first developed sophisticated new tools during the Ice Age in Europe because it was too cold. The lecture, though, points out that sophisticated stone and bone tools were actually developed even earlier in Africa.

Finally, the reading discusses a rock sculpture from Germany that is 35,000–40,000 years old. But the professor claims in his lecture that sophisticated art began as early as 70,000 BC.

Sample Score #1

This essay would probably score very well. The essay has five paragraphs, including an introduction, three body paragraphs, and a conclusion. Furthermore, the writer connects information from both the reading and the lecture by giving the main topic of the reading and accurately describing how the professor challenges each key point from the reading. The writer's language is easy to understand and includes a variety of grammatical structures and vocabulary.

Sample Score #2

This response would likely score poorly. While the essay includes an introduction and three body paragraphs, it does not have a conclusion. In the essay, the writer fails to fully connect information from both the reading and the lecture, and in some places he describes only information from the reading. The essay also lacks specific details from the lecture, which would have made the points easier to understand. For example, in the second paragraph, the writer says that the lecturer partially agrees with the reading but does not describe the details that the professor gives to challenge the point from the reading. The writer uses many of the same grammatical structures from the reading itself, suggesting that he lacks a strong knowledge of English sentence constructions.

Question 2

Sample Essay #1

I disagree with the idea that the best way to learn is by following examples set by others. Figuring things out on your own often leads to a greater understanding of the subject, and you may find a new way of doing something by not following examples. Furthermore, it is more fun to find things out by yourself.

One reason following examples isn't the best way of learning is because you often learn more about a subject when you explore it unaided. For example, I once wanted to learn about origami. I didn't have time to take lessons, so I bought a book and started studying it on my own. I would spend hours looking at the book and practicing, and I ended up learning a lot. I think if I had taken lessons, I wouldn't have explored anything outside of my session, so I wouldn't have learned as much.

Another reason following examples is not the best way to learn something is because it rarely results in finding new ways to do things. When you try to learn something independently, you're more likely to find something nobody has discovered before. Consider my friend who launches homemade rockets as a hobby. Instead of following examples, he decided to figure everything out without help. In the process of doing so, he designed a new rocket fuel that shoots the rocket farther. If he had followed an example, he wouldn't have come up with this new fuel.

Finally, learning new things on your own is better than learning from examples because it's more fun. The feeling you get from discovering something is much more thrilling than what you get from copying an example. For example, a friend of mine once built his own bicycle without any sort of a guide. He was prouder of this achievement than anything else he had done that whole year. I doubt he would have been as excited if he had simply followed instructions.

Sample Essay #2

In my opinion, following the examples set by others is the best way to learn. I think this is true because it's easier to learn from people who know what they're doing. Also, you can learn from the mistakes of others and have someone to help you along the way.

When you follow the examples of others, you are basically just learning from people who have more experience than you. People who have more experience, like teachers, can tell you if you're doing a good job or a bad job. That's very important, if you ask me.

Also, when someone sets an example for you, you know that they've already made mistakes and have learned from them. That way, you don't really have to make the mistakes yourself. Making mistakes is often a part of learning something new. But following the examples of others makes it so you skip this step, and that is convenient, I think.

Last, by following the example of someone else, you have someone to help you along the way. For example, when I was learning how to ride a bike, my cousin rode his bike first to show me how. When it was my turn to try, he was there to give me hints so it wouldn't be so hard. This was really good.

That's why I think it's good to learn by following the examples set by others. It's better because it helps you learn from the mistakes of others and learn from people who know what they are doing.

(Continued)

(Continued)

In conclusion, it's my belief that learning by following examples is not the best way to learn. I think that learning something new on your own is better because it helps you understand a subject more, it can help you find a new way of doing something, and it is more fun than following examples.

Sample Score #1

This essay would likely score very well because the writer provides a clear and well-organized response to the question in the prompt. In the introduction, the writer states her position and briefly summarizes her reasons for holding that opinion. The three body paragraphs each present a distinct reason that supports the main topic. The writer also presents personal details that help clarify her key points and gives a brief conclusion that summarizes her opinion and her reasons for holding that opinion. The language in the essay is clear and includes different types of sentence constructions. The writer uses transition language to improve the flow of the essay, and the response is more than 300 words.

Sample Score #2

This response would probably get a mid-level score. The writer includes five paragraphs and answers the question in the prompt, but it is difficult to understand the writer's meaning at times. The writer could have improved this by adding more personal details to clarify the points. Furthermore, the writer should have included more transition language to indicate the relationship between the sentences in the response. The writer often uses the same words and does not display a broad vocabulary. Finally, at 256 words, the response is too short.

Audio Script

Narrator: Writing Lesson 1: Get Ready

Narrator: Now listen to part of a lecture in an environmental science class.

Professor: As the world's supply of fossil fuels begins to run low, scientists have been exploring alternative sources of fuel for cars and other vehicles. One of the best alternative fuels is vegetable oil. There are a lot of reasons why using vegetable oil is a great idea.

First, it's true that people have to invest a little money at first for conversion equipment. However, if you think about it, the equipment soon pays for itself because the car can be driven many more miles on fuel from vegetable oil. Most cars can drive between 800 and 1,000 miles on just one tank of vegetable oil! Compare this to the average gas engine that gets about 500 miles for one tank of gas. The use of vegetable oil saves a lot of money. In addition, the cost of conversion equipment will come down quickly as more people switch to using vegetable oil.

It's also very true that the use of a converter requires the driver to pay attention. However, it really isn't that hard to remember to turn the equipment switch on and off. After a while, people who use the equipment just do it automatically. Also, with rapid improvements in technology, soon even that won't be necessary. Already there are automatic converters that sense when to turn the equipment on or off. The driver doesn't have to do anything at all.

Finally, it's true that vegetable oil comes from crops that are used for food. However, the vegetable oil that we use for fuel in cars is a waste product. Huge amounts of this waste oil are discarded every day from places like restaurants and potato chip factories. This oil has already been used once for cooking, so using it in a car doesn't interrupt the food supply at all.

🎧 CD1, Track 4

Narrator: Writing Lesson 1: Get Set

Narrator: Now listen to part of a lecture in an archaeology class.

Professor: There's this big debate with historians and archaeologists about the origins of runes. Did they develop independently, or were they based off of some older alphabet system? Our reading from last night suggests that runes developed independently. I don't really agree with that. I think there's a lot of evidence that runes could have developed from another script. In particular, I think they came from Old Italic, a family of alphabets that originated on the Italian Peninsula in the eighth century BC. The Old Italic alphabets spread around Europe and were used to write many different European alphabets.

First of all, it's true that Germanic groups were more isolated than other people in Europe. But they weren't immune to influences from powerful groups like the Greeks and the Romans, who used Old Italic alphabets. Early Romans probably did travel to central Europe, especially for trade. Actually, I believe that trade with Greeks and Italians, and then conquest by those groups, could have really influenced Germanic culture. So the different languages definitely came into contact, and it's likely that runes were based on the Old Italic system.

Also, let's mention the idea about the runes having a basis in mythology. There just isn't strong evidence to support this claim. Yes, runes are mentioned in mythology and in connection with the god Odin, but that doesn't make it impossible that they originated in another alphabet. We know that people who used Old Italic scripts were traveling all over Europe before the Germanic mythology took shape.

I also want to address the claim that there aren't many similarities between runes and other scripts. If you compare runic and Old Italic scripts, it's obvious that these two are related somehow. They all use the same angular letters. And while the reading suggests that anything they have in common is probably random or a coincidence, I think that's pretty unlikely.

🎧 CD1, Track 5

Narrator: Writing Lesson 1: Go for the TOEFL Test

Narrator: Now listen to part of a lecture in an art history class and take notes.

Professor: OK, our reading tries to convince us that the *Venus de Milo* is probably a re-creation of an earlier piece. Personally, I disagree with this stance. I think that the *Venus de Milo* is an original work from the Hellenistic period, not a copy of something from the classical period.

Let's start by looking at style. The article says that the *Venus de Milo* resembles classical works by artists like Praxiteles. Really, though, it depends on how you look at the statue. Yes, some of it looks a lot like classical pieces in certain ways, but that's because the classical period lasted from the fifth century BC until about 330 BC, and the Hellenistic period immediately followed. And actually, the *Venus de Milo* looks very Hellenistic. It's very realistic and detailed, and the body is long and lean. These are features of the Hellenistic era. I don't think the artist was copying classical styles.

Also, there's this claim that the *Venus de Milo* must be a replica because it looks a lot like the *Aphrodite of Capua*, which we know is a replica of an older Greek statue. But this doesn't make much sense, either, if you ask me. I mean, there were many different artists depicting Venus and Aphrodite between the fourth and first centuries BC—so many that of course some of them look similar. So I don't think the similarity between these two works proves anything.

And finally, just because Alexandros of Antioch lived during the Hellenistic period doesn't mean that this image of Aphrodite wasn't his own creation. I think that the Hellenistic period was a little underrated. Plenty of beautiful and unique art came out of that time period. I think, um, we can't assume that the *Venus de Milo* was a replica just because it came from an unknown person at an unlikely time.

WRITING REVIEW TEST

🎧 CD1, Track 6

Narrator: Writing Review Test: Question 1

Narrator: Now listen to part of a lecture in a history class and take notes.

Professor: OK, today let's talk about the Upper Paleolithic Revolution. As you know from the reading, this was a period in which people started exhibiting modern human behavior. By that, I mean that humans started developing tools and culture, which earlier types of humans didn't have. Anyway, some scientists argue that the Upper Paleolithic Revolution took place in Europe about 40,000 years ago. But there's actually a lot of evidence that shows that it took place in Africa a lot earlier than that.

First of all, there's this idea that modern humans emerged in Europe and that's why the European Neanderthals went extinct. But that's not the whole story. I mean, the modern humans had to have come from somewhere, and with the information we have, I'd say they came from Africa. See, it's true that scientists found tools in Europe that date to around 40,000 years ago. But even older versions of those tools have been found in parts of Africa. What does that mean? Well, it means that modern humans migrated from Africa to Europe, and they took their new technology with them when they did.

OK, let's move on. Another theory is that the cold weather in Europe forced modern humans there to develop new tools. Again, I'm afraid this just isn't true. I mean, many stone and bone artifacts appeared in Africa as early as 50,000 years ago. I'm talking about objects like projectile points and engraving tools. So, again, here we have examples of sophisticated human tools that are older than the tools that were found in Europe. It's true that new tools probably allowed humans to flourish in Europe during the period of cold climate, but I don't think the new tools originated in Europe.

Finally, some experts say that the first example of art was found in Europe. But we actually have evidence of much older pieces of art. And guess what? These older pieces were found in Africa. For example, the oldest rock carvings in Africa are two decorated stones that were found in Blombos Cave in South Africa. Amazingly, these were created in 70,000 BC!

Academic Word List

academic⊙ / ækədemɪk, ækədemɪkli /⊙ (academics)

ADJ⊙ (ADJ n) Academic is used to describe things that relate to the work done in schools, colleges, and universities, especially work which involves studying and reasoning rather than practical or technical skills.

Their academic standards are high.

I was terrible at school and left with few academic qualifications.⊙

academically ADV

He is academically gifted.

ⓐ the word you are looking for
ⓑ how it sounds
ⓒ type of word (e.g. noun, adjective, adverb, etc)
ⓓ example sentence

The following 570 words are of the most common word families found in academic texts. These are important to learn and know to ensure academic success. Use the ***Collins Cobuild Advanced Dictionary*** to find definitions, different forms of words, see authentic sample sentences, learn pronunciation, and much more!

Coxhead Academic Word List*

abandon	affect	approximate
abstract	aggregate	arbitrary
academy	aid	area
access	albeit	aspect
accommodate	allocate	assemble
accompany	alter	assess
accumulate	alternative	assign
accurate	ambiguous	assist
achieve	amend	assume
acknowledge	analogy	assure
acquire	analyze	attach
adapt	annual	attain
adequate	anticipate	attitude
adjacent	apparent	attribute
adjust	append	author
administrate	appreciate	authority
adult	approach	automate
advocate	appropriate	available

aware
behalf
benefit
bias
bond
brief
bulk
capable
capacity
category
cease
challenge
channel
chapter
chart
chemical
circumstance
cite
civil
clarify
classic
clause
code
coherent
coincide
collapse
colleague
commence
comment
commission
commit
commodity
communicate
community
compatible
compensate
compile
complement
complex
component
compound
comprehensive
comprise
compute

conceive
concentrate
concept
conclude
concurrent
conduct
confer
confine
confirm
conflict
conform
consent
consequent
considerable
consist
constant
constitute
constrain
construct
consult
consume
contact
contemporary
context
contract
contradict
contrary
contrast
contribute
controversy
convene
converse
convert
convince
cooperate
coordinate
core
corporate
correspond
couple
create
credit
criteria
crucial

culture
currency
cycle
data
debate
decade
decline
deduce
define
definite
demonstrate
denote
deny
depress
derive
design
despite
detect
deviate
device
devote
differentiate
dimension
diminish
discrete
discriminate
displace
display
dispose
distinct
distort
distribute
diverse
document
domain
domestic
dominate
draft
drama
duration
dynamic
economy
edit
element

eliminate	final	incline
emerge	finance	income
emphasis	finite	incorporate
empirical	flexible	index
enable	fluctuate	indicate
encounter	focus	individual
energy	format	induce
enforce	formula	inevitable
enhance	forthcoming	infer
enormous	found	infrastructure
ensure	foundation	inherent
entity	framework	inhibit
environment	function	initial
equate	fund	initiate
equip	fundamental	injure
equivalent	furthermore	innovate
erode	gender	input
error	generate	insert
establish	generation	insight
estate	globe	inspect
estimate	goal	instance
ethic	grade	institute
ethnic	grant	instruct
evaluate	guarantee	integral
eventual	guideline	integrate
evident	hence	integrity
evolve	hierarchy	intelligent
exceed	highlight	intense
exclude	hypothesis	interact
exhibit	identical	intermediate
expand	identify	internal
expert	ideology	interpret
explicit	ignorant	interval
exploit	illustrate	intervene
export	image	intrinsic
expose	immigrate	invest
external	impact	investigate
extract	implement	invoke
facilitate	implicate	involve
factor	implicit	isolate
feature	imply	issue
federal	impose	item
fee	incentive	job
file	incidence	journal

justify	nonetheless	practitioner
label	norm	precede
labor	normal	precise
layer	notion	predict
lecture	notwithstanding	predominant
legal	nuclear	preliminary
legislate	objective	presume
levy	obtain	previous
liberal	obvious	primary
license	occupy	prime
likewise	occur	principal
link	odd	principle
locate	offset	prior
logic	ongoing	priority
maintain	option	proceed
major	orient	process
manipulate	outcome	professional
manual	output	prohibit
margin	overall	project
mature	overlap	promote
maximize	overseas	proportion
mechanism	panel	prospect
media	paradigm	protocol
mediate	paragraph	psychology
medical	parallel	publication
medium	parameter	publish
mental	participate	purchase
method	partner	pursue
migrate	passive	qualitative
military	perceive	quote
minimal	percent	radical
minimize	period	random
minimum	persist	range
ministry	perspective	ratio
minor	phase	rational
mode	phenomenon	react
modify	philosophy	recover
monitor	physical	refine
motive	plus	regime
mutual	policy	region
negate	portion	register
network	pose	regulate
neutral	positive	reinforce
nevertheless	potential	reject

relax	site	terminate
release	so-called	text
relevant	sole	theme
reluctance	somewhat	theory
rely	source	thereby
remove	specific	thesis
require	specify	topic
research	sphere	trace
reside	stable	tradition
resolve	statistic	transfer
resource	status	transform
respond	straightforward	transit
restore	strategy	transmit
restrain	stress	transport
restrict	structure	trend
retain	style	trigger
reveal	submit	ultimate
revenue	subordinate	undergo
reverse	subsequent	underlie
revise	subsidy	undertake
revolution	substitute	uniform
rigid	successor	unify
role	sufficient	unique
route	sum	utilize
scenario	summary	valid
schedule	supplement	vary
scheme	survey	vehicle
scope	survive	version
section	suspend	via
sector	sustain	violate
secure	symbol	virtual
seek	tape	visible
select	target	vision
sequence	task	visual
series	team	volume
sex	technical	voluntary
shift	technique	welfare
significant	technology	whereas
similar	temporary	whereby
simulate	tense	widespread

*Please note, there is no direct correlation between the words found on the TOEFL Test and those found on the Coxhead Academic Word list. This list has been included only as a reference for vocabulary commonly found in academic texts.